Quality Improvement and Evaluation in Child and Family Services

Managing into the Next Century

Edited by Peter J. Pecora, William R. Seelig,
Fotena A. Zirps, and Sally M. Davis

Developed by the Committee on Quality Improvement
and Evaluation of the CWLA National Council on
Research in Child Welfare

CWLA Press • Washington, DC

CWLA Press
is an imprint of the Child Welfare League of America, Inc.

© 1996 by the Child Welfare League of America, Inc.

CHILD WELFARE LEAGUE OF AMERICA, INC.
440 First Street, NW, Suite 310, Washington, DC 20001-2085

CURRENT PRINTING (last digit)
10 9 8 7 6 5 4 3 2 1

Cover and text design by James Graham

Printed in the United States of America

ISBN # 0–87868–606–1

Library of Congress Cataloging-in-Publication Data
Quality improvement and evaluation in child welfare agencies:
        managing into the next century / edited by Peter J. Pecora...[et
        al.]
                p.   cm.
        Includes bibliographical references and index.
        ISBN 0-87868-606-1 (pbk.)
        1. Child welfare--Administration.   2. Social work administration.
        3. Evaluation research (Social action programs)   4. Total quality
        management.   I. Pecora, Peter J.
        HV713.Q35   1996
        362.7'068--dc20   96–15333

Contents

Section IV: Improving Your Services

Foreword

Today's nonprofit organizations operate in a highly competitive environment. While most agencies recognize that it is no longer possible to rely on good work alone, many continue to struggle with the changing world of practice and related reinvention strategies. To succeed as an effective and successful children's service and advocacy organization, every agency today must refocus its energy on structure, product, customer service, and quality improvement initiatives.

Designed as a hands-on tool for agency leaders, this book is filled with practical techniques for moving our agencies into the 21st century. Methods of defining our services and work processes, change strategies, outcome-oriented approaches to practice, program evaluation instruments, a quality improvement toolbox, integrated information systems, and breakthrough planning techniques are among the many tools this important publication provides.

The book was created within the context of today's demanding practice environment. In the mid-'90s, a small group of child and family service professionals met to explore the development of real-world, data-driven measures for evaluating and improving services to children at risk and their families. The group, including most of the authors, had been invited by the Child Welfare League of America (CWLA) to participate in the National Research Council, and had later formed the Subcommittee on Quality Improvement and Evaluation. Its members were an interesting mix of executives, clinical administrators, agency-based researchers, and service system/project evaluators. Most were from well-established, nonprofit child and family agencies. Others came from public research programs and the CWLA staff.

Important program specifications, assessments, outcome models, and change instruments were being developed by individual agencies and agency-university projects around the country. There were also exciting, untapped opportunities within the quality movement for service improvement, yet there was little under-standing of these innovations, and very little direct application at the practice level. Particularly with the advent of managed care, agency administrators were being pressured to provide data documenting their services to children and fami-lies. Many were reluctant to engage in what had often been a costly process that generated little true stakeholder involvement, produced information that was not tied to practice, and had little impact on improving services.

The challenge was clear: The subcommittee needed to build bridges between two worlds. Their first step was developing a vision of what could be: organizations where professionals, parents, children, and payors all participated in data-driven learning environments; where program innovations flowed from benchmarking and outcome studies; and where policies flowed from reliable information re-garding needs and services.

Implementation of this vision, including the development of consumer-focused, outcome-oriented, and payor-driven service delivery approaches, would require significant change in the behavior of board members, administrators, and staff. To be successful, the change process would require careful planning, firm action, and follow-through over a number of years. The authors provide a framework for thinking about, providing for, and implementing the changes necessary for thriving in tomorrow's emerging service world.

Throughout the handbook, the authors draw on the experience and creativity of both private industry and their nonprofit peers. They explore a series of reinven-tion strategies that can prepare agencies for success in the service world of tomor-row. In addition to the aforementioned tools, they explore accreditation as a program improvement mechanism. Their comparative review of the Council on Accreditation of Services for Families and Children (COA) and the Joint Com-mission on the Accreditation of Health Care Organizations (JCAHO) is most informative. Also explored are the benefits of and essential principles involved in creating an integrated agency information system, as well as practical strategies for achieving change through the use of staff teams.

I have had the distinct pleasure of working closely with several of the book's authors in a variety of situations, through my associations with CWLA, COA, and other nonprofit agencies and alliances. In my opinion, all of the professionals who assisted in the development of this handbook have earned the well-deserved respect of their colleagues and peers.

I am able to endorse this publication so completely because I support without qualification the mission statement of the Sub-Committee on Quality Improve-ment and Evaluation:

> To create theoretically sound, practical tools adapted from consumer-driven, data-based paradigms for use by child welfare agencies to strengthen services to children and families.

This handbook will prove to be just such a practical tool for children's service organizations, allowing them to continue developing, providing, and maintain-ing high-quality, responsive services for children and their families.

D. Sharon Osborne
PRESIDENT/CEO
CHILDREN'S HOME SOCIETY OF WASHINGTON

Acknowledgments

This handbook was made possible through the dedicated efforts of the members of the CWLA Committee on Quality Improvement and Evaluation. Patrick Curtis, CWLA's research director, along with Sam Kelman (chair, 1991 to 1995) and Cynthia Pappa-Lentini (the current chair), provided critical leadership to the overall efforts of the CWLA National Council on Research in Child Welfare, which sponsored the Quality Improvement and Evaluation Committee.

We are grateful to the representatives of the Research Council, such as Sally Flanzer and Elizabeth Schnur, and to the outside reviewers, such as Dee Ann Barber, Joann Blaska, David Etzwiler, Thomas Luzzi, Kathy Meeker, Barbara Miller, Anne Nicoll, Deborah Reed, James Traglia, and Karen Vroegh, who read chapters and made helpful suggestions. We especially thank Paul VanOsteberg and his colleagues at the Joint Commission on the Accreditation of Healthcare Organizations (JCAHO) and Pat Topitzer and David Shover of the Council on Accreditation of Services for Families and Children, Inc. (COA) for reviewing the chapter on accreditation.

Doug Klayman was instrumental in organizing the Committee and laying the foundation for its work. Sally Davis co-chaired the Committee as CWLA's representative during the crucial years of handbook development. David Cook provided practical information about the JCAHO accreditation process. Chris Downs helped clarify core concepts of the Deming approach to quality management. Robert Aptekar provided a national perspective on the challenges child welfare agencies face. Jennifer D. Boyd facilitated the development of this handbook by coordinating meetings and communications among committee members and co-authors.

The CWLA Administrative Practices Standards Group, chaired by Sharon Osborne, served as a focus group for an early draft of the handbook, grounding our work in the needs of child welfare agency executives. This group has recently completed its work on the new *CWLA Standards of Excellence for the Management and Governance of Child Welfare Organizations*.

Special thanks to Teresa Patterson of The Casey Family Program for developing the figures and coordinating the communications process with the handbook authors, and to Mary Liepold of CWLA, who helped the manuscript speak in one voice through her excellent copyediting. Finally, we appreciate the executive-level encouragement and support for our work as a committee from David Liederman of CWLA and Ruth Massinga of The Casey Family Program.

This book is dedicated to the staff members of America's child welfare agencies and to the families they serve.

Section I: Preparing Your Organization

Chapter 1

The Changing World of Services
for Children and Families:
Reinventions for the 21st Century

William R. Seelig and Peter J. Pecora

Introduction

In this opening chapter we would like to stand back from the all too consuming, day-to-day issues that confront each of us in the changing world of providing services to children and families and explore the larger, contextual forces that are influencing our ability to provide the best services possible. We begin with a review of the major challenges that face child welfare agencies, including the growing numbers of children and families at risk; the significant shifts in payor, consumer, and employee expectations and investments; and the escalating rate of change. It is our belief that these challenges threaten the survival of many agencies.

We then draw on the experience and creativity of leaders in private industry and our nonprofit peers to explore a series of reinvention strategies that can be employed to transform agencies for success in the service world of tomorrow. Three categories of reinvention are reviewed, with specific ideas and examples given in each area. They include (1) *techniques for focusing the organization* (visioning, developing a mission, strategic objectives, organizational values, and principles for practice); (2) *product, customer service, and organizational imperatives* (continuums of care and affiliations, benchmarking and service re-engineering, product specifications, process and outcome evaluation studies, integrated information systems, and organizational leadership); and (3) *quality improvement initiatives* (continuous quality improvement and total quality management).

This list of strategies, while far from exhaustive, is our attempt to capture the creative energies and the "roll up your sleeves" actions of companies and providers who are committed to making a difference. We conclude the chapter with words of encouragement, a list of references, and an invitation to the wonderful, hands-on, practical, nitty-gritty world of planning, experimenting, evaluating, and refining child and family services that the remaining chapters describe.

Service Paradigm of the Future

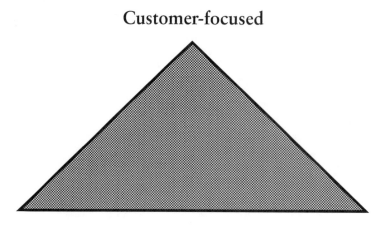

Customer-focused

Payor-driven   Outcome-oriented

Source: Charles Ray (1992), National Council for Mental Health, Washington, DC.

Challenges

The 1990s is a decade of unprecedented change for those of us who are committed to the provision of quality social services to children and their families. The people referred to us for service are at considerable risk, and present an ever-changing array of problems or needs as well as strengths and resources. As consumers, they need to be actively involved in the creation of solutions to their own child and family problems, and as parent/family consumer consultants to service providers they are, appropriately, demanding to participate fully in the development of new programs and services.

Our payors are expecting a full array of high quality services that meet the unique and changing needs of clients. They want new family-focused and community-based programs for seriously disturbed children and adolescents who were once restricted to group and residential care [Monack 1994]. The traditional boundaries between public, for-profit, and not-for-profit providers are disappearing, and a wave of retail-oriented competition has begun. For example, proprietary managed care organizations are "managing" much of the mental health care for children and families, and are beginning to make inroads into child welfare placement programs. Their focus on customer-responsive, time-limited, high-quality, cost-effective services with positive outcomes (see Figure 1.1) may pose a major challenge for child or family service agencies, which heretofore have emphasized traditional service products and services designed primarily by professional staff.

Employees are also redefining their roles. The relationships among workers, management and, where they still exist, unions are undergoing dramatic change. Our child and family agencies face significant challenges in today's service arena. How many of these are you and your agency facing?

Children and Families at Risk

- Growing referrals of children who have experienced prenatal and early childhood deprivation, addictions or trauma, serious physical or sexual abuse, and various forms of familial instability and abandonment.

- Growing referrals of high risk youths who have patterns of dangerous runaway, assaultive, or gang-related behavior and children and adolescents with serious physical health problems, such as untreated dental, vision, and spinal conditions or sexually transmitted diseases.

- Growing referrals of young parents and families who themselves have experienced intergenerational patterns of abuse and neglect, unemployment and poverty, drug and alcohol abuse, and isolation due to the fragmentation of family and community supports.

- Growing referrals of families from diverse ethnic and cultural groups with unique language requirements and needs for assistance with pre- and post-migratory traumas.

Shift in Payor, Consumer, and Employee Expectations and Supports

- Major political challenges to the existing systems of care for children and families, with threats to end or severely limit entitlements, block granting of services to the states, drastic funding reductions, and wholesale program closures.

- Growth in managed care, with the resulting purchase of specialized services by payors for specific populations for predetermined periods of time. A strong shift toward alternatives to group and residential care has already begun.

- A shift from governmental, influence-driven contracting to competitive, entrepreneurial contracting, plus the increased use of customer service patterns, client outcomes, and price in contract decision-making. Yesterday's government driven, "great society" solutions are giving way to tomorrow's data-driven, entrepreneurial contracts.

- Growing competition for service dollars among public, for-profit, and not-for-profit providers. All three are searching for cost-saving service innovations and eliminating non-value-added structures and processes.

- Mandates for consumer (client) involvement in the design, implementation, and evaluation of services.

- Growing competition for skilled and credentialed staff who can work effectively with diverse populations and with a range of individual, family, and macrosystem issues.

Rapid Rate of Change

- To compete successfully, agencies need to respond to opportunities in a proactive manner, on timelines that were unheard of five years ago.

Reinvention Strategies

These changes have far-reaching implications for those of us in the business of serving children and their families. They require a fundamental rethinking of current services and, in many respects, a major transformation of our organizations in preparation for the service world of tomorrow. In *The Virtual Corporation* [1992], Davidow and Malone examined the unprecedented changes that are affecting businesses today, and studied the strategies successful organizations are employing. They explored the development of a vision for the organization and its programs, the sharing of dreams with the customer who is in rather than outside the organization, the upward curve of technology, the future of design with simultaneous and concurrent engineering, the growing focus on time (giving responsiveness the same value as cost and quality), the power of information, the rethinking of management with attention to organizational processes and the cultivation of teams, and the machinery of change through continuous quality improvement (which has been integrated by the Japanese as the process-oriented concept of *kaizen*).

As we translate some of these findings to the child welfare arena, what can result are "virtual services," programs or products that are created quickly and customized in response to customer demand—that is, to individual client, family, and payor needs. Success in this environment depends on our ability to provide timely, high-quality, cost-effective services with demonstrated positive outcomes and customer satisfaction. In reinventing and transforming our agencies into "virtual organizations" capable of delivering these "virtual services," we need to (1) focus our organizations; (2) develop dynamic product, customer service, and organizational resources; and (3) undertake quality improvement initiatives. Let's explore the possibilities of each with examples from private industry and our nonprofit peers.

Focusing the Organization

Visioning

As leaders of the agencies of tomorrow, we are responsible for developing a compelling, energizing vision of an achievable future [Ray 1992]. A vision presents a clear image of the desired end state of the entire system, including such dimensions as our business, our organization, and our ways of working [Beckhard & Pritchard 1992]. It should be positive for all concerned and tap important values. Numerous study processes are available for developing the vision.

One nonprofit agency undertook an environmental scan. Key articles on future trends for the field were examined; national, state, and local leaders were invited to present their thinking on the future; and a retreat for board and executive staff was held to seek input and to build a preliminary consensus on future directions for the agency [Doyle 1992].

Another method, scenario building, involves developing alternative images of the future to create a range of possibilities for the agency [Schwartz 1991]. To accomplish this, leaders seek input from staff and customer visionaries—those with the unique ability to integrate data from different sources and anticipate potential paradigm shifts or new paradigms of service [Barker 1993]. Leaders also commit to personally creating a pragmatic vision that sets the direction for the future, and take personal responsibility for communicating that vision throughout the organization—using the vision to *pull* the organization into the future.

Albrecht emphasizes the importance of an unwavering commitment to a particular direction. He asserts that "No vision statement or mission statement can ever make much sense unless it originates in some valid concept about what it takes to succeed. It is not a platitude. It is not a slogan. It is not an exercise in journalism; it is an exercise in careful, clear, creative, disciplined, and mature thought. It provides a *critical success premise* that leaders can understand, commit to, and dramatize to others" [1994, p. 20]. Staff need to periodically reacquaint themselves with the vision and the mission to remain focused on the key outcomes being sought.

Mission and Strategic Objectives

Having identified the long-term vision, agency leaders carefully compare the desired state with current organizational realities. The gap between the vision and current resources is the basis of a mission statement and the resulting strategic business plan. In a recent document entitled "Principle-Based Practice" [Children's Bureau of Southern California 1993], a contemporary child welfare agency creatively described its transformational vision, mission, and principles of operation. (See Figure 1.2.)

This agency is embedding these values and principles throughout the organization. At orientation and reorientation they involve employees in a "principles game," which challenges them to use these concepts in real-life job simulations. The agency's principles statement is coupled with a striking picture, richly framed in attractive colors, and displayed throughout the agency and its satellite offices in reception areas, over each coffee or snack counter, in meeting rooms, and elsewhere. The executives and managers continually reference the values and principles in agency and team meetings and in their day-to-day interactions with staff. It is also used as a critical frame of reference in problem resolution.

In a recent book on leadership, Haas [1992] shared a combined mission statement and strategy written by Roberto Goizueta, Chairman and CEO of Coca-Cola. There are meaningful lessons for our agencies in this document. Excerpts follow.

- Our Challenge—continuing the growth in profits of our highly successful main business, and those we may choose to enter, at a rate substantially in excess of inflation. Protecting and enhancing the unique position of excellence that the trademark Coca-Cola has attained.

- Our Business—continue to be a leading force in the soft drink industry and become a strong factor in the consumer goods business...tirelessly investigate services that complement our product lines and are compatible with our consumer image.

(**Figure 1.2**)

A Statement of Vision, Mission, and Principles

Principle-Based Practice

(**Vision**)————— To Become an Exemplary Leader In Enabling
Families and Communities to Lay the Foundation for Children
to Become Caring and Productive Adults.

- **Mission:** To Assist Children to Become Caring and Productive Adults.

- Principles

  1. Sound Ethics must guide all agency decisions, policies, and activities in recognition of our stewardship role. "When in doubt, do what's right."

  2. To achieve Excellence, the Children's Bureau must:
     - Strive to Discover and deliver quality, cost-effective services.
     - Measure progress toward specific goals and objectives.
     - Promote improvement in internal and external systems based on feedback and knowledge gained from practice.
     - Search for ways to Prevent impediments to healthy childhood and successful family life.
     - Create a Fair, Family-Friendly work environment.

  3. Excellent services require excellent staff. The agency's goal is to recruit, hire, and train individuals who are mature, competent, eager to learn, able to participate in a team, willing to take risks, and capable of modeling the qualities of caring and productive adults.

  4. Staff, volunteers, caregivers, and clients are expected to treat each other with Respect at all times, and to work toward a productive and cooperative multicultural agency and society.

  5. The Children's Bureau strives to secure input from those affected by decisions and to Educate and Empower staff, caregivers, and clients to make their own decisions—wherever appropriate and feasible.

  6. The Children's Bureau should act *only* in ways that support the agency's mission and the intent of these principles.

Source: Children's Bureau of Southern California. (1992). Reprinted with permission.

- Our Consumers—management at all levels will be committed to serving to the best of its ability our bottlers and our consumers.

- Our Shareholders—remain totally committed to the protection and enhancement of shareholder investment and confidence.

- Our "Bottom Line"—our strong balance sheet and financial position will be maintained to withstand financial windstorms and allow us to take advantage of expansion opportunities.

- Our People—the four ethics of courage, commitment, integrity, and fairness will permeate from top to bottom...so that our behavior will produce leaders, good managers, and, most importantly, entrepreneurs. We will encourage intelligent risk-taking.

- Our Wisdom—as we look back we can say that each of us in our own way displayed the ability to see the long-term consequences of current actions, the willingness to sacrifice short-term gains for long-term benefits, the sensitivity to anticipate and adapt to change, the commitment to manage our enterprise so others welcome us into their communities, the capacity to control what is controllable, and the wisdom not to bother with what is not. [Haas 1992, pp. 125–129]

This for-profit entrepreneurial spirit, which includes customer-focused products and a reasonable return on investment, and our nonprofit pursuit of quality service innovations (including the empowerment of families and the improvement of the quality of life in our communities), taken together, support our missions and promote strategies for business and service success.[1]

Our resulting missions are individualized, providing conceptual road maps for each particular agency. A mission statement should be believable, achievable, and measurable, while offering a future to each person in the enterprise that is better than the present or the past. It is the "culture glue" that focuses the organization, as a collective unity, to accomplish the vision. The mission is also the source for our strategic plan, which details the steps to be taken in filling the gap between our vision and our current operational level [Haas 1992].

In addition to creating a strategic plan to reach our long-term goals and short-term action objectives, it is also important to create a plan and structure for managing the transition. When there is a gap between current services and the services that will be needed for success in the future, changes may result, including the termination of existing services. This program refinement process is often experienced by staff as the death of services as they know them. Yet our accep-

---

1. When child welfare borrows concepts from corporate management, some translation is needed. The translation of relevant concepts from corporate management and social science research is one of the principal goals of this handbook. Much as Coca-Cola needs to balance the competing demands of consumers, stockholders, and the bottom line, child welfare agencies are similarly challenged to forge a vision from the potentially counter-directed demands of service recipients, payors, and legal mandates to ensure the safety of children. The authors acknowledge that the corporate concept of customer responsiveness, as translated to publicly-funded child welfare, must include a variety of customers, including children and families receiving services, public agencies contracting for services, and, ultimately, voters, legislators, and the courts—who may or may not be unanimous in their understanding of what child welfare agencies should do to ensure the safety of children.

tance of these changes as part of the expected program improvement process; our support of staff flexibility and training; and our understanding of the staff reactions that occur as part of a normal change process will help the whole organization move successfully through the stages of mourning (denial, anger, bargaining, depression, and eventual acceptance) to active participation in planning and building for the future [McNair & Liebfield 1992]. A variety of strategies are necessary to support this level of organizational change. [See Chapters 7 and 10 of this book; Beckhard & Pritchard 1992; Bridges 1992.]

Values and Principles for Practice

As agency leaders prepare for the turbulent times ahead, and business leaders reflect on recent abuses in banking and other fields, many of us are returning to and re-examining our basic values and principles for organizational direction and balance. One not-for-profit agency, through broad-based input and dialogue involving both board and staff, created a "Values Constitution." The document includes agency business and social missions, references to professional ethics and standards, and values relating to clients, boards, volunteers, employees, culture, and the environment [Eastfield Ming Quong 1993]. Three excerpts from its business mission follow:

- Our organization is a business and we adhere to sound business principles. We earn more money than we spend, engage in ethical and fiscally sound business practices, and operate from a balanced budget.

- We are customer driven rather than product driven. We monitor and anticipate customer needs and make business decisions based on customer needs and related market forces.

- We recognize that there is an ongoing tension between elements of our social and our business missions, and make a conscious and continuing effort to maintain an appropriate balance between the two.

Another agency, a large treatment center for adolescent boys, adopted a series of "Agency Values and Norms" that guide day-to-day relationships and promote learning at all levels within the organization. Residents, staff members, and board members started with 36 value concepts and narrowed them down, eventually choosing the acronym of THEMES to help staff remember the core concepts. They defined their values carefully, and learned that clarity and simplicity, while difficult to obtain, were well worth the effort. They created a values preamble and identified the core values of trust, helping others, education, mutual respect, empowerment, and self-worth. They then adopted norms to serve as measuring tools. The values became the targets, and the norms the specific behaviors that show whether or not they are hitting the targets [LeRoy Haynes Center for Child and Family Services 1994]. Their norms for self-worth are presented in Figure 1.3. The agency reported that the process of value development had a major, positive impact on the total planning process. Value statements, when embodied in vision and mission statements, become important ingredients in the agency's overall service culture.

Figure 1.3

Norms for Self-Worth

Residents

- We take pride in ourselves and in our cottage.
- We accept where we are today and strive to do better tomorrow.
- We promote a "you can do it" attitude.
- We practice good hygiene and grooming.
- We establish eye contact and greet visitors.
- We give each other compliments for a good effort.
- We encourage our peers to do their best at all times.
- We work daily to achieve our treatment goals.

Staff

- We take pride in our work and in the agency.
- We give residents and each other compliments for a good effort.
- We try to help residents achieve their goals daily.
- We acknowledge the contributions of our peers to the program.
- We give residents the special attention they deserve.
- We role-model appropriate risk taking to build our skills.
- We enhance personal success with daily encouragement and praise.
- We monitor our progress towards work performance goals.

Source: LeRoy Haynes Center for Child and Family Services. (1994). Reprinted with permission.

Product, Customer Service, and Organizational Imperatives

Continuums of Care and Service Affiliations

As we focus our organizations for success in the future, we will confront the emerging role of managed and capitated care in health, mental health, and social service systems. These new service paradigms will dramatically change the way many agencies do business, offering both threats and opportunities. Some of the more obvious changes are summarized below.

Today

- High percentage of single service providers

- Walls between service units & providers

Tomorrow

- Continuums of care and service affiliations within an agency

- Seamless systems of care

• Program-driven services	• Customer-driven services, with clear outcomes by which services are judged
• Innovative service models with traditional training and research methodologies	• Evolving service models, cross-functional team training, continuous quality improvement and outcome studies
• Vague timelines for serving populations at risk	• Specific timelines for services for specific populations
• Funding incentives based on fees for finding and treating problems	• Funding via shared risk in promoting and maintaining health

Responding successfully to these challenges will require internal reinventions, creative affiliations, and collaborations within the larger provider community [Kiser et al. 1994]. Internally, agencies will need empowered, entrepreneurial service teams, service-driven support systems, state-of-the-art communications, and critical indicator feedback mechanisms. These and related agency innovations are discussed in this chapter and in the chapters to follow.

In the managed care sea change that is occurring in the human service industry, a rapid realignment is taking place as agencies position themselves to compete. Affiliations, joint ventures, and mergers, not unlike those that took place in corporate America in the 1980s, are the order of the day. The concept of one-stop shopping is bringing: (1) children's services providers together with adult and geriatric providers; (2) nonprofit agencies together with for-profit providers, health care firms, and public agencies; (3) large facility, bed-based organizations together with small community, office/home-based organizations; and (4) local agencies together with regional, state, and national firms.

Those who are responding to these challenges by creating new service organizations, based on success in our field and in related industries, are creating decentralized, team-based organizations with flexible, interchangeable service continuums. They are empowering staff to provide outstanding service, providing frequent staff training and consultation, and encouraging leadership at all levels. And they are serious about removing barriers. They are providing direction by maintaining a consistent focus on end products and services (for example, on short- and long-term goals and on the results to be achieved by children and families) and are using these as rallying points for quality, productivity, and achievement. [See Chapters 4 and 10 in this volume; Creech 1995; Moran 1995; Peters 1994; Seelig 1995.]

These new service and management affiliations are complex undertakings. They offer opportunities for re-thinking and re-energizing our organizations and, in turn, have the potential of improving services to the children, adults, and families in our care.

Benchmarking and Service Innovating

As we reinvent current services and support structures or develop new service and support technologies, the process of benchmarking can be very helpful.

In one approach to benchmarking,[2] cross-functional teams (including staff, payors, and consumers) carefully define the area needing improvement or development and identify the core, critical process, and service elements within that functional area. Using benchmarking to carefully examine specific program steps and processes, the team explores related best practices within the agency and examines the practices of those who are recognized as leaders within the same field of endeavor. They also analyze the procedures used by those in different fields who are dealing with similar processes and conditions. The data and insights from these surveys often provide new thinking and related improvement opportunities. As improvements or new methods are developed, they are pilot tested against measures that document progress. These step-by-step, cumulative improvements can lead to better services and supports, set the stage for more comprehensive continuous quality improvement (CQI) initiatives, and offer opportunities for new service paradigms and product innovations [McNair & Liebfield 1992; also see Chapters 6 and 7 of this book].

Product Specifications, Service Evaluations, and Outcome Studies

Drawing on the ideas and innovations gained in benchmarking, team members and other staff undertake the task of program specification. They develop specifications by writing out their program philosophy, clinical model, major program components, procedures, activities, and intended results. (See Chapter 2.) This critical process, too often neglected, provides a framework for accountability and utilization review, guidelines for staff training, standards for service, and a foundation for evaluations of services and client outcomes.

The payors of the future will expect process and outcome evaluation findings on our programs that indicate responsiveness, ease of use, and positive results. The ability to produce this kind of information will offer our agencies an enormous competitive advantage in the service world of tomorrow. (See Chapters 3, 4, and 5.)

Outcome effectiveness studies using comparison groups, multiple baseline designs, longitudinal approaches, and qualitative research methods such as intensive case studies can explore the relationship between our services and client outcomes. With careful design and multiple measures, these strategic studies are our best hope for demonstrating client improvement related to program participation. (See Chapter 5.)

Integrated Information Systems (IIS)

Quality information systems are critical to the successful operation of our service organizations. In addition to all the traditional reasons for good systems, human

---

2. *Benchmarking* comes from the Japanese word *dantotsu*, meaning striving to be the "best of the best." "Benchmarking is the continuous process of measuring products, services, and practices against the toughest competitors or those companies recognized as industry leaders" [David Kearns, CEO, Xerox Corporation, Camp 1989]. The objective is to understand existing or planned processes or activities, and then to identify an external point of reference, or standard, by which that activity can be measured or judged. A benchmark can be established at any level in the agency, in any functional area. The ultimate goal is quite simple: to be better than the best [McNair & Liebfield 1992].

service organizations face significant new information demands in today's world. Today's reasons include the advent of managed care, with multiple payors each requesting different client service and billing information; the reduction in organizational layers and major increases in the ratio of workers to supervisors, which requires that staff teams and management be able to tap a central computerized database; and the growing expectation that we will produce reliable, timely service evaluation and outcome information.

To meet these challenges, we need information systems with modular, integrated, relational databases that are designed to move information within and outside the organization in formats that are individualized for the end user [Clarke & Santos 1992; see also Chapter 9.] Staff at all levels need to participate in decisions about what data and critical indicators are needed, assume ownership of the data, and take responsibility for direct data entry. Staff and management, including the CEO, need training in the value and use of critical indicator reporting to successfully manage their growing areas of responsibility. The traditional barriers between the information system and the service staff need to come down in the interests of learning, system development, and maintenance of data integrity.

The rise of technology is an overall environmental factor that will greatly affect the future, although it cannot be addressed in great detail here. For example, will telecommunicating and laptops reduce the need for large office structures? Will counseling via image phones transform some programs? [Personal Communication, James Traglia, May 2, 1995]

Organizational Leadership

Leading the agencies of tomorrow will indeed be challenging. The very structure of our organizations will change—for some agencies, in a dramatic manner. A recent review by Peters [1994] of three emerging models in business and manufacturing provides a glimpse of some possibilities for social service organizations:

1. *Horizontal Models.* In the "horizontal agency," previously separate functional activities are seamlessly linked to provide an uninterrupted flow of production or service. A few key processes (perhaps product development and service delivery) subsume virtually all the previously independent departments (operations, professional development, marketing, finance) and define the agency. Many of the current re-engineering efforts support this model.

2. *Network Models.* The next step beyond the horizontal models creates new ways of linking all agency staff and external partners. These new organizations consist of bits and pieces of various agencies, plus an array of outside consulting firms and contract professionals who gather for limited periods to provide packages of services. They are seamlessly imbedded in larger, hierarchy-free, electronically knit networks. Virtual, modular, and "spider's web" types of organizations fall under this heading.

3. *Self-Designing Models.* This new approach to product development has been dubbed the "rugby scrum" (all tangled at once) or the improvisational theater or jazz combo model. The key is perpetual redesign, not necessarily (or even likely) initiated from above.

In their recent work, Belasco and Stayer [1994] discuss leading the transformational journey by: (1) determining focus and direction; (2) removing the obstacles; (3) developing ownership; and (4) stimulating self-directed action.

This journey will require shifting from our role as managers directing the actions of staff members to a role as leaders helping to establish and ensure the smooth functioning of processes [Davidow & Malone 1992].

Teams will become the primary performance units of our agencies, and will help us meet the growing need for improved service productivity, quality, and responsiveness [Manz & Sims 1993; Reich 1987]. In a recent survey of effective teams, focus on working well as a team and emphasis on key performance areas were inextricably connected. The truly committed team was found to be the most productive performance unit available to management—provided there are specific results for which the team is collectively responsible, and provided the performance ethic of the company demands those results [Katzenbach & Smith 1993].

The self-managing teams that emerged in "quality" manufacturing environments during the 1980s will be common in successful service agencies in the 1990s. Cross-functional teams, which bring staff from diverse functions and parts of the agency, customers, and key stakeholders will design, deliver, and evaluate new service products together [Sashkin & Sashkin 1994]. Skills in meeting management and project leadership will also be critical in this new team-based agency environment [Doyle & Strauss 1982; Shawnee Hills 1993].

A third fundamental shift will be our need as leaders to focus on learning, both during the change process and as a continuous way of life within the organization [Senge 1990]. Learning while doing, through the process of feedback and replanning, is essential for significant change and for the long-term viability of our organizations. The development of policies, procedures, and rewards that place equal value on learning and innovation *and* doing and results may be our most important instrument to assure that learning and change take place [Beckhard & Pritchard 1992]. As we develop measures and continuous feedback mechanisms to monitor and learn from our change activities, we will also need to study how change occurs in process improvements and in actual outcomes. The former might be overlooked in our new emphasis upon outcomes.

Attention to ourselves as learners will be our foundation for successfully developing a learning culture and a learning organization. Maintaining a healthy disrespect for the impossible, learning to work differently from the norm, nurturing our opportunities to learn from living, remaining open to new ideas and feedback, and developing a "learn for living rather than work for living" attitude are all important to maintaining our vitality as agency leaders who are constant learners [Rapp & Poertner 1992; Gowdy & Rapp 1989].

Quality Initiatives

The "quality movement" is fundamental to our success in the future. If we don't have the components of excellence—benchmarking, statistical process control to monitor quality, continuous quality improvement, the constant pursuit of excellence, striving for the capability to do the right thing right the first time—then we won't even be able to play the game in the twenty-first century [Barker 1992]. [3]

Fortunately, progressive child welfare and health care organizations have begun to move beyond traditional quality assurance approaches (such as focusing on detecting and then retroactively correcting problems in the service delivery process) toward adopting continuous quality improvement (CQI) and total quality management (TQM) programs [See Chapters 6-9 of this book; Joint Commission on the Accreditation of Health Care Organizations 1991; Schyve & Prevost 1990; Seelig 1995; Vermillion & Pfeiffer 1993].

Continuous Quality Improvement

In the future our agencies will need to move beyond the bottom line and break-through thinking typical of western companies and cultures. Embracing the concepts developed by Deming [1986] and termed *kaizen* by the Japanese, we will begin taking the longer view, believing the best way to achieve results is to perfect the processes upon which they are based [See Chapters 6 and 7 of this book and Imai 1986]. Successful American businesses and social service organizations are adopting quality improvement (QI) or continuous quality improvement (CQI) efforts that emphasize the pursuit of improvements in service delivery and outcome as a never-ending process. "If you are not getting better, you are getting worse."

This approach calls for involving consumers in program planning, case planning, and case review, as well as convening QI teams and training permanent work teams to study the processes inherent in day-to-day operations. This study of the ways of doing things is at the heart of QI. QI-oriented leaders, however, are cognizant of the time and effort these studies take, and are careful to screen each opportunity for its potential for significant improvement in customer satisfaction or efficiency [Visions 1993].

The "Plan, Do, Check, Act" (PDCA) concept will be central to many of our CQI efforts. These four basic ideas are enormously helpful in beginning a quality improvement program in a service organization (see Figure 1.4). *Plan* involves the beginning and early stages, where you look at the end product and visualize the results you desire. *Do* involves implementing the plan on a small scale or a trial basis. *Check* is the opportunity to review actual results in comparison to the original vision. *Act* is the decision point for full-scale implementation should results match expectations. If the original goals are not met, a new round of planning is undertaken. In fact, in industry, the successful completion of the Act phase usually leads directly to the next Plan to improve the Act, which begins the next iteration of the cycle.

This PDCA cycle is a building block for other important quality tools, such as the Problem-Solving Model and the Nine-Step Quality Improvement Process. QI-oriented administrators make widespread use of statistical tools like check sheets,

---

3. For the purposes of this chapter we are using the following definitions: **Quality**—Meeting or exceeding customer expectations at a cost that represents value to them [Harrington, in Shawnee Hills 1993]; **Continuous Quality Improvement (CQI)**—a systematic, organizationwide approach for continually improving all processes that deliver quality products and services [Brassard & Ritter 1994]; **Total Quality Management (TQM)**—a customer-focused leadership system that creates and sustains a culture of continuous improvement and total involvement [Shawnee Hills 1993]; and **Quality Improvement (QI)**—a general term referring to an integrated set of actions designed to achieve high quality through CQI and TQM.

Figure 1.4

The Quality Improvement Cycle
Plan, Do, Check, Act

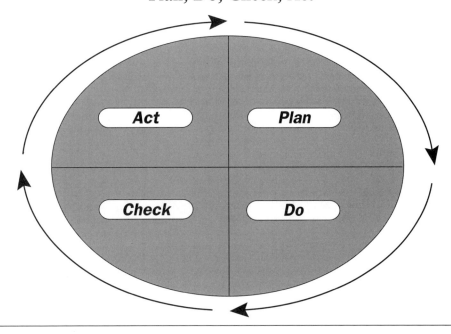

run charts, scatter diagrams, histograms, Pareto diagrams, and control charts. In some organizations these can be found in offices, conference rooms, classrooms, the rooms of children and adolescents in residence, and the family homes of children in care. [For examples of these methods see Chapters 6 and 7 of this book and Joint Commission on the Accreditation of Healthcare Organizations 1992.]

What is required is a total agency emphasis on continuous improvement, with a focus on small, incremental steps, and the relentless pursuit of goals for extended periods of time [Davidow & Malone 1992]. It may be this concept that has most differentiated Japanese from American industry during the last 40 years. The Japanese industrial culture believes that no improvement is too small to make. In contrast, many American industrial organizations have focused on achieving giant improvements, with often relatively long periods of time between innovations.

The students at Mount Edgecumbe High School in Sitka, Alaska, provide us with an encouraging example of QI in action at the consumer level. These 200 students come from all over Alaska, about 90% from rural areas. The majority of them have families with serious social problems, including alcoholism or abuse of some kind. As Native Americans, they have deep ties to their heritage, and struggle to maintain the traditional values and pride while adjusting to another language and to the different cultures of the larger world. Assisted by their teacher, David Langford, they used Continuous Process Improvement (their term) to prepare for and argue at a student-faculty assembly on the need for dormitory rule changes. The presentation was built around QI, and factual information was gathered by using selected concepts from the Deming [1986] method of QI. Faculty and administration were won over by the students' enthusiasm and the quality of their ideas.

From this beginning the school dorm has been improved, class schedules have been rewritten, and the traditional grading system has been replaced. Students trained in statistics track their own performance, using "grade calcs." Curriculums and school administrative policies were similarly affected. One student says "It's made people work harder, and I think it's practically done a miracle in this (English) class." Another adds, "Really, it smokes!" [Dobyns & Crawford-Mason 1991, pp. 221-224].

Thus, while QI is not a panacea, it will provide approaches to problem-solving, analytical tools, significant data, and other supports for implementing many of the components of success discussed in this chapter and in the remainder of this book.

Total Quality Management

The quality movement is also transforming management within our agencies. It brings a customer-focused leadership system that creates and sustains a culture of continuous improvement and total involvement [Shawnee Hills 1993]. A QI or TQM approach brings a passionate commitment to customer success and organizational survival [Clemmer 1992]. It also brings a passionate approach to supporting frontline staff and explains the need to involve them, and customers, in all phases of product (program) development.

Deming, one of the early innovators of TQM and the quality movement, approached the subject from both scientific and humanistic perspectives. He applied a variety of statistical approaches to quality improvement while maintaining an emphasis on supporting employees through substantive involvement in design, production, and refinement [Walton 1986]. Significantly, Deming stressed that TQM must start at the top of the organization. He argued that most TQM efforts failed because the whole effort was initiated by or implemented by middle management without the full and complete buy-in of senior management [Personal Communication, A. Chris Downs, May 2 1995]. Deming's classic 14 Points to TQM will be helpful to aspiring programs that seek guidelines for measuring their overall progress toward total quality involvement [Deming 1986][4].

In a recent seminal work on the comprehensive application of TQM by leading companies, Creech [1994] described five dynamic interrelated variables or pillars of success. (See Figure 1.5.) In this model the *Organization* has a decentralized, team-based, quality-oriented management system and structure. The *Product* provides the focal point for the team and the organization. This product mindset is a "pivot point" for quality, productivity, and all the other TQM ingredients.

---

4.   Deming's 14 points are as follows: (1) Create constancy of purpose for the improvement of products and services; (2) Adopt the new philosophy; (3) Cease dependence on inspection to achieve quality; (4) End the business of rewarding business on the basis of price tag alone; (5) Improve constantly and forever the system of production and service; (6) Institute on-the-job training; (7) Institute leadership; (8) Drive out fear; (9) Break down barriers between departments; (10) Eliminate slogans, exhortations, and numerical targets; (11) Eliminate work standards (quotas) and management by objective; (12) Remove barriers to pride of workmanship; (13) Institute a vigorous program of education and self-improvement; and (14) Put everyone in the organization to work to accomplish the transformation [Deming 1986].

Figure 1.5

The Five Pillars of TQM

Source: Adapted from Creech, W. (1994). *The five pillars of TQM: How to make total quality management work for you.* New York: Truman Tally Books.

The *Process* pillar is the series of progressive and interdependent steps by which the end is attained. Process improvement steps and measures of effectiveness are included.

The *Leadership* pillar supports involvement, empowerment, and cultural shifts that bring leadership alive at all levels. Leaders are highly involved in developing working teams, promoting leadership thinking, and creatively involving everyone. They are not involved in micromanagement. *Commitment*, the degree of employee commitment to its ideals and goals, is the heart of the organization. Inclusion of frontline workers in the business of the broader organization is critical here.

In their work with service companies, Clemmer and Sheehy [1992] have adapted TQM concepts to build high performance service systems, similar to our child and family service organizations of tomorrow. Prior research had shown that 85% of quality problems lie not in workers per se but in entrenched organizational practices. In response, they list tasks that agencies will need to accomplish if their organizations are to achieve and sustain ever higher levels of service and quality, including:

- Organizations must continuously monitor the changing needs of external customers and use their priorities to establish service/quality objectives and indicators for success.

- Senior executives must *visibly* and *actively* lead the cultural change process and the continuous improvement journey. This starts with the senior management team being able to answer these questions *in unison:* (1) What business are we in (our strategic niche)? (2) What do we believe in (the values that will guide everyone's behavior)? (3) Where are we going (the vision of our *preferred* future)?

- Management and staff support groups at all levels need to begin serving the frontline producers, deliverers, and supporters of the organization's basic products and services. In turning our organizations upside down, our management and staff groups need to establish a system of continual data collection and feedback for the service they are providing. This activity needs to be tied to their compensation.

- The organization needs to provide all staff with a thorough introduction to the following concepts: why service/quality is critical; how to define service/quality for the organization and the team; how service, quality, productivity, and cost relate; the deep implications of the 85/15 rule; what the organization, teams, and team members personally need to do and in what order to maximize quality; and what tools, techniques, and skills must be developed—and why.

- Continuous learning must become entrenched at all organizational levels.

- All our organizational systems (financial, human resource, planning, and so on) and structures must be aligned to serve customer and front-line team needs ahead of serving management.

- Everyone at all levels, throughout our organizations, needs to be an active and contributing member to his or her work team and process improvement and/or project teams. Leaders need to assume ownership and operational responsibility for product development, marketing, administration, and other key processes, while delegating the management of the work to teams closest to the action.

- Our sales, marketing, or public relations strategies need to be aligned continually to move our organization closer to our strategy niches. [Clemmer & Sheehy, pp. 97–98].

These efforts can succeed. In 1987 a national demonstration project on quality improvement in health care paired industrial quality experts with groups from 21 health care providers. The results were impressive. One by one the teams reported simple, elegant stories of successful applications of the basic tools. These stories illuminated processes and revealed causes of unnecessary service variation that lowered agency effectiveness. New insights into old and familiar problems resulted [Berwick 1990]. While quality will only be one part of the total management/service equation, it will be a critical building block to success in other areas. For agencies that have begun or are about to begin QI programs, Appendix A offers a summary of critical implementation issues.

Conclusion

For those of us in the business of serving children and families, the future is replete with challenges and opportunities. In this chapter we have attempted to stand back from our day-to-day work to examine the future for child and family serving agencies. We explored the growing list of challenges our clients are facing and the many new demands that will be made by current and future customers. We attempted to identify the key components of the "virtual agency" of tomorrow, one that will be able to provide timely, high quality, and cost-effective services with demonstrated positive outcomes and customer satisfaction. We also discussed agency reinvention strategies, and reviewed methods to focus our organizations; techniques to grapple with product, customer service, and organizational imperatives; and examples to assist in developing successful quality initiatives. We drew on the experience of both for-profit organizations and our nonprofit peers. We attempted to cover the waterfront of challenges and invited our readers to explore a series of interrelated strategies for turning those challenges into winning opportunities for the children and families they served and their payors, staff members, and volunteers.

The chapters that follow provide practical, user-friendly applications of many of these strategic ingredients for successful change. The next chapter helps agencies define their customers and specify the programs and services that they provide. This process is a critical building block to future evaluation efforts and continuous quality improvement processes.

References

Albrecht, K, (1994). *The northbound train: Finding the purpose, setting the direction, and shaping the destiny of your organization.* New York: Amoco.

Barker, J. (1993). *Paradigms: The business of discovering the future.* New York: Harper Collins.

Beckhard, R., & Pritchard, W. (1992). *Changing the essence: The art of creating and leading fundamental change in organizations.* San Francisco: Jossey-Bass.

Belasco, J., & Stayer, R. (1993). *Flight of the buffalo: Soaring to excellence, learning to let the employee lead.* New York: Warner Books.

Berwick, D. (1990). *Curing health care: New strategies for quality improvement.* San Francisco: Jossey-Bass.

Brassard, M., & Ritter, D. (1994). *The memory jogger II: A pocket guide of tools for continuous improvement & effective planning.* Methuen, MA: Goal/QPC.

Bridges, W. (1993). *Managing transitions: Making the most of change.* Reading, MA: Addison-Wesley.

Camp, R. (1989). *Benchmarking: The search for industry best practices that lead to superior performance.* Milwaukee: Quality Press, p. 10.

Children's Bureau of Southern California. (1992). Principle-based practice [Mimeograph]. Los Angeles, CA: Author.

Clarke, R., & Santos, N. (1992). Management information systems for community mental health settings, *R & E: Research and Evaluation in Group Care, 2,* 14-18.

Clemmer, J. (1992) *Firing on all cylinders: The service/quality system for high-powered corporate performance.* Homewood, IL: Business One Irwin.

Creech, W. (1994) *The five pillars of TQM: How to make total quality management work for you.* New York: Truman Talley Books.

Davidow, W., & Malone, M. (1992). *The virtual corporation: Lessons from the world's advanced companies.* New York: Harper Business.

Deming, W. E. (1986). *Out of the crisis.* Cambridge, MA: Massachusetts Institute of Technology Center for Advanced Engineering Study.

Dobyns, L., & Crawford-Mason, C. (1991). *Quality or else: The revolution in world business.* Boston: Houghton Mifflin.

Doyle, M., & Straus, D. (1982). How to make meetings work: *The new interaction method*. New York: Jove Books.

Doyle, M. (1992). Visioning, reinvention consultations. Michael Doyle & Associates, San Francisco, CA.

Eastfield Ming Quong. (1993). Values Constitution [Mimeograph]. Campbell, CA: Author.

Gowdy, E., & Rapp, C. A. (1989). Managerial behavior: The common denominator of effective community-based programs. *Psychosocial Rehabilitation Journal, 13* (2), 31-51.

Haas, G. (1992). *The leader within: An empowering path of self-discovery.* New York: Harper Collins.

Joint Commission on Accreditation of Healthcare Organizations. (1991). *The transition from QA to CQI: An introduction to quality improvement in health care.* Oakbrook Terrace, IL: Author.

Joint Commission on Accreditation of Healthcare Organizations. (1992). *The transition from QA to CQI: Performance-based evaluation of mental health organizations.* Oakbrook Terrace, IL: Author.

Katzenbach, J. R., & Smith, D. K. (1993) *The wisdom of teams: Creating the high-performance organization.* New York: Harper Business, pp. 43-64.

Kearns, D. (1989). Benchmarking. In Camp, R., *Benchmarking: The search for industry best practices that lead to superior performance.* Milwaukee: Quality Press.

Kiser, L., Moran, M., Seelig, W., & Gruppo, A. (1994). Establishing a successful continuum of ambulatory mental health services (Core Seminar). American Association for Partial Hospitalization.

LeRoy Haynes Center for Child and Family Services. (1994). Agency values and norms {Mimeograph]. LaVerne, CA: Author.

Manz, C. C., & Sims, H. P. (1993). *Business without bosses: How self-managing teams are building high-performing companies.* New York: John Wiley & Sons, pp. 1-22.

McNair, C. & Leibfield, K. (1992). *Benchmarking: A tool for continuous improvement.* New York: Harper Collins.

Monack, D. (1994) Themes identified—Leadership challenges and crossroads. *Focus (Newsletter of the Foster Family-based Treatment Association), 3*(2), 6,11. New York: The Foster Family-based Treatment Association.

Moran, M. (1994). Choate Health Systems: The interchangeable system of care (Training Outline). Woburn, MA: Choate.

Peters, T. (1994). *The Tom Peters seminar: Crazy times call for crazy organizations.* New York: Vintage Books.

Peters, T. Organizational models show shape of business is changing. *San Jose Mercury News* (March 14 1993).

Rapp, C. A., & Poertner, J. (1992). *Social administration: A client-centered approach.* New York: Longman Inc., pp. 1-28.

Ray, C. (1992). *Futures consultation.* National Council for Community Mental Health, Washington, DC.

Reich, R. (1987, May-June). Entrepreneurship reconsidered: The team as hero. *Harvard Business Review.*

Sashkin, M., & Sashkin, M. (1994) *The new teamwork: Developing and using cross-function teams.* New York: AMA Publications.

Schwartz, P. (1991). *The art of the long view: Planning for the future in an uncertain world.* New York: Doubleday.

Schyve, P. M., & Prevost, J. A. (1990). *From quality assurance to quality improvement.* Psychiatric Clinics of North America, 13, 61-71.

Senge, P. (1990) *The fifth discipline: The art and practice of the learning organization.* New York: Doubleday.

Shawnee Hills. (1993). *Total quality management training guide.* Charleston, West Virginia: Shawnee Hills Total Quality Training Center.

Shawnee Hills. (1993). *Visions team handbook.* Charleston, WV: Shawnee Hills Total Quality Training Center.

Vermillion, J. M., & Pfeiffer, S. I. (1993). Treatment outcome and continuous quality improvement: Two aspects of program evaluation. *The Psychiatric Hospital, 24.*

Walton, M. (1986). *The Deming management method.* New York: Dodd, Mead & Company.

For Further Information

Belasco, J. & Stayer, R. (1993). *The flight of the buffalo*. New York: Warner Books. A personal book of expertise, insight, and passion. The authors offer practical strategies and examples for agency leaders who want to create an atmosphere of quality, customer satisfaction, and business success.

Creech, W. (1994). *The five pillars of TQM: How to make total quality management work for you*. New York: Truman Talley Books. Provides a comprehensive approach and a set of well documented strategies for implementing a successful total quality management program. Written by someone who succeeded where others have failed.

Davidow, W., & Malone, M. (1992). *The virtual corporation* A fascinating book that integrates current product development, customer service, and management concepts into successful business (and agency) standards for our fast approaching future.

Deming, W. E. (1986). *Out of the crisis*. Cambridge, MA: Massachusetts Institute of Technology Center for Advanced Engineering Study. This book outlines the major concepts of QI as developed by one of the eminent pioneers in the field.

Joint Commission on Accreditation of Healthcare Organizations. (1991). *The transition from QA to CQI: An introduction to quality improvement in health care*. Oakbrook Terrace, IL: Author. An extremely clear synopsis of essential QI concepts and some of the implications for health care and social service organizations.

Selected Quality Improvement Implementation Issues

Peter J. Pecora and William R. Seelig

Several issues related to the implementation of the Quality Improvement (QI) methods need to be monitored and analyzed early in the implementation process to provide either early warnings or confirmation that the design and implementation process is on track. First, QI planning and implementation teams would be wise to compare how their intended or operating QI systems promote some of the attributes of managerial and organizational excellence discussed in Chapter 1.

A number of earnest QI efforts have been unsuccessful, casting doubt on the viability and value of this approach to management and organizational functioning. The following sections present specific examples of the implementation issues related to QI that should concern agency staff. This is by no means an exhaustive discussion, but is intended to provide some practical cautionary notes to consider as readers learn about the application of QI methods.

Adherence to Central Organizational Philosophy and Values

As a QI effort is planned and implemented, you need to determine if and how the effort supports or undermines key elements of the organization's vision, mission, philosophy, and core values. For example, a new or renewed emphasis on consumer satisfaction should not be allowed to interfere with essential child advocacy efforts, even if certain "customers" (such as referral agencies) or consumers (such as biological parents) are angered by valid staff efforts to protect children from harmful actions by their parents. To use another QI principle as an example, a focus on cost effectiveness should not be pursued to such a degree that families are not receiving necessary services. A balance of rigor and customer needs must be maintained.

Involvement of Consumers and All Levels of Staff

One of the keys to success in quality improvement efforts is the involvement of consumers, board members, administrators, supervisors, and line staff in designing, implementing, and monitoring programs. For example, consumer and staff feedback is critical for helping to identify areas needing service improvement and strategies for program refinement. Without meaningful involvement of a variety of stakeholders, change efforts are likely to be blocked, hampered, or neutralized.

Method Integrity

It is important to know whether QI methods and new service delivery models are being implemented as originally designed or unauthorized variations are occurring. Program implementation experts and program evaluators have coined the term *model drift* for the process by which an original design becomes muddled over time in unplanned and unregulated ways.

Balance between Program Process and Outcome

To what degree is the focus of the QI effort on analyzing and refining internal service delivery processes, such as errors in service planning or provision, rather than on examining the results of the service? The child welfare field cannot afford to support programs that efficiently deliver an ineffective service.

Balance between Internal Agency Needs and the External Agency Environment

Child welfare agencies operate in turbulent, constantly changing organizational environments with shifting client needs. QI efforts should be monitored to be sure that the agency focus has not shifted too greatly toward improving internal processes to the neglect of new consumer needs. Harari [1993, p. 33] quotes a manager who experienced this situation: "Before we invested in Total Quality Management, the rap on our company was that we churn out poorly made products that customers don't want. Now, after Total Quality Management, things have changed. We now churn out well-made products that customers don't want."

Bureaucracy and Paperwork

Administrators must consider the degree to which the QI effort is creating new layers of agency bureaucracy and/or burdensome new paperwork demands. The Peters and Waterman [1983] concept of "lean form" would underlie this enquiry. Staff support can be quickly undermined by the development of elaborate committee structures and unnecessary service delivery checklists and reports.

Staff Compensation

Another issue is to what extent service quality is tied to staff compensation and merit pay. While staff may find QI efforts intrinsically rewarding because of increased effectiveness and higher consumer satisfaction, it may also be helpful to tie compensation to the success of implementation efforts. (There are those, however, who feel that most financially based personnel incentive plans are not effective motivators. See, for example, Kohn [1993].) From another perspective, defining staff competencies as a foundation for employee recruitment, training, supervision, and performance appraisal can be a vehicle for emphasizing worker actions that support a QI approach [Personal Communication, Barbara Miller, May 12, 1995].

Focus on Excellence

What usually distinguishes truly effective child welfare agencies is a focus on service excellence rather than on meeting certain minimum contract or accreditation standards. Agencies must consider the extent to which the QI effort helps the organization develop and deliver innovative services that are responsive to consumer needs.

Development of Cross-Functional Teams

As with other types of organizations that operate in competitive and turbulent environments, organizational responsiveness is partially dependent on the ability of the staff to work across department and discipline lines (the breakdown of "functional foxholes," as discussed in Harari [1993, p. 35]. The frequency and ease of working in cross-departmental or matrix management teams should be examined. Staff efforts at service refinement may be hampered by departmental lines of authority and/or lack of interdepartmental communication and cooperation.

Consumer Satisfaction and Complaints

Agencies need to address the extent to which the QI effort has resulted in a decrease in customer complaints or a change in the nature of these complaints. For example, do consumers voice fewer complaints about intake staff? Do they feel that their most important concerns are being met, and that staff members are accessible by phone? It is imperative to be obsessed with customer satisfaction [Peters 1994].

Service Outcomes

With a successful QI approach, organizational effectiveness in one or more areas should improve. One challenge of the program implementation effort is to be specific about the expected changes and to design an evaluation that is able to determine whether or not the desired results are obtained. This design should also differentiate, to the extent possible, between quality-driven improvements in organizational functioning and other sources of organizational change.

Relationships with Allied Agencies

Child welfare agencies interact with a variety of other agencies for client referrals, ancillary services, and follow-up support for families and children. The extent of change in the working relationships with these agencies as a result of the program emphasis on quality and customer satisfaction should be assessed.

Summary

Selected implementation issues for QI efforts in child and family services were described, with an emphasis on determining if the QI efforts are having the intended effects in key areas such as service delivery quality, staff functioning and morale, increased outcome effectiveness, and higher consumer satisfaction. These areas must be high priorities for planning and monitoring.

References

Harari, O. (1993, January). Ten reasons why TQM doesn't work. *Management Review,* 33-38.

Kohn, A. (1993). Why incentive plans cannot work. *Harvard Business Review, 71* (5), 54-63.

Peters, T. J., & Waterman, R. H. (1982). *In search of excellence: Lessons from America's best run companies.* New York: Harper & Row.

Peters, T. J. (1994) *The Tom Peters seminar: Crazy times call for crazy organizations.* New York: Vintage Books.

Section II: Defining Your Services

Chapter 2

How Do We Propose to Help Children and Families?

Sue Ann Savas

Introduction

Before an agency can effectively develop or refine services that meet the needs of clients, program staff must first identify whom they are serving, what these clients' needs are, and how the program will meet their needs. Program specification is the first step in the process of providing appropriate, effective services and evaluating your program. The program specification process is part of being customer oriented (defining who your internal and external customers are) and outcome based (defining what you want to accomplish). This process includes defining the target population, program activities, and expected client gains (see Figure 2.1). These elements will become the foundation for the design of an evaluation plan. Program staff participating in the specification of the program and the design of the evaluation will gain an improved understanding of why they are providing a service and why they need to track certain activities. Chapters 3 and 5 will specifically describe how to design process and outcome evaluations.

This chapter will describe how to specify your program and what can be gained from the process.* The specification process is recommended for new and existing programs. Often the staff of new programs are so busy with program startup that they don't take the time to clearly describe the target population and the intent of the program. Within existing programs, changes in staff and unplanned adjustments to the intervention model over time may result in a program that

---

* The program specification process described in this chapter draws from Boysville of Michigan's experience in applying concepts developed by Chen and Rossi [1989] and Wholey [1979]. Special thanks to Boysville of Michigan, the members of the Program Development Department, Laura Lee for her feedback, and Steve Kapp for initiating the process.

Figure 2.1

Evaluation and Program Improvement Process

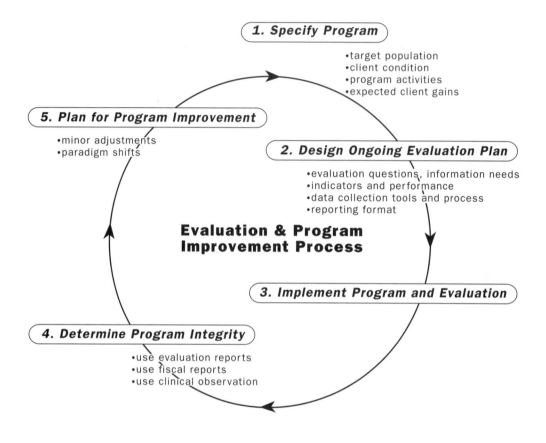

1. Specify Program
- target population
- client condition
- program activities
- expected client gains

5. Plan for Program Improvement
- minor adjustments
- paradigm shifts

2. Design Ongoing Evaluation Plan
- evaluation questions, information needs
- indicators and performance
- data collection tools and process
- reporting format

Evaluation & Program Improvement Process

3. Implement Program and Evaluation

4. Determine Program Integrity
- use evaluation reports
- use fiscal reports
- use clinical observation

no two staff members could describe in the same way. This program specification process can be completed without the help of external consultants. The time spent specifying the program will be worth the investment.

By comparing the intended program model with actual program functioning, staff members gain what they need to determine program integrity. To answer the question: Are we providing the service we promised?, staff should refer to policies, operational guidelines, evaluation results, fiscal information, and their own observations. Armed with this information, staff members can identify factors that may promote or obstruct implementation efforts and develop action plans to improve specific program areas. Program improvements could be minor adjustments, such as changing the content in a psycho-educational multifamily group to include developmental issues specific to adolescence. In contrast, major program improvements generally involve paradigm shifts. For example, paradigm shifts are required when agency values shift from serving youths in residential settings to serving youths and their families within their communities.

The program specification process is based on the following assumptions:

- Program designs are best implemented when they are grounded in theory and/or in empirical evidence that the intervention approach can be effective.

- Program staff can best implement a service when all of its components, activities, values, beliefs, and assumptions are documented and clearly identified.

- Program staff must be collaboratively engaged in all program specification and evaluation processes if these activities are to be effective.

- A flexible program specification process is most effective when it is designed to meet the work styles of the participants.

Rationale for the Program Specification Process

Programs are increasingly asked to produce data that substantiates the appropriateness and effectiveness of their services. Information about program efforts, such as family contacts, is tallied to demonstrate that the service was delivered as promised. Performance indicators, such as the percentage of youths living a legal lifestyle after release from a residential program, are monitored and used to determine which program is qualified to provide services in the future. Agencies in a position to produce these data and use the information to improve the quality of service will have a competitive advantage. These agencies can demonstrate their accountability and cost-effectiveness. The program specification process will enable agencies to appropriately use the type of evaluation approaches that work best for them (see Figure 2.2). Agencies that use the program specification process described in this chapter will be closer to the competitive edge because they have:

- a description of the target population, including the client or system conditions that led to the need for the program;

- clearly defined program components and activities (what the program is promising to do with the clients);

- a description (in measurable terms) of what clients will gain after successfully completing the program; and

- an explanation of why staff believe this service will lead to client gains (the theory behind the program model).

Steps toward Program Specification

The program specification process is flexible, and can be adjusted to meet the work styles of the participants. As diagrammed in Figure 2.3, there are four basic steps to follow in specifying programs.

Figure 2.2

Summary of the Five-Tiered Approach to Program Evaluation

Evaluation Level	Title of Evaluation Tier	Purpose of Evaluation	Audiences
Level 1	*Pre-implementation tier*	1. To document the need for a particular program within community 2. To demonstrate the fit between community needs and proposed program 3. To provide "data groundwork"	1. Potential funders 2. Community/ citizen groups
Level 2	*Accountability tier*	1. To document program's a. utilization b. entrenchment c. penetration into target population 2. To justify current expenditures 3. To increase expenditures 4. To build a constituency	1. Funders, donors 2. Community leaders, media
Level 3	*Program clarification tier*	1. To provide information to program staff to improve the program	1. Program staff 2. Program participants
Level 4	*Progress toward objectives tier*	1. To provide information to staff to improve program 2. To document program effectiveness	1. Staff members 2. Program participants 3. Funders 4. Other programs
Level 5	*Program impact tier*	1. To contribute to knowledge development in the substantive fields of child development, family process, and organizational theory and/ or to the refinement of evaluation practices 2. To produce evidence of differential effectiveness among alternative program approaches 3. To suggest program models worthy of replication	1. Academic and research 2. Policymakers at federal, state, and local levels 3. General public, through the media 4. Potential program directors and funders

Tasks	Types of data to be collected/analyzed
1. Detail basic characteristics of proposed program 2. Conduct community needs assessment to support establishment of such program 3. Revise proposed program to coordinate with assessed needs	1. Locally generated statistics that describe populations and needs for service (including public/personal costs of not providing the program) 2. Interviews with community leaders on seriousness of problem 3. Interviews or survey data from prospective participants

1. Accurately describe program participants and services provided
 	
2. Provide accurate cost information per unit of service
	1. Client-specific monitoring data
	
	2. Service-specific monitoring data
	
	3. Case material
	    a. Data from interviews with clients indicating clients' needs and responses
	    b. Community (nonuser) reactions to program

1. Question basic program assumptions: what kinds of services for whom and by whom? 2. Clarify and restate program's mission, goals, objectives, and strategies	1. Content of staff meetings, supervision sessions, interviews with staff 2. Observation by staff of program activities and staff process 3. Previously collected staff and service data 4. Interview data from parents on desired benefits of program 5. Client satisfaction information
1. Examine outcome (short-term) objectives 2. Derive measurable indicators of success for a majority of the outcome objectives 3. Decide on data analysis procedures 4. Assess differential effectiveness among individual clients 5. Assess community awareness among individual clients	1. Interview material regarding individual client's progress toward objectives 2. Standardized test scores for clients, where applicable 3. Client-specific information from criterion-referenced instruments 4. Client satisfaction data 5. Evidence of support for/resistance to program in community
1. Delineate specific impact objectives that are to be achieved, presumably through success in achieving short-term objectives 2. Identify measure(s) that can assess enduring and/or lifestyle changes among participants 3. Develop evaluation plan that reflects common understandings among evaluator(s), program personnel, and contractor (if outside program)	1. Quantifiable client-specific data, including standardized test results collected over time (longitudinal client data) 2. Control group data or comparison group standards 3. Qualitative client data, including record reviews, client interviews, etc. 4. Cost-effectiveness information, necessary for planning program replication

Source: Jacobs, F. H. (1988). The five-tiered approach to evaluation: Context and implementation. In H.B. Weiss and F.H. Jacobs (Eds.). *Evaluating family programs,* pp. 52-55. Hawthorne, NY: Aldine de Gruyter. Reprinted with permission.

Figure 2.3

Steps Toward Program Specification

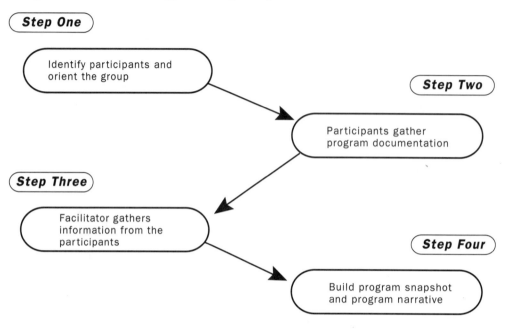

Step One
- Identify participants and orient the group

Step Two
- Participants gather program documentation

Step Three
- Facilitator gathers information from the participants

Step Four
- Build program snapshot and program narrative

Step 1
Identify who will participate in the program specification process.

Participants often include program staff, clients, managers, evaluators, and funders. A team facilitator is needed to manage the process, document the responses, and make sure that everyone is heard. A team facilitator who has little experience with the program is often in the best position to ensure that the program is described completely and clearly. Once participants are identified, they need an orientation to the process. This orientation should include the purpose of the project, roles and responsibilities of the participants, meeting times, and the establishment of group norms.

Step 2
Gather existing program documentation, such as licensing rules and regulations, COA standards, and copies of the contract, budget, and staffing pattern.

If it is accessible, recent client profile, service, and outcome data should be generated for this process. Also, participants should initiate a brief literature review and discussions with other agencies to identify best-of-the-best treatment approaches and program models that have worked before with this population. This process is called benchmarking (see Chapter 1). Participants will need to identify factors, both theoretical and empirically based, that contribute to client gain. All of this information should be organized into a reference notebook for easy access and for the historical record.

Figure 2.4

Interview Guide: Summary of Questions Used to Complete the Program Snapshot

Client and System Conditions	Major Program Components	Program Processes or Activities	Immediate Client Outcomes	Long-Term Client Impacts
1.1 Why are these clients in need of the service?	2.1 What will the program offer to whom?	3. 1 What program activities will occur within each major program component?	4.1 What will the clients gain when the services are terminated?	5.1 What long term changes or impacts do we expect to see with the clients?
1.2 What system conditions will the program address?	2.2 When?	3.2 What will we see when the activity was completed successfully?	4.2 What will a "successful" client look like at the end of the program?	5.2 What do we mean by *long term*?
	2.3 For how long?			5.3 What did the clients gain that was unexpected?

Step 3

Develop a series of questions to help the team with the specification process and the development of a program snapshot.

The major components of the program snapshot (a one-page summary diagram) are listed in Figure 2.4, along with some key questions. Detailed suggestions for these interviews are given later in this chapter. The facilitator directs the interview process, which is similar to that of a focus group. The answers to the questions will lead to the development of the program snapshot and narrative. Because the process is intense, half days tend to be more productive than full–day sessions.

Step 4

Draft a program snapshot and a program narrative that will be reviewed and approved by the team and by agency administration.

The facilitator will use the team's answers to prepare this draft. It is important to make sure that the final product represents what was actually said: to work towards a *complete* picture of the program rather than a neat but overly simplistic picture. The format in Figure 2.4 is recommended. Program specification participants have reported that this format is effective in describing the program on one page. The program narrative is a more detailed description of each piece of the snapshot. An example appears later in the chapter.

Program Specification: A Detailed Look

This section will describe in greater detail the interview phase (step 3) and the completion of the snapshot and narrative (step 4). Boysville of Michigan's Day Treatment Program for adjudicated youth will be used as an actual program example throughout this section. The Day Treatment Program was developed as an alternative to removing youths from their homes and placing them in a campus–based residential program or a group home. Youths live at home with their families while participating in day treatment six days a week.

The answers to the questions listed in Figure 2.4 are organized and summarized to present the program on one page. In this chapter, the one-page diagram is referred to as a *program snapshot*. In the literature, Wholey [1979] and Hawkins and Nederhood [1987] refer to it as a *logic model*, because it displays logical relationships among client needs, program efforts, and outcomes. Readers move through the program from left to right. The client and system conditions (left side of snapshot) should be addressed by the program activities (center), which were designed to achieve the intended outcomes (right side of snapshot). The numbering scheme on the snapshot matches the numbers on the narrative, where the program is described in greater detail.

Client and System Conditions

The first phase of program specification results in a description of the target population and the client/system conditions behind the target population's need for services. Determination of who should receive services can be made by the contractor, the provider, and/or the policymaker; however, frontline service providers need to understand and be committed to serving the target population, as well as working with the client and system conditions that drive the need for service.

In the framework of today's multiple service systems, many programs are developed in response to *system* conditions. For example, a case management program might be developed in response to a fragmented service delivery system. The clients' needs have not changed, but because the original system is not responding to their needs, an additional layer of service is added. It is important to carefully specify the client population in relation to client needs, funder requirements, and the intervention model of choice. The following questions were developed to guide program staff through the process of articulating client and system conditions:

- Why are we providing the service? What problems will the program address? Who will be served? What are their needs and strengths? How many individuals and families are in need of the service?

- How are the clients identified? Where are the clients living? What are the referral streams by which clients come into the agency? What are the payment sources? What are the acceptance criteria or eligibility requirements? Are these preventing clients from getting needed services?

Figure 2.5

Client and System Conditions for a Day Treatment Program

1.1   Need for in–home service alternatives for juvenile delinquents from Genesee County who were rated as low or medium risk.

1.2   Need for in–home service alternatives for Genesee County adolescents in foster care homes

1.3   Need to increase community supports and resources for youths and their families participating in in–home service alternatives.

- Are there service gaps within the delivery system? Are other agencies providing a similar service? Are clients able to access this service in their own community? If not, why not?

- As an agency, what experience do we have in serving this population? How can we collaborate with other providers to strengthen the service?

Figure 2.5 presents a sample set of answers to these questions.

Client Outcomes

Despite the position of expected client gains (outcomes) on the chart, participants generally find it easier to generate this section *before* describing the activities that will be implemented with clients to achieve those gains. Discussion of outcomes should occur after the client and system conditions have been identified but before discussing the service model and activities. Some useful questions to address are listed below.

- What will the clients gain from the program or service? What is the program trying to accomplish? If the program reached its highest level of success, what would the clients look like? What knowledge, attitudes, and behaviors would they exhibit?

- Have the funders set program performance standards? Are there internal program standards that would apply to this client group? Are there outcomes specific to an identified client that are different from those for other family members? What indirect gains are anticipated from the program?

- How do the outcomes achieved address the needs identified in the conditions section? What are the expected outcomes for system conditions?

- How do the short-term gains differ from the long-term gains? What gains will the clients maintain after the service has been completed? Will other indirect gains be achieved after the program is implemented successfully?

Figure 2.6

Day Treatment Program Outcomes

	Immediate Outcomes		**Intermediate Outcomes**
4.1	75% of youths shall complete all/most of treatment goals.	5.1	75% of youths living in a home placement.
4.2	75% of youths shall be living in a home placement.	5.2	60% of youths enrolled in school or employed.
4.3	75% of families shall complete all/most of family goals.	5.3	60% of youths living a legal lifestyle.
4.4	75% of families will demonstrate less reliance on professional support and increase informal social support networks.		

- How will this program impact the service delivery system or public policy? Will this program activate resources within the community or enhance advocacy efforts?

Boysville's day treatment staff worked with Michigan Department of Social Service staff to develop a set of youth and family outcomes (see Figure 2.6). Standards have been set for each outcome measure. Clearly, the challenge in this step of the process is to specify program outcomes that are reasonable and can be measured. Notice that the outcomes are measured immediately at program release (month 12) and again three and twelve months after program completion (months 15 and 24 respectively).

Program Components and Activities

Understanding the prevalence and etiology of a problem is a critical step to program model development, and provides a framework for evaluation. For example, program administrators' beliefs about the causes of adolescent chemical dependency dictate their approach to treatment. Proponents of the 12–step medical model use education as the primary intervention, because their theory suggests that once the adolescent learns about the disease and how to live a sober lifestyle, he or she will abstain from drugs and alcohol. In comparison, structural family therapists would argue that the adolescent's substance abuse is a symptom of family disorganization and rigidity. Intervention based on this theory would be directed toward negotiating closeness/distance between family members and clarifying boundaries and roles; once the family unit has been reorganized, the symptom will diminish. Participants in the program specification process should de-

> **Figure 2.7**

Day Treatment Program Activities

Program Components		*Activities*	
2.3	Intensive In–Home (6–8 months)	3.3a	Re–entry into home school
		3.3b	Vocational/job placement
		3.3c	In–home family sessions
		3.3d	Parent training
		3.3e	Recreation
		3.3f	Wraparound services and flexible funds
		3.3g	Respite care—youth
2.4	Aftercare (6 months)	3.4a	Monitor community adjustment
		3.4b	Monitor community networking
		3.4c	In–home family sessions
		3.4d	Termination of services

scribe program activities and take the time to discuss why these activities are included in the program. (See Figure 2.7.)

Explaining why a particular set of activities or program efforts will lead to the desired outcome is the next step in this process. During this phase of the process, programs are organized into major components and detailed activities, or processes, that fall within each program component. Sample questions for completion of this section include:

- What are the major components of the program? How was the model for this program developed? What theory and/or research findings support this program model? What other services or treatment approaches have been tried, within the agency or elsewhere? What does the research tell us about effective service strategies? (Again, this is part of a benchmarking process.)

- How long is the service provided? Who will provide the service? How many clients will be served? What administrative supports are needed? What clinical supports? Clerical supports?

- How will the program be funded? What program components or activities are mandated by contract? By licensing standards? By accreditation standards?

- How will the program activities bring about the desired client change? What specific program processes are included within each component?

(**Figure 2.8**)

Program Narrative for Two Components

(**3.11 Assessment Case Planning**)

Program staff assess the youth and the family within 30 days of referral. Program staff make at least one visit to the family home. If appropriate, program staff make use of the Department of Social Services "Needs Assessment Scale." In accordance with licensing requirements, case plans identify youth and family treatment goals, activities to meet those goals, time frames for goal completion, and plans for aftercare services. The case plan is completed within 30 days of intake. Plans are updated every three months to reflect progress.

(**3.12 On-Site Education**)

Classroom instruction by a certified teacher and aide is provided five days per week, five hours each day at the Corcoran facility. In partnership with the parents, an Individualized Education Plan is developed for each youth. WISC–R test scores are provided by Genesee County DSS. Woodcock-Johnson Achievement Tests are administered by education staff. Youths are assessed for special education services and, if appropriate, the certification process is initiated.

Establishing Connections

After the answers to the questions have been developed into a program snapshot, staff members should step away and review the overall program. These five questions have proven helpful in ensuring that the program logic is sound.

1. How are program activities connected to the identified needs described in the conditions sections?

2. How are the activities connected to the desired outcomes?

3. Does the picture represent how the program is intended to work? Review the program snapshot.

4. How does the program reflect the agency's mission and values?

5. How feasible is the program? Given the available resources, is there a clear link between clients, program, environmental conditions, and intended results? Will this program achieve the anticipated results?

The Final Product

Agency administrators and staff have found that the program snapshot is most effective when used in concert with the program narrative. Two components of Boysville's Day Treatment Program Narrative are illustrated in Figure 2.8. The

Figure 2.9

Boysville of Michigan: Corcoran Day Treatment Program

Client and System Conditions	Program Components	Activities	Immediate Outcomes (Month 12)	Intermediate Outcomes (Months 15 and 24)
1.1 Need for in-home service alternatives for juvenile delinquents from Genesee County who were rated as low or medium risk.	2.1 Day Treatment (4-6 Months)	3.1a Assessment and Case Planning 3.1b On-Site Education 3.1c Respite Care—Youth 3.1d Youth Group Therapy 3.1e Family Therapy and Parent Training 3.1f Recreation 3.1g Work With Home, School 3.1h Vocational/Job Placement 3.1i Wraparound Services and Flexible Funds	4.1 75% of Youths Shall Complete All/Most of Treatment Goals 4.2 75% of Youths Shall Be Living in a Home Placement	5.1 75% of Youths Living in a Home Placement 5.2 60% of Youths Enrolled in School/Employed
1.2 Need for in-home service alternatives for Genesee County adolescents in foster care homes who were referred due to parental neglect.	2.2 Ongoing Tracking	3.2a Telephone, Face-To-Face, Collateral Contacts 3.2b 24-Hour Service	4.3 75% of Families Shall Complete All/Most of Family Goals 4.4 75% of Families Will Demonstrate Less Reliance on Professional Support and Increase Informal Social Support Networks	5.3 60% of Youths Living a Legal Lifestyle
1.3 Need to increase community supports and resources for youths and their families participating in in-home service alternatives.	2.3 Intensive In-Home (6-8 Months)	3.3a Re-entry into Home School 3.3b Vocational/Job Placement 3.3c In-Home Family Sessions Using Structural Family Therapy 3.3d Parent Training 3.3e Recreation 3.3f Wraparound Services and Flexible Funds 3.3g Respite Care—Youth		
	2.4 Aftercare (6 Months)	3.4a Monitor Community Adjustment of Youth 3.4b Monitor Community Networking by Family 3.4c In-Home Family Sessions Using Structural Family Therapy 3.4d Termination of Services		

narrative describes each program area, including what will be accomplished, by whom, how often, and within what time frames.

Benefits of the Program Specification Process

After completing the process described in this chapter, you will have: (1) a summary of the information above, presented as a program snapshot (see Figure 2.9) and (2) a more detailed description of your program in the form of a program narrative (see Figure 2.8). The products of your efforts will guide the following:

Quality Programming

- Develop program performance standards
- Implement an ongoing program improvement process
- Build a relevant and feasible evaluation that is based on program parameters
- Identify the combination of program components best suited to produce the intended outcomes
- Prevent unnecessary "model drift"

Staff Development

- Reach consensus on program functioning with managers and staff
- Create a professional staff development and training program
- Engage staff as experts in the program specification and evaluation process, enabling them to gain more understanding of program design and evaluation
- Improve staff morale

Funding and Marketing Efforts

- Provide specific intervention models for requests for proposals
- Renew contracts, licenses, and accreditation
- Educate new board members, donors, and other stakeholders
- Market innovative program models

How Program Specification Leads to Evaluation

Once the program is specified, the program evaluator or identified facilitator continues to work with program staff to develop an evaluation. The evaluation should provide staff with the information they need to monitor and determine program integrity, effectiveness, and efficiency. The development of the program evaluation includes:

Figure 2.10

Evaluation Plan and Program Timeline

Evaluation Plan

Evaluation Questions	Information Needs	Data Collection Tools	Frequency
1.1 – 1.3 Who are we serving?	Youth and family profile information, including demographics, juvenile justice history, educational status, previous placements	• Intake Data Sheet	At intake
2.1 – 3.4d What services are we providing?	Tracking activity, family contact activity, critical incidents, and truancies	• Tracking Form • Family Service Contact Form • Incident Data Sheet	Ongoing
4.1 – 4.4 Have the clients achieved the program outcomes at the end of In–Home?	Completion of treatment goals, education gains, improvements in behavior, increasing social support	• Closing Data Sheet • Pre and post Woodcock–Johnson Achievement scores • Pre and post Behavior Evaluation Scores • Pre and post Social Support Network Maps	At the beginning of Day Treatment and at the end of Intensive In–home
5.1 – 5.3 Have the clients achieved the program outcomes at the end of Aftercare?	Living in a home placement, enrolled in school and/or working, living a legal lifestyle	• Youth follow–up survey	Completed three and twelve months after Intensive In–home phase is completed

Program Timeline

Day Treatment	Intensive In-Home	Aftercare	Follow-Up
(phase 1)	(phase 2)	(phase 3)	
4–6 months	6–8 months	6 months	End of program
Intake			

Follow-Up Survey →   Follow-Up Survey →

1. Developing indicators for each item in the program specification snapshot (process and outcomes). For example, random tracking contacts will indicate the extent to which youths in the Day Treatment Program are following their daily schedule while in the community.

2. Identifying measures. For example, occurrence, location, time, and type of daily tracking contacts with youths, parents, or collateral sources that staff will record on the Tracking Form.

3. Stating program standards. For example, 100% of the youths will follow the daily schedule as indicated by tracking contacts.

4. Reviewing the feasibility of the evaluation plan, given the program's resources (staff time, processing time, funds for data collection instruments).

The information presented in Figure 2.10 is an example of an evaluation plan and timeline that can be developed as an outgrowth of the program specification process.

Conclusion

Program specification is a capacity building process that works best in a safe, positive, teaching/learning environment. For most agencies, existing program staff and resources are sufficient to produce a complete and logical program model. Consultants are not essential to engaging in this analytical process; program and agency staff have successfully completed the process on their own. Program specification should be repeated throughout the life of every program within an agency as well as in the agency overall. The process can be conducted during mission statement reviews, during annual reviews with pre-existing programs, along with new program development, and during accreditation. Agencies involved with the development or implementation of a quality assurance or quality improvement process would be well advised to complete a program specification first, one program at a time. The evaluation and planning techniques presented in the chapters to follow assume that the program specification step has been taken.

References

Hawkins, D., & Nederhood, B. (1987). *Handbook for evaluating drug and alcohol prevention programs: Staff/team evaluation of prevention programs (STEPP)*. Office of Substance Abuse Prevention DHHS: No. (ADM), 87–1512.

Jacobs, F. (1988). The five–tiered approach to evaluation: Context and implementation. In H. B. Weiss & F. H. Jacobs (Eds.), *Evaluating Family Programs* (pp. 37–68). Hawthorne, NY: Aldine de Gruyter.

Wholey, J. (1979). *Evaluation: Promise and performance*. Washington, DC: Urban Institute.

For Further Information

Gabor, P., & Grinnell, R. (1994) *Evaluation and quality improvement in the human services*. Boston: Allyn & Bacon. Provides a useful overview of program evaluation concepts with some attention paid to quality improvement as well.

Wholey, J., Hatry, H., & Newcomer, K. (1994). *Handbook of practical program evaluation*. San Francisco: Jossey-Bass Publishers. Presents the fundamentals of program evaluation in a clear manner.

Chapter 3

Closing the Gap: Does the Program Match the Blueprint?

Sally M. Davis and Sue Ann Savas

Introduction

"Most organizations do not figure out what they want to measure, and why, soon enough" [Fenwick 1991].

Does this sound familiar? In this chapter we address process evaluations, the day-to-day operational evaluations that often precede the outcome evaluations discussed in Chapter 5. While we acknowledge that the term *process* has a specific meaning pertaining to the strategies and procedures a program follows, we are using it more broadly to include a number of other types of evaluations that are useful for studying the day-to-day operations of a child welfare agency.

At the heart of continuous quality improvement and total quality management is evaluation of the processes inherent in the day to day operations of a child welfare agency. This chapter is intended to help you review which aspects of these operations should be evaluated, and how.

We discuss five types of process evaluations that help child welfare program staff determine: (1) what services are provided, (2) why they are needed ("prevalence/incidence" and "coverage and bias" studies), (3) how services are provided ("service provision" studies), (4) how services are experienced or received by clients ("consumer satisfaction" studies), and (5) what can be learned from program implementation that informs future efforts ("implementation" studies).

Our discussion will answer these questions:

- What can you gain from these evaluation studies?

- How do you decide which evaluation methods to use?

- How are the data collected?

- What are the common pitfalls, and how can they be avoided?

An agency administrator who undertakes an evaluation wants to know: Did the program work? This is what stakeholders also want to know. But to fully answer this question, we need to be clear about the specific aspect of the program being focused on and to determine that it is being implemented with integrity. In child welfare, as in other human service fields, it is a rare case in which program "treatment" is clearly identified, implemented as planned, and consistently delivered so that changes experienced by clients can be unquestionably attributed to program involvement. So agency staff must focus on describing exactly what happened to participants through the course of their involvement with the program [King et al. 1987]. The following scenarios, while simplistic, demonstrate how results gathered from an outcome evaluation are often incomplete without other information.

Scenario #1

An agency received funding to provide substance abuse prevention services to families. Findings from an outcome evaluation demonstrated that parental substance abuse increased among program participants. Clearly, this was not the intent of the program. What contributed to the results?

Possible explanations for *poor* outcomes include:

- Families did not participate as consistently as expected.

- Staff did not implement the program according to plan.

- Families who were accepted for prevention services had more serious needs than the program was designed to accommodate.

- The programmatic assumptions were flawed.

What would you, as the leader, do next?

- Cancel the program?

- Adjust the model? Increase the "dosage?"

- Retrain the staff?

- Tighten the eligibility criteria?

- Re-evaluate the data to select some possible explanations, or to at least rule out as many of the above explanations as possible?

- Fire the evaluator?

Scenario #2

An agency provides in-home services to families with a child returning from out-of-home placement. The program outcomes have been successful and consistent over the last three years. The agency is interested in replicating the program in three other communities. But first administrators need to know what contributed to the results.

Possible explanations for *successful* outcomes include:

- An exceptional worker was able to engage the families.

- Community resources provided extra support to the families.

- Youths and families participated fully in all family sessions.

- The communication and discipline skills taught matched family needs.

What would you, as the leader, do next?

- Replicate the model as is?

- Select communities that are similar to the first?

- Ask the exceptional worker to train the new program staff?

- Accept only those families that have demonstrated their commitment?

The scenarios above are only two of the reasons why process evaluations make sense for child welfare agencies. In scenario #1, a process evaluation would help the leader identify causes for program outcomes [King et al. 1987]. A leader faced with scenario #2 would use a type of process evaluation, along with analysis of outcome evaluation data, to characterize a program for replication and dissemination.

What Can Be Gained from Process Evaluations?

Process evaluations allow an agency to monitor program implementation and determine quality, prepare for an outcome evaluation, describe a program whose goals are not immediately measurable, and understand the theory underlying the program.

Monitor Program Implementation and Determine Quality

A very simple form of process evaluation that is familiar to child welfare agency administrators is monitoring [Rossi & Freeman 1993]. Monitoring is an essential management function that determines whether a program looks or operates as planned. This type of evaluation is synonymous with quality assurance in terms of the routine, ongoing collection of information describing services provided and clients served. Evaluations conducted for this purpose collect information on the types of program activities and the "dosages," mix, or order of services necessary to accomplish program goals in a particular stage of program development, as demonstrated in Figure 3.1.

Prepare for an Outcome Evaluation

Process evaluations are also conducted as a preliminary step to conducting outcome assessments. In order to say that specific services resulted in desired outcomes, program staff must be very clear about what services were actually delivered. For example, it is not possible to say that parent aide services resulted in better parenting practices unless it's clear what is meant by parent aide services. A

Figure 3.1

Monitoring Family Service Activity

Information Need	Program Characteristic
How frequent is the service?	Two contacts per week per family
What is the type of contact?	One face-to-face contact and one phone contact
What is the duration of contacts?	Between 15 minutes and 90 minutes each
Where do the contacts occur?	50% of the contacts should occur in the family home
Who attends?	At least one adult family member should attend each contact

An agency example: Family workers record their contacts on a Family Service Contact Sheet. Each month, family workers and program managers receive a report listing the name of the family, and the date and location of the contact. First, we must determine if the service is occuring before we can assess the quality of the service. This family contact information is used to determine which families are recieving the predetermined service. Routine case reviews are conducted to determine the quality of therapy sessions. In addition, the monthly reports lead to discussions on which types of families are not participating and how threats to worker safety in some neighborhoods impact their efforts. (For more information on family contacts as a process measure see Savas et al. [1993]; Whittaker et al. [1993]; Finch et al. [1991].

client whose parent aide provides transportation to medical appointments once a week did not receive the same service as a client who sees a parent aide four days a week for intensive parent education and homemaker services. Efficient use of an external evaluator's time begins with an agency collecting specific information on the services provided. It is best not to assume that a service is provided as planned or that it is interpreted and implemented consistently across cases.

Describe a Program Whose Goals Are Not Immediately Measurable

Child welfare agencies also conduct process evaluations to describe programs whose outcomes are not easily measured [Henerson et al. 1987]. Practitioners in the human service field are familiar with the challenge of demonstrating that prevention services in fact prevented an undesirable situation when that situation is either too far in the future to measure or so confounded by other presenting problems that no one can say with certitude that without the service it would have occurred. This is why we need experimental designs that randomly assign participants to control and comparison groups, and also need long-term follow-up studies.

We recommend being creative about these issues and making the best possible effort to use control groups and long-term follow-up. (See Chapter 5 for more on this). Unfortunately, there are times when control groups and long-term follow-up are prohibitively expensive. The reality, for many child welfare agency-based researchers, is a two-year demonstration project with evaluation requirements attached, or yearly reporting requirements for clients served through per diem dollars. While it may not be possible to show that long-term goals were reached in the limited time a demonstration project was in operation, it is possible to document why the agency believes specific efforts will lead to the attainment of specific program goals [Wood 1993]. Further, it is also possible to document program effort and monitor the achievement of interim goals.

Understand the Theory Underlying the Program

Theory is, to put it simply, "All the things that have to happen in a program, in what order and sequence, to achieve the various outcomes and impacts" [Wood 1993, p. 90]. Often, practitioners in a program are operating under variations of a theory of intervention, but they have not articulated that theory to the point that all practitioners in the same program are in agreement. Program specification, discussed in Chapter 2, creates a blueprint; comparing the blueprint to the actual program allows program staff to see areas that are implemented according to the model and areas that are not. Where there are gaps, there are opportunities for program improvement, and ultimately theory development.

For example, when parental substance abuse, domestic violence, and child abuse coexist, what needs to happen and in what order to ameliorate these problems? A demonstration project designed to link substance abusing parents with alcohol or other drug treatment was unsuccessful at addressing the substance abuse treatment needs until team members realized they needed to address the domestic violence issues first. This type of information can be used to modify program theory, train new staff, and provide booster trainings to veteran staff.

What This Method Can and Cannot Do

To attribute client successes or failures to agency services, two things are needed: a solid understanding of services provided, and control or comparison groups. A process evaluation study can provide the first. It cannot provide the second.

It is possible to describe client successes or failures (outcomes), but impossible to make claims about the relationship between the agency's efforts and client outcomes without control or comparison groups or the use of sophisticated time series designs. However, descriptions of client outcomes (or descriptive research) can be very useful; the data they generate will usually satisfy the requirements of accrediting bodies. At the program level, decisions can be based on data rather than gut feelings. For example, if post-discharge surveys reveal that many clients drop out of school within six months of discharge, an agency may decide to link clients with advocacy services for six months. Or, an agency may decide to compare or *benchmark* a particular outcome over a period of years with another facility known to be very successful in that regard, while emulating their strategies. To describe outcomes, simply aggregate information such as client background variables and risk factors, disposition at discharge, or post-discharge status.

It is also possible to go one step further and determine whether certain client outcomes are associated or correlated with client background variables or services provided. For example, correlational research is useful for determining if clients receiving one type of service are more likely to drop out of school within six months of discharge than other types of clients, or if clients with one given profile are particularly likely to be unhappy with their group therapy program. Correlational research uses the same information as descriptive research, as long as individual information is coded in such a way that it can be linked to individual clients.

How to Select an Evaluation Method That Meets Your Needs

Decision-Making Criteria

Selecting the process evaluation method that meets your needs can seem like a very difficult task, given all the different evaluations from which to choose. Begin the selection by assembling a team to answer critical questions about information needs, resources, and duration of effort.

What information do you need?

Program leaders and evaluators must always keep in mind this precaution: Find out just what you need to know, not everything that would be nice to know. You must have a reason for collecting information, and your information needs must be specific. Even when you have specific information needs, they must be prioritized, and some may need to be eliminated due to financial and human resource constraints or to limit the degree of intrusiveness for clients and staff. This may mean looking at one program at a time or looking carefully at information that is already in client files. Perhaps with only minor modifications you can collect different or additional information—just by directing copies to a central processing office or adding a face sheet with a checklist to process note records.

Who needs the information? How will the information be reported? How will the information be used to enhance program services for clients?

First, determine who requires the information. In some cases, the answer may be straightforward. A funder requires you to document how many clients were served and which families received services in accordance with the grant. In another case, an agency executive might receive a call from an unhappy parent who is not satisfied with aftercare services. The call leads the executive to ask whether this situation is an exception or not. Requests for information may also come from within the agency. For example, a clinical supervisor who needs to complete social support network maps with families may request a Tickler Report to notify workers of due dates.

Next, work with the consumer to create a rough draft of the report. Identify the pieces of information needed to complete the report. Information can be reported in a number of different formats (see Figure 3.2) depending on how the consumer will use the information. For example, in order to respond to the funder's question, you would need the client's name, first day of service, last day of service, and units of service provided. This information is aggregated to produce the total number of families served during the grant period and the total units of each type

Figure 3.2

Sample Questions, Information Needs, Sources, and Reporting Formats

Evaluation question	Information need	Source	Reporting format
How many families were served in 1994? Which services did the families receive?	First day of service, last day of service, types of services received	Intake and closing forms, Family Services Checklist	Statistics and narrative provided in annual report to funder
How do parents feel about the aftercare service?	Parental satisfaction	Parent Consumer Survey	Quotes are listed quarterly by each program site. Client names are not used.
To what degree are clinicians completing neighborhood assessments?	Completion of assessment and quality of assesssment	Case file	Results are verbally shared with clinicians at next team meeting.

of service provided. A request for information about parental satisfaction could be organized as a narrative, with quotes, themes, and patterns drawn from the parents. It could also include quantitative ratings in certain areas.

What resources are needed and available?

Resources will constrain the evaluation efforts of any child welfare agency. Typically, resources are limited; therefore, evaluations need to be designed as economically as possible. This means taking into consideration the qualifications necessary for data gatherers and the extent of intrusiveness and time commitment for clients and staff. For example, some tools require the person administering the questions to a client to have a significant amount of training, and some require significant amounts of time to administer and score.

Is this going to be an ongoing or one-time effort?

Decide whether the information will be gathered for a limited time (for example, for the duration of a demonstration grant) or on an ongoing basis. Keep in mind that it may be useful to collect data for a short time about a comparable established program to augment the evaluation of a demonstration project.

From what source will the information be obtained?

See Chapter 9 for some strategies that enable a program to establish comprehensive, ongoing data collection efforts. These would be especially useful to programs that are in the process of establishing integrated information management systems.

If resources exist for putting an information system in place, the process outlined in Chapter 2 will help you define and prioritize appropriate indicators of worker effort and client gain. According to its prioritized information needs, an agency may need to develop or refine its existing recordkeeping procedures. Possible resources to consider include the following:

- Clients' time and privacy;

- Staff time required to collect the data;

- Staff time needed to locate missing data and verify and process data obtained;

- Staff time needed to write reports;

- Leader or evaluator's time to design and monitor the project; and

- Staff time (including that of leaders and evaluators) to read, interpret, and use the data to refine program operation.

Specific Types of Process Evaluation Projects

There are several types of process evaluation projects. Some are time limited and others use information collected on an ongoing basis. For each type of project, we have summarized the questions to be asked and the corresponding information to be collected and suggested data collection methodologies to be followed. The list of projects is not exhaustive, nor are any of the projects mutually exclusive. An agency with a comprehensive data collection system may decide to collect information and use it for a variety of purposes. An agency just beginning with evaluation can select one project and move ahead slowly.

Prevalence and Incidence Study

A prevalence study answers questions like: (1) To what extent is substance abuse a problem for agency clients?; or, from a community perspective (2) Is domestic violence an issue our agency should address, because of the number of maltreated women in our community? An incidence study answers questions like: (1) Has the number of people the agency serves who are affected by substance abuse increased?; or, from a community perspective (2) Has the number of children with fetal alcohol syndrome increased in our geographic area?

As particular problems are identified, child welfare agencies often need to assess the degree to which these problems affect their clients. Prevalence and incidence studies are similar but distinctly different. *Prevalence* tells what percentage of an existing population is affected with a particular problem, while *incidence* gives the rate of occurrence of a problem among new cases [Rossi & Freeman 1993]. While prevalence and incidence studies are, strictly speaking, population studies, the concepts of prevalence and incidence are important to the agency-based evaluator. As child welfare agencies become aware of existing or emerging issues among their clients, they need to make decisions about programming and training based on systematic assessment.

Some agencies routinely screen for or assess such issues as child maltreatment, substance abuse, sexual abuse, domestic violence, communicable diseases, fetal alcohol syndrome, or learning disabilities at intake. If the information is systematically maintained, a program can access prevalence information. Other agencies may not conduct such assessments, but may need to determine the incidence of a given problem among incoming clients. If an agency or program is just beginning to consider an issue, it is more than likely that it is not systematically collecting information on that issue. In such cases, a screening tool is probably needed.

A number of tools have been tested for identifying and measuring such issues as depression, substance abuse, and child maltreatment [see Daro et al. 1990, Magura & Moses 1986, Pfeiffer et al. 1992]. The resources section at the end of this chapter can help agencies identify available measurement tools.

Coverage and Bias Study

A study of coverage and bias answers the following questions:

- Who uses agency services?

- Does a program attract and retain the clients it was designed to serve?

- Do certain types of clients use agency services more or differently than others?

This kind of process evaluation assesses the extent to which the agency achieves the levels of participation specified in the program design for a target population (coverage) and the degree to which subgroups of the target population participate differentially (bias). Evaluation experts analyze coverage and bias as a measure of program efficiency [Rossi & Freeman 1993]. A program may fail to serve its target population because of recruiting practices or rejection by potential clients. For example, one youth service program designed to serve runaways found that although minority youths comprised a sizable percentage of the city's runaway population, few minority youths used the program. Seeing the bias toward Caucasian youths alerted program staff to needed changes in staffing patterns, outreach practices, and program model.

To assess coverage and bias, an agency needs to determine the number of people in need of a particular service and the numbers of people in need who are served and not served. This information can often be obtained from program records, surveys of program participants, or community and epidemiological surveys. While measures of the number of people needing a particular service and the number receiving services may not be immediately available to an agency, community needs assessments conducted by area agencies may prove useful.

In the example of minority participation in a runaway program, described above, the program examined available intake information on the racial/ethnic characteristics of program participants and compared them to police reports for status offenses and census data on race for their city. Other demographic indicators of interest might include sex, age, zip code, or family income level. Program staff may have other ideas about client characteristics that distinguish degrees of program participation. These characteristics may be more subtle than race, sex, or age, and may include indicators of functioning or other aspects of case history.

Agencies often use the concept of coverage or bias when preparing grant proposals or conducting strategic planning. Used in this way, the concept equates with needs assessment. For example, a particular agency was interested in providing services to one inner city community. At the time, the agency had limited knowledge of what services were available in that community. Program staff worked with evaluators to complete a community profile and assessment. Information was drawn from phone books, resource directories, census data, state agencies, police precinct reports, public health reports, high schools, phone contacts with community service providers, and the local library. Geomapping databases and software are becoming useful tools for some studies of this type. On the basis of the information collected, the agency was able to assess the degree to which existing services covered the area. The final product included the following:

- A street map of the defined community;

- A demographic profile of residents (breakdown of race/ethnicity by census tract, high school dropout rates, crime statistics, health information, economic characteristics, ages);

- A list of agencies and services within the area;

- A list of agencies and services outside the area but available to the community;

- A list of religious institutions and affiliated schools; and

- A list of informal resources (block clubs, community groups).

Service Provision Study

A service provision study answers the following questions:

- What happens during treatment?

- What do staff members do [How do staff perform] in relation to established standards?

- What activities are prescribed for program participants?

- What services are provided to clients?

To answer these questions, one typically gathers information about case goals and plans, services offered, services utilized, levels of participation, types of clients participating in specific activities, referrals made, follow-up on referrals, amount of staff time devoted to certain activities, and differences in services provided across project locations. An agency that already has an information management system can access these data fairly readily. The next task is to tabulate and summarize the information in a format program staff can easily understand.

If service information is not already being collected on a systematic basis, there are at least two options available that require modest investment of resources. First, an agency can conduct a case study of service planning and utilization. To do so, systematically select a limited number of cases (maybe every tenth case for a six-month period) and analyze all case notes, abstracting from the case record information such as indicators of each client's case goals, referrals, and participation in services. Alternatively, an agency can conduct a time-and-motion study, a short term (two or three week) data collection effort in which staff keep detailed logs of the services they provide, the amount of time they spend with clients, the time required for each task (for example, to conduct a group and to complete the associated preparation and follow-up activities), and other data. In both cases, the findings can be used to develop or refine measures of service provision and utilization, describe case flow through the program, identify commonly received services, examine trends in activity attendance, or establish rough estimates of the amount of staff contact program clients experience.

Consumer Satisfaction Study

A consumer satisfaction study generally answers the following questions:

- What do the participants want from the program?

- How do clients characterize their experience in the program?

- What do program participants perceive to be the most and least helpful aspects of the program?

- What would clients like to see changed about the program?

Consumer satisfaction studies are difficult to do well, in part because dissatisfied consumers are hard to locate and engage, and all kinds of consumers tend to respond in socially desirable ways. Client mobility and literacy are also issues to be considered. Often, without questions about specific areas needing change, findings from consumer satisfaction studies are simply glowing testimonials about the virtues of a program that fail to capture valid criticisms or needed recommendations for change. To obtain candid, useful information, child welfare agencies can take advantage of tested survey instruments and experienced interviewers. Of course, the agency should also be willing to regard anything less than a glowing testimonial as an opportunity for program improvement.

A number of consumer satisfaction surveys have been developed and tested over the years, and are available for use by child welfare agencies [e.g., LeProhn 1993; Magura & Moses 1986; Pecora et al. 1992; Reid & Grundlach 1988]. Typically administered to program participants as they exit the program, these surveys provide easily tabulated information on consumer satisfaction with many aspects of service.

Existing tools tend to ask what consumers thought about the services—"How convenient is the location of our building?" or "Are you satisfied with the fee that was charged for the services you received?" Questions should also focus on client functioning or change—"What aspects of supervising your children have changed since you received our services?" or "Since you first talked to someone from this agency, have there been any changes in your personal life or personal difficulties?" Program leaders need to decide which types of information are most useful and research survey tools carefully. (See the end of this chapter for a list of supplemental resources.)

The agency that considers creating its own consumer satisfaction survey should conduct a focus group with current or former clients first. It is especially helpful to take into consideration the viewpoints of clients who refused services or exited early. A focus group can help you craft survey questions that are meaningful to consumers, thereby increasing the likelihood that consumers will respond to the survey and provide useful information. A focus group will not reveal how all clients perceive agency services, but it will, if properly conducted, identify a select group of meaningful issues and shed light on why these issues are important.

What do consumers want? It's a crucial question to ask. A proactive purpose for consumer focus groups is to gather consumers' input on the design of proposed services. If your agency does not already have a mechanism for consulting consumers, a focus group may provide an opportunity for starting to include client input in the design of new services.

Implementation Study

An implementation study answers the following questions:

- Were the services delivered according to the program plan? (See Chapter 2, Program Specification.) Note that the focus is less on the exact nature and number of services than on how the program is being implemented.

- What were the barriers to implementing the program? How were those barriers overcome?

- Which supports and services were most available to and best utilized by families?

Information needed to answer these questions includes the time required to recruit and train staff, successes and failures experienced in setting up the program (building referral networks, putting collaborating relationships in place, and conducting community education and outreach efforts), the number and types of presenting problems at intake for the first year, and any factors within the community that may have enhanced the program. This information is typically collected through interviews with program staff at all levels of the project and with staff at collaborating agencies. Consumer interviews provide important supplemental data.

Information is also gathered from documentation, such as grant proposals, minutes from planning meetings, client referral forms, and program policy manuals. These information gathering efforts are often conducted by someone who is not directly tied to program operations. This increases the likelihood that the report will be unbiased and thorough.

After collating the input, the evaluator or interviewer constructs a narrative that describes the conditions experienced in the process of implementing the program, the timeline for project implementation, successes or barriers, unexpected accomplishments or challenges, and explanations for any discrepancies between the project proposed and the project actually implemented. Where appropriate, the evaluator may suggest organizational modifications or revisions to the project design.

This implementation information is useful for a variety of purposes. For example, findings about difficulties faced in establishing referral networks and obtaining appropriate referrals may point to a need for increased community education efforts and refined intake processes to screen for appropriate clients. Findings about difficulties in recruiting volunteers or paid staff may suggest modifications to the program design or enhanced efforts to identify and train staff within the organization.

Data Collection Strategies

Most service providers are already collecting data to meet external information demands. State licensing entities, contractors, funders, and accrediting bodies require the routine collection of specific information, such as critical incident reports, assessment data, lists of services provided, and numbers served. However, service providers rarely draw on these data for their own purposes, in part because the information may not be stored in an accessible place. (See Chapter 9 for information about integrated information systems.) The trick to using this information for the agency's internal purposes is to clearly articulate the questions the agency wants answered, as demonstrated above and in Chapter 2. This point cannot be emphasized enough: *Evaluations should be driven by specific evaluation questions.*

Once these questions are articulated and agreed upon, agencies are often surprised to find how easily they can be answered by information already on hand.

Having taken stock of what is already collected, however, you may find that still more information is needed. Before you jump into conducting a consumer satisfaction survey, take a close look at the data collection techniques available. In the discussion above, we have described some of the numerous social science research methods that are used to evaluate the processes involved in the day-to-day operations of a child welfare agency:

- Documentation reviews (such as client case file peer and utilization reviews, grant proposals, agency policy manuals, and public relations materials);

- Interviews and focus group interviews;

- Case studies;

- Time and motion studies;

- Secondary data analysis (census data, police records, and state or national child welfare statistics, such as those collected by the National Child Abuse and Neglect Data System or the Adoption and Foster Care Analysis and Reporting System);

- Observational scales;

- Paper and pencil checklists and tests; and

- Standardized instruments.

At the end of this chapter, we have included a preliminary list of resources on data collection.

Common Pitfalls, and How to Avoid Them

An evaluation cannot accomplish the goals identified above unless it is designed with careful attention to the information to be collected, the needs of those collecting the information, and the use the findings will be put to. In our experience, child welfare agencies typically encounter a range of difficulties when conducting both process and outcome evaluations.

First, it is all too easy to collect too much information and still not find out what you want to know. There are few situations more heartbreaking to program staff who have invested their time and energy into logging their activities and surveying their clients than finding out that the data was never used or did not answer their questions. For example, an agency might begin an evaluation with the idea of understanding client characteristics, but at the end of the evaluation might decide that they really wanted cost-benefit information to defend the program. The information needed to justify the program in terms of costs will seldom be available unless it was included in the original design of the evaluation. Chapter 2 outlines an effective process for defining what information is needed and why. That process should include as many levels of staff as possible to be sure that all relevant data elements are identified and prioritized.

Regular review of the findings may show that certain data elements should be added or dropped. Don't be surprised if staff, through the course of the project, become aware of other factors that appear relevant. The evaluation design and data collection instruments may need to be modified to allow for such changes. For example, during the course of a study of child abuse and neglect prevention programs, staff realized that the information collected on children's school attendance did not tell them what they wanted to know about Head Start participation. Because they believed Head Start is an important indicator of families' linkages to community programming and the well-being of children, modifications were made to allow for more detailed descriptions of Head Start participation.

Unless program staff provide input, an evaluator ends up defining the program objectives through his or her choice of data collection instruments, which may not have been designed for purposes that sufficiently match those of the program under review [Rutman & Mowbray 1983]. As a result, data may be collected that do not accurately describe the services provided or measure the context within which the program operates. In such cases, "buy-in" by those actually collecting the data is a minimal requirement to avoid jeopardizing the accuracy of the project.

Interested parties may attempt to use information gathered for an evaluation for purposes for which it was not intended, such as personnel review or accounting of expenditures [Rutman & Mowbray 1983]. The surest way to sabotage an evaluation, especially one that depends on staff to collect information on the services they provide or on their clients, is to make their job security conditional on getting the "right" answers.

Another potential evaluation pitfall is asking for a level of detail that is too time-consuming, invalid, or inappropriate. Even the most conscientious service provider may lapse into jargon or fail to give complete information when time is at a premium. The result is poor quality data, and it is difficult and time consuming, if not methodologically unsound, to "fix" bad data.

Keep the level of detail in check by starting with clear evaluation questions and revisiting them every time a new data element is proposed. For example, it may not be necessary to measure a particular item every month. Every six months may suffice. Or, if you only need to know whether or not something occurred, it is not necessary to find out how or how many times it occurred.

Not all information is difficult to obtain, but unless everyone involved in the project is clear about what specific terms mean, information collected may be unreliable, and therefore, unusable. For example, a youth-serving program attempted to log "community outreach contacts." Some workers counted the number of people who attended community presentations (which numbered in the thousands), and some workers counted the number of clients recruited to the program as a result of the presentations (which numbered approximately 100).

Even the best attempts to identify and define the most appropriate indicators need to be reviewed and modified. Misunderstandings are inevitable, staff turnover results in new people joining the evaluation effort, and definitions need to be modified to reflect the circumstances data collectors face. Furthermore, unless the people involved in the evaluation have the opportunity to see the findings that result from their efforts, even the most conscientious will lose interest.

Conclusion

Did the program work? Before asking the question, leaders need information about what happened to participants through the course of their involvement with the program. This chapter listed questions about the processes inherent in the day-to-day operations of a child welfare agency:

- To whom are services provided?

- What services are provided to clients, and why?

- How are services provided?

- How are services experienced or received by clients?

- What can be learned from program implementation to inform future efforts?

The techniques described in this chapter are descriptive rather than prescriptive. They describe program participation, service provision, and consumer satisfaction, but do not attempt to attribute clients' successes or failures to anything the agency did or did not do. We hope that the information presented will help you sharpen the focus of an evaluation by identifying these and other commonly asked questions and logically grouping them into projects. This chapter also provided tips for conducting evaluations with limited resources. Leaders are encouraged to limit the scope of their initial evaluation efforts to one aspect of a program, and to consider methodologies such as focus groups or case studies, which are less resource-intensive than other data collection techniques such as surveys.

Chapters 2, 3, 4, and 5 of this handbook are interrelated components of an overall evaluation strategy: (1) Specify the purpose and principal beneficiaries of a program; (2) Describe and analyze program operations; (3) Implement an outcome-oriented approach to management and practice; and (4) Draw conclusions about its effectiveness. Chapter 4 highlights issues relating to outcome-oriented management and service delivery. Chapter 5, Do We Make a Difference?, presents a rationale for outcome evaluations, describes how they are designed, and illustrates how the resulting information can be used to improve program services.

References

Daro, D., Abrams, N., & Casey, K. (1990). *Parenting program evaluation manual* (2nd ed.). Washington, DC: National Center on Child Abuse and Neglect.

Fenwick, A. C. (December 1991). Five easy lessons. *Quality Progress*, 63-66.

Henerson, M. E., Morris, L. L., & Fitz-Gibbon, C. T. (1987). *How to measure attitudes*. Newbury Park, CA: Sage Publications.

King, J. A., Morris, L. L., & Fitz-Gibbon, C. T. (1987). *How to assess program implementation*. Newbury Park, CA: Sage Publications.

Le Prohn, N. (1993). *Relative foster care: Role perceptions, motivation and agency satisfaction*. A dissertation submitted in partial fulfillment of the requirements for the degree of Doctor of Philosophy. University of Washington School of Social Work, Seattle, Washington.

Magura, S., & Moses, B. S. (1986). *Outcome measures for child welfare services: Theory and applications*. Washington, DC: Child Welfare League of America.

Pecora, P. J., Bartlomé, J. A., Magana, V. L., & Sperry, C. K. (1991). How consumers view intensive family preservation services. In M. W. Fraser, P. J. Pecora, and D. A. Haapala (Eds.), *Families in crisis: The impact of intensive family preservation services*. New York: Aldine de Gruyter.

Pfeiffer, S. I., Soldivera, S., & Norton, J. (1992). *A consumer's guide to mental health outcome measures*. Devon, PA: Devereux Foundation.

Reid, P. N., & Gundlach, J. H. (1983). A scale for the measurement of consumer satisfaction with social services. *Journal of Social Service Research*, 7, 37-54.

Rossi, P. H. & Freeman, H. E. (1993). *Evaluation: A systematic approach* (5th ed.). Newbury Park, CA: Sage Publications.

Rutman, L. & Mowbray, G. (1983). *Understanding program evaluation*. Sage Human Services Guides #31. Beverly Hills, CA: Sage Publications.

Wood, M. M. (Fall 1993). Using practitioners' theories to document program results. *Nonprofit Management and Leadership*, 4(1), 85-106.

For Further Information

General

Carl, J., & Stokes, G. (1991, July/August). Ordinary people, extraordinary organizations. *Nonprofit World*, 9(4), 8-12.

Fitz-Gibbon, C. T., & Morris, L. L. (1987). *How to design a program evaluation*. Newbury Park, CA: Sage Publications.

Hamel, J. (1993). *Case study methods*. Qualitative Research Methods Series. Newbury Park, CA: Sage Publications.

Herman, J. L., Morris, L. L., & Fitz-Gibbon, C. T. (1987). *Evaluator's handbook*. Newbury Park, CA: Sage Publications.

Morris, L. L., Fitz-Gibbon, C. T., & Freeman, M. E. (1987). *How to communicate evaluation findings*. Newbury Park, CA: Sage Publications.

Morris, L. L., Fitz-Gibbon, C. T., & Linkheim, E. (1987). *How to measure performance and use tests*. Newbury Park, CA: Sage Publications.

Patton, M. Q. (1987). *How to use qualitative methods in evaluation*. Newbury Park, CA: Sage Publications.

Reichheld, F. F. & Sasser, W. E. (September-October 1990). Zero defections: Quality comes to services. *Harvard Business Review*, 105-111.

Savas, S. A., Epstein, I., & Grasso, A. J. (1993). Client characteristics, family contacts, and treatment outcomes. *Information systems in child, youth, and family agencies*, 125-137. New York: Haworth Press, Inc.

Stecher, B. M., & Davis, W. A. (1987). *How to focus an evaluation*. Newbury Park, CA: Sage Publications.

Terrill, C. A. (February 1992). The ten commandments of new service development. *Management Review*, 24-27.

Measurement Tools

Close Conoley, J., & Impara, J. C. (Eds.). (1994). *The supplement to the eleventh mental measurements yearbook.* Lincoln, NB: University of Nebraska Press, Buros Institute of Mental Measurements.

Corcoran, K., & Fischer, J. (1987). *Measures for clinical practice.* New York: Free Press.

Finch, S. J., Fanshel, D., & Grundy, J. F. (1991). *Data collection in adoption and foster care.* Washington, DC: Child Welfare League of America.

Kramer, Jack J., & Close Conoley, Jane, Eds. (1992). Th*e eleventh mental measurements yearbook.* Lincoln, NE: University of Nebraska Press, Buros Institute of Mental Measurements.

Murphy, L. L., Close Conoley, Jane, & Impara, James C., Eds. (1994). *Tests in Print IV,* vols. 1–2. Lincoln, NB: University of Nebraska Press, Buros Institute of Mental Measurements.

Shontz, F., Goldman, R., Hellmer, T., & Troxel, M. (1993). M*issouri Children's Trust Fund: Evaluation manual.* Jefferson City, MO: Children's Trust Fund 1993. [To order, contact Vivian Murphy, Children's Trust Fund, P.O. Box 1641, Jefferson City, MO 65101-1641, 314/751-5147.]

Touliatos, J., Perlmutter, B., & Straus, M. (Eds). (1990). *Handbook of family measurement techniques.* Newbury Park, CA: Sage Publications.

Weiss, H., & Jacobs, F. (1988). *Evaluating family programs.* New York: Aldine De Gruyter.

Whittaker, J. K., Tripodi, T., & Grasso, A. J. (1993). Youth and family characteristics, treatment histories, and service outcomes: Some preliminary findings from the Boysville research program. *Information systems in child, youth, and family agencies,* 139-153. New York: Haworth Press, Inc.

Consumer Satisfaction

Bush, M., Gordon, A. C., & LeBailly, R. (1977, September). Evaluating child welfare services: A contribution from the clients. *Social Service Review,* 491–501.

Client Satisfaction Questionnaire (CSQ): CSQ-8, CSQ-18A and CSQ 18B. Contact: C. Clifford Attkisson, Ph.D., Professor of Medical Psychology, Department of Psychiatry, 401 Parnassus Avenue, CPT, San Francisco, CA 94143-0984, 415/476–7374.

LeProhn, N. S., & Pecora, P. J. (1994) *The Casey foster parent study: Research summary.* Seattle, WA: The Casey Family Program.

Madison, A. (unpublished). Client participation in health planning and evaluation:An empowerment education strategy. Presented at the Annual Meeting of the American Evaluation Association, November 2-5 1994, Boston, MA. [Copies are available from Dr. Madison at the University of North Texas, Department of Public Administration.]

Magura, S., & Moses, B. S. (March-April 1984). Clients as evaluators in child protective services. *Child Welfare,* 63(2), 99-112.

Magura, S. & Moses, B. S. (1986). Parent outcome interview. In *Outcome measures for child welfare services: Theory and applications* (pp. 203-241). Washington, DC: Child Welfare League of America.

Nguyen, T. D., Attkisson, C. C., & Stegner, B. L. (1983). Assessment of patient satisfaction: Development and refinement of a service evaluation questionnaire. *Evaluation and Program Planning,* 6, 299-314.

Service Satisfaction Scales. Contact: Thomas Greenfield, Ph.D., Alcohol Research Group, 2000 Hearst Avenue, Suite 300, Berkeley, CA 94709-2167, 510/642-5208.

Focus Groups

Morgan, D. L. (1988). Focus groups as qualitative research. *Qualitative Research Methods Series, 16.* Newbury Park, CA: Sage Publications.

Krueger, R. A. (1994). *Focus groups: A practical guide for applied research.* Newbury Park, CA: Sage Publications.

Section III: Assessing the Impact of Your Services

Chapter 4

Implementing an Outcome-Oriented Approach to Case Planning and Service Improvement

James J. Traglia, Ruth Massinga, Peter J. Pecora, and Glen B. Paddock

Introduction

Child and family service agencies across the United States, Canada, and Europe are working to better define the service delivery outcomes they are accountable for achieving [e.g., American Humane Association 1993, Magura & Moses 1986, Maluccio 1979, Rapp & Poertner 1987, Parker et al. 1991]. Outcome-oriented program management and case planning are not new to child and family services or mental health. What may be new, however, is agencies' recognition that they need to reinvigorate their implementation of these approaches by infusing the entire organization with an outcome-based culture, so that administration and practice reinforce each other.

An outcome orientation to the work of a child and family services program is both a conscious way to approach day-to-day administrative tasks and a specific methodology for case management and clinical practice. In an environment characterized by such an orientation, meetings begin with a review of outcomes that the leader wishes to achieve; reports chart progress made in implementing program-wide or systems goals and methods for identifying the achievement of positive outcomes by the agency's clients. Everyone is able to see clearly how the administrative and system outcomes support client outcomes and/or are an outgrowth of those client outcomes.

An outcome-oriented approach to individual cases is powerful when it:

- is embedded in a teamwork environment that seeks to establish a *common* understanding of the desired outcomes among major stakeholders in the case;

- views the agency's desired outcomes as a consistent aggregation of individual case successes; and

- includes a system of resource allocation that is based on hard data about desired results, rather than one that counts and rewards the accumulation of processes and service delivery activities alone.

Of primary importance is an emphasis on achieving specific outcomes that is present and supported throughout the organization, including line staff, supervisors, managers, and executives. The casework part of the process begins with how staff members assess children and families, engage them in setting case goals, and develop service plans to meet those goals. That process ends with casework recording forms that are consistent with, and therefore support, the same approach to service delivery planning and implementation [McDevitt 1994]. In addition, the organization must create an environment that defines and visibly rewards successes as measurable outcomes, not as quantities of activity performed. It demands the same outcome and results orientation, and critical thinking approach, at administrative levels of the organization as at the clinical level.

This chapter will discuss what is involved in using an outcome orientation in administration and practice in child and family services, and how to incorporate an outcomes perspective with a service provision perspective. It forms a bridge from the previous chapters, which focus on program models and the service delivery process, to the outcome evaluation chapter that follows.

Administrative Aspects of Applying an Outcome Orientation to Service Delivery

Foundation Components

In Chapter 2, Savas emphasized that to be successful, agencies need to carefully specify the client and system conditions of the community they are serving, along with the program components, program processes, immediate client outcomes, and long-term client outcomes. This specification results in careful program planning, effective interventions, and clarity regarding program specifications. The next two sections of this chapter illustrate the importance of these steps, with special emphasis on how management practices and service delivery processes need to be embedded with key outcomes in order to evaluate cost effectiveness and document client improvement.

Young et al. [1994, p. 7] articulate the importance of a client-focused outcome orientation, especially with the advent of managed care systems and other forms of services collaboration:

> We believe that greater emphasis upon the client-focused outcomes of collaborative efforts is vital. As funders increasingly and rightfully demand accountability for spending, client outcomes data becomes increasingly significant. Showing that programs can help clients is ultimately the only way we can counter the shift toward a narrow emphasis upon cost efficiency that is emerging from some versions of managed care and from budget pressures at the state and local levels. We can only defeat a narrow push for fiscally-defined outcomes if we can show broader services effectiveness measured in terms of client outcomes. In addition, a greater emphasis upon client outcomes offers a hope of redirecting the efforts of the systems and programs that seek to help children and families to their real goals—changes in the lives of these clients—rather than organizational goals that sometimes overwhelm well-intentioned efforts to help clients.

The authors highlight the most often used argument for an outcome approach: It is a way to develop accountability in a field that has traditionally asked for society's support on the basis of its firmly held good intentions. An equally important, although much less heard, argument is that an outcome orientation can free an agency, and thus its staff, from an ineffective attempt to manage work that is essentially interpersonal through the meticulous regulation of administrative processes. This basic incompatibility between a bureaucratic control model of work management and the humanistic, relationship-driven nature of the work meant to be performed in a social service agency is a familiar criticism. An outcome orientation, however, can support the empowerment of service units and workers to reestablish their concern for the *ends* of their work, rather than the *means* by which it gets done. Charles Handy, in a recent article entitled "Trust and the Virtual Organization," asks the question: How do you manage people you can't see? His position is that an organization must trust its employees, not blindly but within the bounds of shared commitments to the purposes of the organization [Handy 1995, as cited in Fukuyama 1995].

Child and family social services practice has traditionally concentrated on methods social workers employ—planning them, implementing them, measuring them, and evaluating them from a process perspective. Practice has seldom reached beyond the activities of the social worker to determine what difference those methods have made in people's lives, what role they have played in reaching goals that society deemed desirable, and thus to what extent they are worthy of financial and moral support. Child and family services practice has in many cases come to act as if the means *were* the ends. Providing a service—well planned, well executed, well evaluated—seems to be *the* goal of the activity, rather than a means to a greater personal or social end.

Failing to identify the specific outcomes that service methods are to achieve can misguide the measurement of efficacy. Those with a fiscal interest can learn that a method is or is not applied, but will not know if a particular method resulted in the desired outcome. By first defining the desired social end, and then outlining the steps that will achieve that end, practitioners can measure both ends and means for achieving them, and report on both for fiscal analysis in a meaningful way. Without the linkage to ends, a discussion about methods—having more or fewer services, increasing or decreasing a budget—becomes purely an exchange of opinions unrelated to any means to validate positive or negative judgments.

At the most basic level of a social service organization, practice must reorient itself outward, shifting focus from the agency's internally controlled processes to its externally accomplished social results. The individual practitioner is a change agent: team-based, self-critical, results- and consumer-oriented. By helping the client to envision the desired outcome first, a worker creates a frame for his or her work and a partnership with the client in the service of its accomplishment. Through the use of open, interactive teams, reliance on feedback from clients, and opening of progress assessments to other specialists, the worker also creates the standards against which success will be judged and manages case progress without an elaborate information system and research studies. While these more formal support systems are important, the changes in practice described above need to occur at the most basic level so that information management and research can support, rather than drive, the practice approach.

This kind of practice environment requires a nontraditional organizational culture. The agency must move away from both the bureaucratic and the private practice models of professional work, and toward an organizational ethic that seeks to unleash the powerful creativity and independence of staff members in the service of organizational goals. In the absence of an outcome orientation, organizations increasingly rely on the stultifying control of detailed processes as the basis of organizational leadership. This reinforces the pre-existing tendency for individuals, in fields with vague and difficult to measure outcomes, to concentrate on internal processes that are relatively easy to manipulate and control. The result can be goal displacement, substituting a means for an end, which then tends to be reinforced by administrative practices that reward large quantities of activity while ignoring the achievement of changed behaviors.

The creation of an outcome-oriented agency environment is not straightforward because of the complex contexts in which social service organizations work. As discussed in Chapter 1, the agency vision, mission, and major program objectives form the context for managing with an outcome orientation. At the same time, those outcome ideas must be organically related to an overarching, and strongly articulated theoretical framework that explains how the outcomes are linked to the specific work of the agency at the client level, thus serving as a road map for anticipating steps in an overall work process, for the analysis of problems, and for the choice of solutions. They must be clearly articulated; compatible with each other; realistic within the constraints of the organization's resources, knowledge, and technology; and increasingly assimilated by staff as guides to day-to-day thinking, decision making, and behavior. (See Figure 4.1).

These desired outcomes are only partially defined by the agency. They should also be an expression of the community environment, client strengths and needs, service delivery process, and outcomes that both payors and consumers desire.

Achieving an outcome-based approach to service delivery is a complex endeavor, one that gives rise to *hope, fear,* and *confusion,* according to Schorr et al. [1994, p. 13]:

Hope that result-based accountability could be the key to:

- freeing schools, health care, social agencies, and other human services from the rules that prevent them from operating flexibly in response to the needs of those they serve,

- restoring the public's faith that both public and private human service institutions can accomplish their intended purpose, and

- encouraging communities to be more planful, more intentional, in how they support children and families.

Fear that result-based accountability will be misused and bring about:

- the abandonment of attempts to better the conditions of disadvantaged children whose effects are difficult to measure or take a long time to occur,

- the erosion of essential procedural protections and neglect of concerns for equity,

- a smoke screen behind which further funding cutbacks will be made, or

- decisions that penalize individual professionals, institutions, and agencies who may not be achieving hoped-for results, but are trying hard and doing the best they can.

Confusion about how to devise, and obtain agreement on, a set of goals and outcomes and reliable ways of measuring results that could justify the hopes and quell the fears of the many concerned constituencies.

There are a number of key management issues and principles that must be addressed in implementing an outcome-oriented approach to service delivery. These principles will help achieve what is hoped for and avoid what is feared. Other chapters in this book begin to address some of the confusion. The next sections of this chapter will discuss how an outcome orientation can be applied in case planning and service delivery, before addressing some of the management principles necessary to support this approach.

How an Outcome-Oriented and Developmentally Focused Framework Can Guide Service Delivery

For many years, the human services literature has emphasized the importance of formulating clear and behaviorally specific treatment goals. Research findings attest to the value of social worker and client establishing agreed-upon goals that will frame and guide their change-oriented relationship toward the desired outcomes.

The Importance of Goal-Setting

Rhodes [1977] observed that ambiguities about the goal-setting process, and the poor specification of treatment goals that result, account for a consistently high percentage of unplanned client withdrawal from service. Wood [1978], after reviewing several outcome studies on the efficacy of direct practice, reported, among other findings, that in studies reporting negative outcomes, practitioners had not employed explicit outcomes with explicit treatment goals. However, practitioners in studies reporting positive outcomes typically used contracts that spelled out the goals to be achieved in the helping process.

Reid [1970] concluded that social work practitioners were overly general in specifying goals, leading to "unrealistic aspirations and to repeated shifts in direction" (p. 145). Similar conclusions were articulated by Wood [1978] who cautioned direct service workers about the dangers of setting vague and unreasonably high goals for those they work with. Clearly, goal-setting in the case planning process is central to the successful achievement of the desired case outcomes.

Goals specify what clients wish to accomplish. They are an essential ingredient in the contract for service that outlines what the agency and/or the caseworker commit to in trying to help achieve these goals, and what the client will do. Inherent

Figure 4.1

Logic Planning Model for Child and Family Services

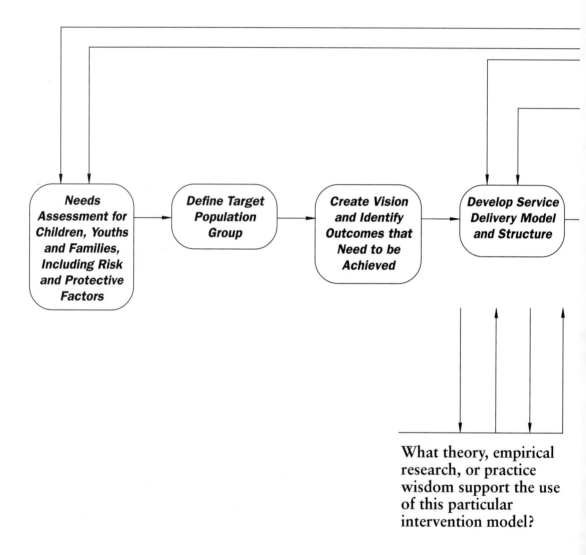

What theory, empirical research, or practice wisdom support the use of this particular intervention model?

Sources: Adapted from Savas, this volume; and Committee on Prevention of Mental Disorders. (1995). Division of Biobehavioral Sciences and Mental Disorders, Institute of Medicine. (1994). Appendix A— Summary. In Mrazek, P.J., & Haggerty, R.J. (Eds.), *Reducing risks for mental disorders—Frontiers of preventive intervention research,* p. 505. Washington, DC: National Academy Press.

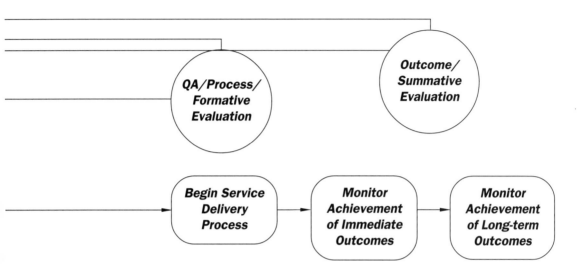

in the goals should be desired outcomes—changes in life situations, abilities, and environmental pressures that correspond to particular problems identified through a focused assessment process. In order for the casework process to be outcome focused, the caseworker and client need to understand there are intervening goals and outcome goals. Intervening goals, or goal indicators, are steps in the pathway that lead to the achievement of the larger outcome goal. In this approach, having an intervening goal that is a small achievement (reducing tantrums in the home by one per week as a start) is a milestone or step towards the desired end, not the end itself. Is locating a resource the desired outcome, or is the accomplishment of some salutary effect in the client's life the outcome? The latter is always preferred: it is focused on client accomplishment and desirable social results, not on the good working of internal agency processes, which may assist the client in outcome achievement but are not outcomes themselves, and are only of interest to the degree that they assist in outcome achievement.

For example, in family foster care, the client is a youth who is being cared for by someone other than immediate biological parents. Setting goals for short and longer range outcomes is often a team effort involving the foster parents, the youth, the agency social worker, community representatives (the court or the tribal authorities) and, whenever possible, the birth parents and other relatives. The establishment of behaviorally clear goals serves many valuable functions for the youth, birth family members, foster parents, and social workers:

- Assures that all parties are in agreement about the intervention and the long range outcomes to be achieved, thus increasing the motivation of the participants;

- Specifies desired behavior changes clearly, thus providing direction and continuity to helping efforts and an understanding of what success will look like;

- Provides the raw material (the content), around which the youth, foster parents, and worker build their partnership;

- Facilitates the development and selection of appropriate treatment and intervention strategies;

- Helps the youth, birth family, foster parents, and social worker monitor their progress towards the desired long-range outcomes so that each will know when and where achievements have been made and where effort needs to be focused;

- May help staff, youth, family members, and foster parents understand what and how much a particular youth, developmentally, is able to accomplish in the near future as distinct from the distant future;

- Permits agency staff members to determine if they have the skills, competencies, interest, and time for working with the youth, or whether the youth should be referred to someone else for best service;

- Permits youths and families to determine their own commitment to the agency's goal priorities and approach to services and their willingness to participate in the roles expected of them;

- Promotes a conversation that elicits more information, so that staff members gain knowledge of the family context, the larger ecological issues that may be present, what is and is not working, and how people feel about it—all of which can be used to promote better assessment and more focused goal-setting as part of the natural case-planning process.

- Provides outcome criteria in evaluating the effectiveness of specific interventions and of the overall helping process.

Employing goal-setting to achieve the above functions requires knowledge on the part of the social worker about types of goals, and the ability to distinguish and help others distinguish between goals and processes and skills in goal negotiation and conflict management. These are some of the core competencies necessary for implementing an outcome-oriented approach to practice. In the next section, some of these core competencies will be discussed, beginning with the ability to set long-term goals via vision statements.

Setting Long-Range Goals

A program that sees its mission as the raising of a child to adulthood, working with families (such as those involved with severe neglect) over a long period of time, or establishing some sense of continuity in understanding a child and planning for his or her progress despite a disjointed service delivery process has a special responsibility for being clear about its expected long-range results. Such programs can have a profound effect on the direction and quality of a client's life. Clarity of direction, and direction-setting shared by the affected party, are ethical, not just methodological, requirements. Moreover, the ability to make sound decisions, with reasonably full knowledge of the consequences associated with various options, is one of the key indicators that the consumer of the service has attained the requisite skills to take charge of his or her own life in a responsible way. All of these considerations should undergird a practice focus in which joint staff and client definition of the expected results is the most significant element of the agreement to work together.

In programs truly geared to the provision of short-term services, a concentration on short-term service goals may be appropriate. In a program that takes on long-term parental responsibility for a child's development and future success, such a concentration is not adequate. Most effective long-term family foster care and group care programs have adopted long-range outcome measures that guide overall practice with the youths and families they serve.

The primary outcome is helping youths to lead successful, independent lives by developing physically, emotionally, cognitively, socially, and in other ways. For example, because The Casey Family Program delivers long-term family foster care, its long-range outcomes are concerned with safe emancipation of youths, and are referred to collectively as the "Program Vision for Children." One or more of these long-range outcomes can be used to develop a "Vision for a Particular Child," which is constructed individually for each child in the care of a program. A vision for a child can be described in terms of the quality, or characteristics, of the eventual adulthood seen as appropriate for that youth.

A dual level of vision is present, as the program's view of positive *agency/system* outcomes parallels the view of outcomes that is developed for each *individual child*. Thus, programmatic achievement of safe emancipation is interpreted as having been met when a high proportion of program graduates meet a range of success criteria. Those criteria are interpreted to fit the unique circumstances of the particular child. This level of vision attempts to mirror the mental picture that a parent or guardian creates for his or her own child, even if it sometimes is not fully articulated in words. Such a vision pulls together the family's sense of how a successful adult thinks and lives, and strives to create the experiences that will lead the child to realize that vision.

For many agencies the focus is on a parent or an entire family. In these situations, the family can be involved in discussing long-range goals for themselves, such as employment or more stable housing, as a way of gaining a perspective on their situation and moving to develop more short-range goals that will enable them to achieve their long-range plans.

In outcome-oriented service planning, case outcomes are the expected end states to be achieved (child developmental milestones or key areas of improvement in parental functioning, such as having an adequate food supply or abandoning the use of severe corporal punishment). This work is done within the context of a theoretical base that explains the nature of the development cycle for individual or family change by establishing a predictable order to the steps in the change process. Within that framework, one begins by partializing broad outcomes into narrower *case goals*, a term used to designate the types of outcomes that generally may take a year to two years to accomplish.

Case *indicators* are the more immediate changes or improvements expected to occur as a result of some action or service, using a one- to six-month time frame. (Indicators can also be thought of as the smaller milestones on the path toward accomplishment of case goals.) The term *indicator* is therefore used in the specific manner adopted by many other human service programs, which have implemented the Mission—Goal—Objectives/Indicators paradigm. But in all cases— mission, goal, and indicator—we are dealing with outcomes, not processes; end states, not activities related to end states.

Components of Case Planning

Three major components pertain to professional case planning in many family service agencies (See Figure 4.2). Some of these components are assumed and not explicitly described in program training manuals or operating guidelines, yet they are critical to an outcome approach to service delivery. The role of each of these components in case planning is illustrated by Figure 4.3 and is briefly described in the next sections, along with examples for case planning purposes.

Assessment

Assessment is an ongoing clinical activity. The formal recording of assessment data occurs initially during the intake process, and generally every six months as part of case reviews. The purpose of this activity is to assess child, parent, or family development, progress toward identified outcomes, the continued appropriateness of identified case goals, and the effectiveness of the service plan and service delivery. A variety of assessment approaches can be used, including client self-observation. Intake is a time to learn about family strengths and problems, to

---

Figure 4.2

Components of Case Planning

I. Assessments

    A. Child and family intake assessment; and

    B. Periodic case review and assessment

II. Outcomes

    A. Program vision for children and families

    B. Vision for a particular child, parent, or family;

    C. Case goals for a particular child, parents, or family that are outcome-oriented; and

    D. Indicators that mark the progress made towards case goals;

III. Methods

    A. Development of the service plan (including case resources and case methods); and

    B. Services provision

---

determine the environment that would best support family member growth and development, and to develop a vision or long-range goals for the family.

The child's or family's development, progress toward achievement of the long range outcomes, achievement of previous case goals and indicators, and the effectiveness of the service plan and delivery are assessed every six months. This review and analysis of case outcomes and plans is essential for future planning. Following a well-defined process of assessing progress and reviewing outcomes means that case planning is done with careful consideration of the ongoing and changing needs of the child and family. In this way, a long-range plan can be implemented incrementally, yet continuously. Some agencies review the case goals and service plan every three months, to provide a less intensive but nonetheless essential review of youth progress. This review, documented in the contact or case notes, also helps meet Council on Accreditation (COA) and Joint Commission on Accreditation of Healthcare Organizations (JCAHO) standards. (See Chapter 8.)

Service Outcomes

An outcome is an end state that is desired. In planning, one must be able to specify the desired long-range outcome(s) by envisioning the program outcomes for all families or individual consumers being served, specifying those in terms that are relevant for individual consumers, and creating the goals and indicators

Figure 4.3

One Model of Outcome-Oriented Case Planing

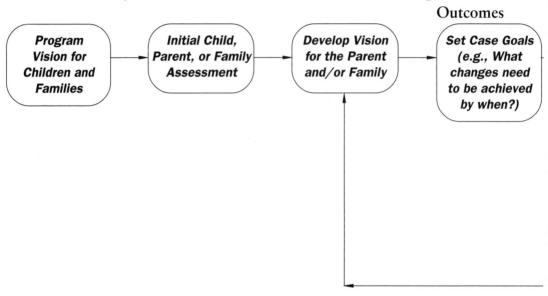

Outcomes

Program vision for families and children (Life-long generic outcomes for all those served

Child, parent or family, vision (Life-long outcomes for a particular youth,

Case goals (6-month to 2-year

Indicators of

Child, parent, and family developmental frameworks provide the critical frame of reference by enabling the worker to assess the youth, parent, or family within a context of specific developmental milestones that must be achieved for healthy growth and development.

Service Methods

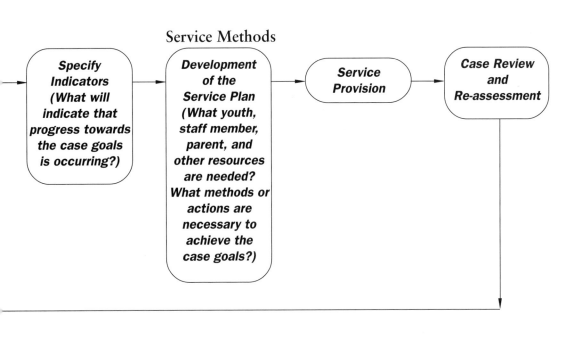

parent, or family)

goals for a particular youth, parent, or family)

progress toward goal achievement for a 1–6-month period

Achievement of Program Vision

Source: Adapted from Traglia et al. (1994). *The Casey Family Program.* The Casey Family Program, 1300 Dexter Avenue North, Suite 400, Seattle, WA 98109.

that form the developmental milestones that must be reached along the way. Listed below are four types of outcomes for families and children in family foster care that would fit with this case planning framework.

Program Vision for Children and Families

For most children, the goal of a family foster care program is to reunite them with their biological parents or relatives or to place them in an adoptive home. For children who are not likely to be reunited or adopted, a long-term foster care program is dedicated to raising children to safe emancipation by maximizing child development in a variety of areas, always reconsidering the possibility of family reunification or adoption, as well as the important role played by birth families, a child's cultural milieu, and the community within which the child is rooted.

Programmatic outcomes desired for all these children are set through policy. Such outcomes answer the questions: What does the program try to do? What is the point of our work? What is the fundamental mission or purpose of the agency as it works with youth?

For example, when a long-term foster care program or an independent living transition program say that they "raise" or "emancipate" children, they use short-hand to summarize their desired outcomes. What does it mean to "raise" children? A number of child welfare agencies have defined this outcome generally as the achievement of safe emancipation. All of the activities should be understandable in relation to this outcome. Some activities are directly related—such as providing a safe home in which the child will live; some are indirectly related—such as ensuring that the agency fundraising and contracting process provides sufficient income to continue the work until the child in care reaches emancipation.

Embedded within the notion of safe emancipation are more concrete outcomes that define the phrase. These are based upon the field's and the program's knowledge of what youths need for adulthood:

- a sense of belonging,

- an acknowledgment and honoring of one's cultural genesis,

- an accommodation to one's birth family,

- an ability to form and maintain healthy relationships,

- an ability to participate in the life of the community,

- an ability to support oneself economically, and

- a sense of self-worth and mastery.

These outcomes are not problem focused. They are focused on growth, on the future, and on the child's potential. They should be seen as requiring a search for, and a concentration on, the strengths of the child first, and only secondarily on identifying and overcoming problems. Thus, the work of the program and its staff members is to create the conditions within which the growing child can achieve these outcome prerequisites to safe emancipation. A classic quotation from Goethe illustrates the importance of establishing a long-range vision for children: "If you treat an individual as he is, he will remain as he is. But, if you treat him as if he were what he ought to be and could be, he will become what he ought to be and could be." [pointed out by Anne Nicoll, personal correspondence]

During intake, the worker translates the program's overall desired outcomes to the level of the individual case by creating a vision that is tailored to meet the unique needs of each child or family. That vision is an outgrowth of careful child and family assessment. Assessment of child and family functioning in a variety of areas is the primary method for determining that family and child's strengths and needs. The Casey Family Program, for example, uses eight case planning factors as assessment areas: emotional health, family adjustment and other relationships, cultural identification, competence and achievement, physical health, educational development, self-sufficiency, and legal involvement.

Using this or another assessment framework, workers ask themselves such questions as: How does this child or family's unique circumstances inform and define their need to feel a sense of belonging? Given that assessment, what should the vision be for this particular child related to his or her sense of belonging? Each consumer of service in this area must have such a vision developed, recorded, and continuously referenced and updated throughout his or her life in care. A social worker and a 13-year-old Native American girl developed this vision jointly:

> Angie will learn to speak her language and learn to participate in ceremonies. Angie will graduate from high school and pursue educational goals beyond high school. Angie will be integrated into the Lewis family through a Hunka ceremony when she is finished with high school. Angie will learn the roles and responsibilities of being a woman in preparation for womanhood and motherhood.

The outcomes are the criteria by which we measure our success at the end of the process. All of our intervening work concentrates on how to create, with the active participation of the parents and child, an environment within which the family can address, master, and assimilate the tasks that are the signposts of their growth and development.

Case Goals

The worker must then translate this vision into a form that is useful for planning work. This requires a further level of analysis, one that is repeated throughout the life of the case. Most child welfare agencies use a three- to six-month planning cycle for setting and monitoring case goals, with a longer horizon of one to two years for more comprehensive planning. Clearly, the length of the cycle is dependent upon the needs of the family or child and the particular goals that are being set.

And yet, how should the worker translate the lifetime case vision into a set of manageable, one- to two-year case goals? First, the worker must have a frame of reference, a generic life plan as a starting point in analyzing the family today and indicating where that child or family needs to go next. These questions seem best answered by using a child, adult, or family development frame of reference.

The worker therefore assesses the child, parent, or family by placing them in a developmental range, both by age and by observation of their behaviors. This in turn gives the worker a partial, but important, picture of the client's past, present, and future in relation to the work that must be accomplished in order for the them to reach his or her personal manifestation of the outcomes that the program has determined are essential.

Then the worker sets a one- to two-year case goal that links his or her assessment of the particular child or family to what their next achievable developmental horizon needs to be.

Some examples of case goals are listed below:

1. Mary will improve her behavior in school, reducing physical fights and stealing from students, as measured by the Achenbach Teacher Report Form, by April 1995.

2. John will improve his school performance in terms of reading level by achieving a fifth-grade reading level by June 1996.

3. Mary's relationship with her husband will improve by January 1995, so that both parents note violent disagreements only one or two times per month.

Case goals are measurable, expressed in the form of an observable end state consistent with the child's particular developmental strengths and needs, and appropriate to the social and cultural circumstances of the child and his or her family. Therfore, while a child, parent, or family development frame of reference is an aid, the worker's job of translating that generic life plan into the concrete circumstances of the particular client is a formidable analytic task. In summary:

- The term *case goal* is used to designate achievements that generally take one to two years to accomplish, but might be set for a shorter period of time, such as three to six months.

- Case goals lead to major outcomes or achievements for the youth, such as finishing an educational program, developing a healthy network of friends, and increasing self-sufficiency skills with respect to decision making.

- Case goals are derived from the assessment, and either represent the developmental milestones that must be achieved to make progress toward the vision developed with the child, or address particular needs of the child or family that, if not addressed, would be a barrier to development.

- Case goals specify the results to be achieved by a certain date. More specifically, they name the changes or improvements expected to occur as a result of some action or service. What do you expect to happen as a result of the services provided? What behavioral changes or other changes are desired?

- Case goals are stated in clear and, to the extent possible, measurable (i.e., operationally defined) terms. Sometimes the measurement method is specified, while in other cases it is implied. Measurements may take a variety of forms, such as validated tests or observations by knowledgeable individuals involved in the child's life.

Outcome-Oriented Case Indicators

Indicators are also derived from the assessment, because they represent what must be achieved during the next one to six months to eventually reach a particular case goal. They might include the acquisition of a particular skill or the attainment of a more immediate developmental milestone. Specifically, indicators refer to the interim changes or improvements expected to occur to reach a case goal.

The indicators form a bridge between the goals to which they lead and the service plan through which they are accomplished. For example, the completion of daily homework (indicator) may be an outgrowth of weekly tutoring sessions (service), in turn leading to successful completion of the school semester (goal).

Some examples of indicators of progress toward achieving the case goal of improved anger management for a parent or child might include the following:

1. Mary has learned how to describe different feelings.

2. Mary is able to assess how her emotions can change over time, using a feelings scale and other methods.

3. Mary can use two self-relaxation methods to control angry feelings.

Service Methods

Services are first planned, using available assessment data, and then provided by the social worker or another person. The following sections describe the components of service.

The Service Plan

Only after the outcomes for the child, parent, and/or family and the interim case goals related to them have been established can a service plan be developed. It is tied directly to the identified needs and outcomes for that family, and ultimately to the agency and youth/family/worker vision for that child. The service plan describes what will be done to help achieve the case goals, and it often includes the case resources and case methods that will be involved.

Case resources (also known as input goals) are most often referred to while planning a program or service, because they describe the necessary organizational components or supplies. Case resources focus on the staff, materials, and other components used to provide the program or service.

For most case plans, describing case resources will not be necessary, but in some situations social workers use statements of this type to identify what will be needed to provide a service or treatment intervention. For example:

1. Locate and purchase drawing materials and other group activity supplies by May 1.

2. Contract with a therapist for Marcia by August 1.

3. Find a new foster home for Susan by July 15.

Case methods (also known as process goals) are typically incorporated within a service plan for a child or family. Case methods refer most often to activities, plans, tasks, or services that will be provided and worker actions that will be taken.

Case resources and case methods are rarely referred to by name in case planning materials because they are imbedded within the service plan. Examples of case methods would include:

1. Provide two hours of individual therapy per week, beginning March 2, with a formal review of progress every six months.

2. Provide one hour of tutoring in reading every week, beginning late April.

3. Enroll Matthew in the YMCA camp for two weeks this summer.

Services provision. Services provision includes the actual activity and tasks that the worker performs through the use of various case resources and case methods, all of which is described in the service plan.

Putting It All Together

The relationships among assessment, planning, and specifying outcome-oriented case goals, indicators, case resources, and case methods can be described in various ways. One phase builds upon another, with the overall program mission or vision, the child/parent/family assessment, and rigorous critical thinking forming the foundation for effective practice. More specifically, the *program vision* sets the context for the long-range outcomes to be achieved, while the *client vision* grows out of the individual assessment process, so that specific *case goals* are set in a sensitive manner for a particular youth, parent, or family.

One of the core tasks of a family service worker is to translate the case goals into a plan of action. The worker's job is a constant, dynamic interplay among observation, analysis, action, and evaluation in the here and now, while maintaining a focus on the ultimate outcomes desired. Progress toward the accomplishment of case goals is assessed by focusing on the attainment of certain specific and time-limited *indicators*.

Many child welfare programs view the case planning horizon as a rolling process of yearly or half-yearly goal setting, broken into quarterly planning and analysis segments based upon the duration of service delivery. Agencies frequently, however, misname the three to six month time interval a "reporting" cycle. In fact, the report is only an external sign or documentation of a much more important process: the review and revision of case goals through an analysis of continuously recorded facts, observations, and impressions—gathered from personal contact, written reports, and expert evaluations—within a child, parent, and/or family development frame of reference.

The six-month review is an opportunity to mutually assess client functioning and achievement of outcomes with the youth, the family, and collateral resources using an historical and current perspective. But it is also a future-oriented document, in that it is where the service plan for the next six months is developed and recorded. The worker has several important tasks:

- Interacting with the child and with significant people in the child's life, including birth parents, extended family members, foster parents, and other professionals involved with the child.

- Interpreting and recording those contacts in a contact log.

- Establishing developmentally focused case goals based on the range of data gathered and analyzed, with a specific time horizon.

- Disaggregating those goals into one- to six-month intervals. This involves establishing indicators or milestones toward case goal achievement. The important point is that these indicators must be clearly related to the developmental case goals set for the child, parent, or family.

- The yearly cycle calls for an in-depth reexamination of the case goals and progress made towards meeting those goals, to include the child, birth parents, foster parents, and administrative staff (as appropriate) in a formal, evaluative way.

The above process results in the worker creating or revising the case goals and indicators for the next six months on the basis of a developmental framework. Finally, a new or revised service plan is developed. Most, if not all, of the service plan relates directly to the case goals and indicators. The focus is on activities, services (case methods and case resources), and the creation of opportunities that will lead to the attainment of the indicators set out in the plan. The service plan, however, may describe worker, client, or agency actions that do not directly relate to a specific case goal but are necessary prerequisites for the case management process and outcome achievement, such as ongoing medical treatment of an allergic condition.

Key Management Issues and Principles

None of these outcome-oriented concepts and processes can be implemented overnight. Unless the governing body and key executives demonstrate that they value this approach, model critical thinking and outcome orientation in the ways they perform their functions, and provide incentives to support achievement of program and individual child and family outcomes over methods, there will be inadequate or incomplete implementation of this approach. Commitment will be demonstrated over time through the active leadership and support of everyone in the management team. Management has at least seven key tasks in this process:

- Creating a climate that champions this vision-driven, outcome-based approach;

- Building interagency communication systems that promote the sharing of breakthroughs in process and technique;

- Insisting that agency services, whether therapy, tutoring, or health care, are all outcome oriented;

- Building reward and compensation systems for staff that are tied to results attained and contributions to interagency effectiveness;

- Valuing and promoting consumer assessments and active contributions to the evolving program design by placing consumer feedback in a prominent position in the publicly described hierarchy of evidence of program efficacy, and acting promptly upon client suggestions for program or case-specific improvements;

- Providing regular clinical consultation and training to staff based on practice models that are outcome-oriented and consumer focused; and

- Using supervision methods that focus on the key components of this model and supervisors who are capable of providing the proper feedback and skill-building.

Implicit in all of these approaches is the responsibility of administrators to create and maintain an organizational culture that values excellence in service design, execution, and results. Staff members and program participants alike should know that the organization is striving for and will reward work that demonstrates congruence between the collective vision of program and individual child and family success. Of course, this means that the staff development efforts of the organization must be geared to the cultivation of skills, knowledge, and attitudes that are complementary to the organizational culture, and that the human resource systems (compensation, benefits, etc.) reflect organizational goals.

In short, the more the organizational infrastructure reflects an intentional approach to achieving the desired results, the more likely that the outcomes will be achieved. Organizations, however, do not operate in a vacuum, but in a larger community environment. Administrators must appreciate the necessity for their organization to be an active player in developing and supporting an external environment where its values and approaches can thrive. Active and ongoing work to cultivate significant stakeholders within the business, policymaking, and fund development circles of the community, for example, is an important function of the executive, as well as the line staff and program participants.

These stakeholders must be given a real role in defining the program goals and identifying ways they can help the program meet them. The risks and opportunities involved in this approach cannot be understated. Professional staff may hear unpleasant truths about how others see their methods and approaches. At the very least, the definition of *team* will have to be expanded to include the work effort of people who are not under the direct control of the agency. The potential benefit, however, is quite significant—a greater investment in achieving the program's mission and in the aspirations of program participants, who may start to be viewed as people with active potential to be tapped rather than limited, passive beneficiaries of the largess of others.

These management approaches are consistent with the currently evolving concept that building social capital is a necessary feature of healthy social organization—facilitating collaboration and cooperation between individuals and sectors to achieve common goals [Putnam 1993; Fukuyama 1995]. Applying the work of involved people who have multiple roles and functions in varied settings, all of them integral to achieving positive outcomes for individuals as well as social institutions, requires creative leadership of the systems that create, sustain, and rely upon the organization. These tasks are undoubtedly complex, but must be mastered if the program vision, as well as the visions for individual consumers of the service, are to be achieved.

Conclusion

This chapter described what is involved in applying an outcome orientation to administration and practice in child and family services. It discussed how to redefine what you provide from a service provision perspective to a broader perspective that also incorporates outcomes. We hope that it will help bridge the concepts discussed in the previous chapters, which focused on the program model and service delivery process, with those discussed in the outcome evaluation chapter to follow.

References

American Humane Association. (1993). *First National Roundtable on Outcome Measures in Child Welfare Services*. Englewood, CO: Author.

Fukuyama, F. (1995). *Trust*. New York: Free Press.

Magura, S., & Moses, B. S. (1986). *Outcome measures for child welfare services: Theory and applications*. Washington, DC: Child Welfare League of America.

Maluccio, A. N. (1979). Perspectives of social workers and clients on treatment outcome. *Social Casework, 60*(7), 394-401.

McDevitt, S. (1994). Case records in public child welfare: Uses and a flexible format. *Child Welfare, 73*(1), 41-55.

Parker, R., Ward, H., Jackson, S., Wedge, P., & Aldgate, J. (1991). *Looking after children: Assessing outcomes in childcare*. London: HSMO Books.

Putnam, R. (1994). The prosperous community: Social capital and public life. *The American Prospect, 13* (Spring), 35-42.

Rapp, C. A., & Poertner, J. (1987). Moving clients center stage through the use of client outcomes. In R.J. Patti, J. Poertner, & C.A. Rapp (Eds.), *Managing for service effectiveness in social welfare organizations*. (Special issue) *Administration in Social Work, 11*(3-4), 23-38).

Reid, W. (1970). Implications of research for the goals of casework. *Smith College Studies in Social Work, 40*, 140-154.

Rhodes, S. (1977). Contract negotiation in the initial stage of casework. *Social Service Review, 51*, 125-140.

Schorr, L., Farrow, F., Hornbeck, D., & Watson, S. (1994). The case for shifting to results-based accountability. In N. Young, S. Gardner, S. Coley, L. Schorr, & C. Bruner (Eds.), *Making a difference: Moving to outcome-based accountability for comprehensive service reforms*. Falls Church, VA: National Center for Service Integration Clearinghouse.

The Casey Family Program. (1994). *Practice guidelines for clinical practice and case management*. Seattle, WA: Author.

Wood, K. (1978). Casework effectiveness: A new look at the research evidence. *Social Work, 23*, 437-458.

Young, N., Gardner, S., & Coley, S. (1994). Getting to outcomes in integrated service delivery models. In N. Young, S. Gardner, S. Coley, L. Schorr, & C. Bruner (Eds.), *Making a difference: Moving to outcome-based accountability for comprehensive service reforms (pp.* 7-12). Falls Church, VA: National Center for Service Integration Clearinghouse.

For Further Information

Mrazek, P., & Haggerty, R. (Eds.). (1994). *Reducing risks for mental disorders: Frontiers for preventive intervention research.* Washington, DC: National Academy Press. Presents an excellent summary of the theory and research-based design of prevention programs.

Parker, R., Ward, H., Jackson, S., Wedge, P., & Aldgate, J. (1991). *Looking after children: Assessing outcomes in childcare.* London: HSMO Books. Discusses an innovative approach to using developmental milestones and other areas of focus to guide practice in child welfare.

Young, N., Gardner, S., Coley, S., Schorr L., & Bruner, C. (1994). *Making a difference: Moving to outcome-based accountability for comprehensive service reforms.* Falls Church, VA: National Center for Service Integration Clearinghouse. Provides a concise summary of some of the major concepts of an outcome orientation to service delivery within a larger systems and agency context.

Chapter 5

How Do We Know We're Making a Difference?

—Miriam P. Kluger and Gina Alexander

Why Do an Outcome Effectiveness Study?

Are your services making a difference? How have they changed your clients' lives? Outcome effectiveness studies get to the heart of these questions in a formal, documented way. Also referred to as impact assessments [Rossi & Freeman 1993], outcome effectiveness studies measure whether a program has attained the goals that service staff members set for their clients.

Proving a service's worth or effectiveness has become increasingly necessary in the funding arena. Third party payors, foundations, and all levels of government are scrutinizing the results of the services they are funding and calling upon providers to become more accountable with respect to outcomes. Outcome effectiveness studies are often a prerequisite for receiving basic funding or service contracts. The United Way recently began to require that organizations demonstrate service outcomes. With the advent of quality principles (QI, CQI, TQM) and customer-driven service, assuring the effectiveness of our services becomes even more important. Yet relatively few child welfare agencies know how to actually measure service effectiveness.

Outcome effectiveness studies focus on a specific service or program rather than on the agency as a whole. From an agency leadership perspective, information on the effectiveness of individual services is critical when making decisions regarding strategic and long-range planning, budgeting, continuous quality improvement, and right-sizing. The major technical considerations discussed in this chapter include allowing enough time to carefully define what effectiveness means for the particular service; using multiple measures from multiple sources to capture client, provider, and other relevant perspectives; and incorporating an assessment of any extenuating circumstances or factors that may account for positive changes noted. The resources that must be devoted to these considerations, such as time given by provider staff, evaluators, and clients, make these endeavors costly! However, a "quick and dirty," single-measure assessment, such as a client satisfaction survey, is not adequate to credibly assess a program's effectiveness.

Chapters 2 and 3 provided information on how to define the components of a program and what steps are necessary for evaluating various aspects of the program. This chapter describes some of the major approaches to outcome effectiveness and what is involved in implementing these kinds of studies.

Illustrations from outcome effectiveness studies in child welfare are used in the hope that the reader may freely adapt these examples to his or her own work. But first, for those readers still skeptical about their value, we present our Top Six List of reasons for conducting an outcome effectiveness study.

The Top Six Reasons for Conducting An Outcome Study

Reason #6: Assists the agency in meeting licensing and accreditation standards.

Reason #5: Improves the chances for success when applying for grants. An outcome study can describe the impact of the service in a quantified, objective manner.

Reason #4: Provides the board of directors, agency administrators, and line staff with information for planning and budgetary decisions that affect the survival of programs.

Reason #3: Empowers clients and consumers as they supply critical information and participate in studies. Respects their thinking and input as important to the provision of top-notch, customer-driven services.

Reason #2: Provides agency leaders with reliable information to respond to growing payor requirements for quality outcome data.

Reason #1: Helps program directors identify what is most effective and what needs to be improved in order to manage and improve services.

What Is an Outcome Effectiveness Study?

Unlike some agency approaches to evaluation research, outcome effectiveness studies are not primarily concerned with unearthing a program's weaknesses. Nor are outcome effectiveness studies synonymous with client satisfaction surveys, where consumers are queried regarding their likes and dislikes about aspects of a service they received, although client satisfaction surveys may be a component. Rather than relying on information provided solely by the client, as a client satisfaction survey does, outcome effectiveness studies often seek information from multiple sources, including the service provider.

As their name implies, outcome effectiveness studies focus on the outcomes rather than the processes of service. Instead of focusing on how the services are delivered, they examine the impact these services have on clients at various points in a program, including at termination and follow-up. They attempt to determine whether the client system (youth, parent, family, community) has changed in a way targeted by the service.

At the individual, family, and systems levels, they attempt to assess the net impact of the service after controlling for other possible explanations. For example, clients might be randomly assigned to two different kinds of service (e.g., one experimental, one "business as usual"); or clients might be matched with comparison group clients on the basis of certain characteristics, such as age, gender, race, and social functioning.

It is frequently impossible to use random assignment in a child welfare setting. This does not excuse child welfare agencies from conducting rigorous outcome research. One of the most important concepts underlying outcome evaluation is the idea of comparison. One cannot simply say that clients are better for having participated in a program; the skeptic will ask, "better than what (or better than whom)?" The answer is either that they are better than they were before (determined by assessing them before and after the program), or they are better than others who did not participate (determined by assessing participants and nonparticipants). In research jargon, these comparisons constitute a *design*. The design of an evaluation lays out who is being compared to whom. Children receiving a service are compared to children who are not receiving the service, and other factors being equal, any gains observed in the first group are believed to result from the service.

When it is not possible to randomly assign clients to treatment and control groups, it is often possible to involve a comparison group in some other way [Campbell & Stanley 1963; Cook & Campbell 1979]. One may be able to identify a similar group of children who are not part of the program being evaluated (comparison group or matched sample design), or one may be able to compare children participating in a program to those on a waiting list (case overflow control group design). The use of randomly assigned control and treatment groups, however, is considered the most rigorous approach for quantitative evaluations.

It is frequently possible to strengthen the evaluation design of an existing program. For example, if there is a waiting list for the program being evaluated, these people could be included in the evaluation as a case overflow control group, and they could be assessed at regular intervals, using criteria similar to those for clients accepted into the program. Or, if all the people on a waiting list are ultimately offered services, an assessment might be made while each client is on the waiting list and then again at the regularly scheduled times for clients in the program [see Bingham & Felbinger 1990, Cook & Campbell 1979, Grinnell 1993, Rubin & Babbie 1993].

The least rigorous approach is to assess clients before and after program participation (pretest-posttest design). Without comparison groups or longitudinal time-series designs, it is difficult to determine what causes the change. Note that the evaluation steps described in the next section are not exhaustive, but rather are intended to outline the major phases and to provide some key principles or cautions.

Steps in Conducting an Outcome Effectiveness Study

At this point, the reader should be familiar with what an outcome effectiveness study is. In order for an agency to successfully undertake such an effort, the

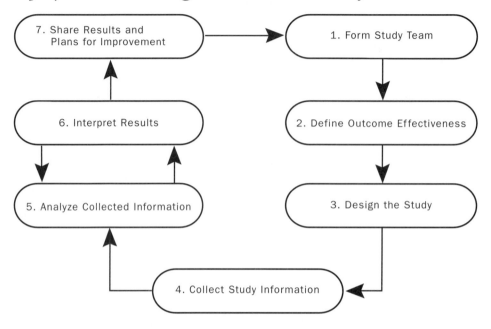

Figure 5.1

Steps for Conducting an Outcome Study

7. Share Results and Plans for Improvement

1. Form Study Team

6. Interpret Results

2. Define Outcome Effectiveness

5. Analyze Collected Information

3. Design the Study

4. Collect Study Information

executive director needs to believe in the value of outcome effectiveness studies and support them by providing adequate resources to conduct such studies, as well as speaking knowledgeably and favorably about the practical benefits of these endeavors.

While the executive director—particularly in a large organization—is unlikely to be involved in the details of planning and implementing the study, he or she should monitor the progress of outcome effectiveness studies through periodic (perhaps quarterly) progress reports. Perusing brief descriptions of related activities that occurred during the quarter will reveal if any sensitive issues are creating particular challenges or if any of the critical steps (summarized in Figure 5.1) have been omitted. It is beyond the scope of this handbook to describe in detail all of the concepts relevant to these steps. For further information see Rubin and Babbie [1993] and other program evaluation texts.

For agencies with more than one program, a decision must be made regarding which program to study first. In most cases, select a program that has been well implemented, has a clear intervention model, and is stable. Also consider which group of staff have the time to engage in data collection and other evaluation activities. A good place to start may be with a program whose external funder requires a formal outcome effectiveness study. However, an agency may have a program that is fairly new, and staff and management want to know "how we're doing" before deciding whether or not to expand. While some believe that a program should be working well before any attempt to study its effectiveness, there may be an upcoming grant proposal that would be strengthened by including effectiveness data. Further, knowing which components of a program seem promising (i.e., yield supporting effectiveness data) is valuable in shaping a new endeavor. But remember, outcome evaluation must be used cautiously in cases where program models are not stable.

Step 1. Form the Study Team

Once the program is selected, the team needs to be formed. Usually the program or service director and one or two other service providers are on the team. A lead evaluator and perhaps a research assistant (who might be a student intern or a college volunteer) may also be on the team. Agencies without internal evaluators may include a staff member responsible for planning and with an interest in assessment. Alternatively, a consultant experienced in outcome effectiveness studies may be hired. A tentative meeting schedule should be drawn up and plans made to communicate the team's progress in designing the outcome effectiveness study. The composition of the team will be determined partly by the scope and nature of the study (e.g., qualitative vs. quantitative, longitudinal vs. experimental).

Step 2. Define Outcome Effectiveness

Once the team has been formed, the group must agree on the key research questions the study will address. This task includes developing a definition of what constitutes program effectiveness and what short-term and long-term outcomes are being sought.

What does it mean for a particular program to be effective? It is one thing to want to assess whether a service is accomplishing its goals; it is another thing to define how it is having an impact on the client's life. The ideal outcome of a program is influenced by different philosophical frameworks and viewpoints. These disparate perspectives make it all the more important to have a uniform definition of effectiveness that is accepted by all the service providers within a particular program and by clients/customers and third party observers of service effectiveness. An important aspect of outcome studies is consensus among team members—particularly service providers—on the definition of effectiveness. Clients could also be asked what outcome they would consider effective. Input from clients on the definition of effectiveness is a step in achieving client-driven services.

As discussed in Chapter 2—which described how to develop a program specification document—brochures, program announcements, accreditation guidelines, and licensure materials are helpful in determining the mission, purpose, and goals of the program. Many agencies already have a clearly defined mission and written program goals that are regularly reviewed through a strategic planning process. Speaking with staff members may identify program philosophies that have evolved over time, have never been codified in writing, and yet are at the heart of the service. Agency documentation may lag behind program innovation. Keep in mind that defining effectiveness for a program is a lengthy process that must be done carefully and early. Hastily written, incomplete, or inaccurate definitions can jeopardize the value of a study.

Start with a brainstorming session, where individual ideas related to effectiveness may be generated in a comfortable environment. The program specification summary (if it exists) and relevant materials such as brochures or program mission statements may provide additional ideas. Effectiveness should be linked to program goals and objectives. The evaluator may also speak with program staff individually to see if the list seems complete to them. After intensive discussion, the team's resulting definition should be clear and concise. Team members must agree that this is the right definition of effectiveness for this program.

Outcome criteria also flow from a formal program specification process. See Chapter 2 for a detailed explanation of this process.

Step 3. Design the Study

Once the definition of program effectiveness has been written and agreed to, the next step is figuring out how to know when this definition has been met. In child welfare, it will almost always take more than one measure and source of information to determine whether a program is effective. During this step, you will need to select your research design. For example, will some kind of control or comparison group be formed? From whom will you obtain information, and when? Will there be a follow-up measure? Other questions to answer include whether there will be an assessment after service has ended. All information must be collected during a specific period—two weeks, two months, six months, twelve months, or more. See Appendix B, at the back of this chapter, for a summary of some of the major types of research designs, written by noted researcher Mark Fraser.

Part of the design process involves choosing measures that will be sensitive enough to detect the expected changes in client, family, or system functioning. Sometimes existing standardized measures or scales may fill the bill. In other cases the right choice is a structured interview with a set of predetermined questions as a guideline. Another potential source of information is case records. If the program has information stored on a computer, or bookkeeping has relevant information, these may also provide sources of information for assessing outcome effectiveness. Yet other possible sources of information are teachers, other service providers, and anyone else in an ancillary or collateral role.

Step 4. Collect Study Information

Once the measures and procedures are piloted, revised, and piloted again, the actual collection of study information can get underway. How long the data collection phase takes depends on the study design. A period of time as brief as a month could be chosen, and program effectiveness assessed for all clients seen during that one-month period. The information may take longer to gather if clients have completed receipt of service before outcome effectiveness is evaluated. Another possibility is to do assessments of effectiveness six months after service delivery has ended.

Step 5. Analyze Collected Information

Once the information has been collected, it must be converted to a usable format. This step, called data analysis, begins with a predetermined plan. However, it also has a give-and-take feel to it. (The reader is referred to Chapter 6 for a discussion of different levels of statistical analysis.) After some data analysis has been completed, the team will look at the results and try to make sense of them. From this initial data analysis, the team will likely identify new questions that require further data analysis. The team then looks at these additional results, which again generate further questions. This iterative analysis-review-further analysis process may go on for an extended period of time, until all team members are satisfied that the findings have been explained as fully as possible. These aspects of the study can be complex, and, clearly, specialized expertise is needed.

Step 6. Interpret Results

This step answers the question, What does it all mean?, and alternates with the previous data analysis step. Early interpretation of findings leads to additional questions to support or disprove various explanations. During this step it becomes glaringly obvious why the team should not be small and narrow in its scope, because various interpretations of the results need to be considered. The purposeful involvement of administrators, line staff, consumers, and others can help to interpret the meaning of the data.

Step 7. Share the Findings

Documentation of the study effort in the form of a written report occurs at this step. The report outlines why the outcome effectiveness study was done, how the team defined effectiveness for this program, what the sources of information were, what the measurements were (e.g., survey, interview), a summary of the results, and how these results were interpreted. Preparing an executive summary of a full-scale study for wider distribution is often helpful.

With studies that have a long time frame for collecting information, such as a six-month follow-up, it is helpful to prepare interim reports midway through. The reports are a reminder that the outcome effectiveness study is still in existence, and for those involved in providing information for the study, they are a reassuring sign that the information they take time to provide has not gone into a black hole.

A brief summary of the findings should be sent to clients and any others who have provided information for the study. If appropriate and requested, separate reports may be sent to program staff, summarizing findings for their clients.

For those not receiving written reports, or who prefer to hear rather than see a report, presentations of the study may be given at meetings of staff members, of top leadership, of the full organization, and of the board. It is also beneficial to share not only the study findings, but the methodology, or way in which it was done, with colleagues at other agencies. This can be done by speaking at conferences or by publishing the study in a professional journal or newsletter.

Special Challenges in Outcome Research

Assessment Measures

Assessing effectiveness in the child welfare arena is a complicated proposition. Once a definition of a desirable outcome has been developed, appropriate instrumentation must be found to measure it. Few measures are objective and comprehensive by themselves, and established systems with standardized instruments are rarely in place to gather objective data. One helpful strategy is to use multiple measures from as many sources as realistically possible. For example, to assess a mother's parenting skills, one may ask a caseworker if she or he observed particular behaviors, and one may also ask the client to assess her own parenting. Information from two or more sources is often better than asking only the client or only the caseworker.

Measuring Client Outcome

A client outcome is a change (or lack of change) in the problems or functioning of a client that can be attributed to the program or service [Magura & Moses, 1986]. Outcome studies focus on the goals a program has set for its clients. Choosing ways of measuring these goals, as discussed earlier, can be a time consuming process. When choosing measures, it is important to consider the following:

- Do they measure what you intend to measure?

- How realistic is the time needed to gather the information?

- Will use of the assessment method interfere with, or enhance, service delivery?

- How relevant is the information obtained from the measure to decision making about program changes or improvements?

- How will the data be used?

- Do you really need it?

There are many ways to measure outcomes, ranging from simple numerical counts (number of clients employed, number of reports of further child maltreatment, length of placement, etc.) to standardized measures of development, achievement, personality, behavior and so forth. In between may be an array of staff developed measures such as questionnaires, interview schedules, and rating forms. Numerical counts are usually the simplest to collect and the easiest for people to understand. Staff-developed measures are generally program specific—no other instruments can be found that will do the job. If you decide to develop your own measures, it is wise to use an internal or external evaluation consultant to advise you.

There are literally hundreds of standardized measures (see for example, Bloom & Fischer [1982] and Pecora et al. [1995]). Many programs use a variety of such measures as part of the treatment process. If your agency already uses specific standardized measures, data collection is simplified and staff acceptance is probably high. If a new measure is to be introduced as part of an outcome study, it is important that the study team and management communicate the benefits to service providers and get feedback as to its usefulness. An example of a widely used standardized measure in child welfare is the Child Behavior Checklist or CBCL [Achenbach 1991a, 1991b]. The Child Behavior Checklist is a standardized rating scale of observed behavior patterns that aids in determining appropriate treatment interventions, and measures behavior change in response to interventions. It is a useful tool for practitioners or service providers, and it is frequently used in research and evaluation. In response to the call for outcome based programming in child welfare, many new measures have been developed, including the Child Well Being Scales and the Parent Outcome Interview. A discussion of these and other measures can be found in *Outcome Measures for Child Wel-*

fare Services [Magura & Moses 1986]. Again, in selecting standardized measures for outcome evaluation, it is best to first get expert advice. Even if the collected information points to positive changes in clients' lives, other factors must be checked before credit can be given to the program. The improvement may have happened without the client's receipt of services or participation in the program, because of a change in the client's home environment, changed employment circumstances, and/or services provided by some other service organization or community resource, such as a church or a self-help group, that coincided with receipt of services from the program being studied. One way to deal with this situation is to anticipate this question and address it during the study. For example, clients can be asked to rate how a whole host of factors (including the service being assessed) may have contributed to an improvement in their situation. Alternately, negative changes in client's lives also demand scrutiny before changes are made to the program. Further, it is important to record the client's status on the outcome variables before a period of service, and the nature and intensity of the services received.

Length of the Assessment

Realistically, and certainly initially, outcome effectiveness tends to be assessed for a finite time period. But ideally, assessment of outcome effectiveness is an integral part of all programs. Outcome measures are most useful when they are incorporated into the program as a permanent component. Outcome effectiveness studies require time to complete, perhaps two to six years. Further, a shift from preoccupation with billable units of service delivered or program output to an outcome, value-added orientation often takes a good deal of time to develop. In addition to answering the question, How many clients took part in Program X, the executive must also ask: Were they helped by Program X? Did the program achieve its goals? Did the payor receive added value?

Outcome effectiveness studies require time to plan, especially when an agency is first attempting to do such a study, as perspectives often differ on what it means for a program to be effective. It may take time to distinguish what program staff hope to accomplish from what they actually accomplish. Outcome studies often have a follow-up assessment built into them that extends the period of information collection substantially.

Using the Team Approach

In order to design and execute a study that will yield useful information, service providers and evaluators must work together. Taking a team approach to an outcome effectiveness study is essential to implementing total quality/continuous quality improvement. Evaluators have technological expertise in such areas as instrument development, and service providers know about client-related factors that influence what information to collect and how to collect it. The cooperation of program staff is also essential to the success of any outcome effectiveness study. All team members should be involved in the development and selection of measures and study design, and should also be available to discuss results and their interpretation.

For the core project team to work smoothly, however, roles and responsibilities must be clearly designated. Whether the agency uses an internal evaluator or a consultant, team members need to be clear on who has final responsibility for what aspects of the study. There must be consensus around roles and responsibilities.

A team size of three or four generally works well. If many more people are on the team, it can be a lifetime job to find meeting times. Decision-making can slow to a crawl when there are too many points of view. On the other hand, not having enough team members can limit exposure to different perspectives, resulting in a focus that may be narrow, incomplete, or "out in left field."

Fortunately, there are ways of gathering ideas from staff members without increasing the team size, such as soliciting suggestions through memos and occasional large group meetings to share progress and gain ideas. Team members should act as representatives of their colleagues, asking for reactions to ideas and offering brief progress reports. This strategy can also be used to gain client/customer input into the design and structure of the study.

Providers and Consumers as Sources of Outcome Data

Service providers are a valuable source of information. They have regular contact with clients and they observe change through experienced eyes. Staff members in child welfare programs are usually busy, and may question why they have to provide information if data will also be collected from clients. But they have an important role: In addition to all the good reasons for collecting information from both sources, as outlined earlier, not every client solicited for the study may choose to participate. Clients ordered by the courts to receive services, for example, may not want to fill out optional surveys or be interviewed for the study. This may also be the case with dissatisfied clients, who are so disgusted that they do not want to be bothered. Missing information could lead to a selection bias and nonrepresentative or nongeneralizable results. Incentives to participate, such as modest gift certificates to food or department stores, may make a difference. But contact with staff members is crucial to this process.

Some clients who want to participate may be unable to do so because of a literacy problem or difficulty in understanding the questions being asked. Special interview strategies can be used to help compensate. Information from program staff however, may be the only way to evaluate outcome effectiveness for those clients. Program managers need to acknowledge the extra effort that program staff members make to provide information. Every effort should also be made to collect information in as unobtrusive and rapid a manner as possible.

One difficulty, however, with providers' assessments of program efficacy is that their judgments may be consciously or unconsciously influenced by the desire to make a difference in clients' lives. Some providers may consider assessing outcome effectiveness synonymous with assessing their own professional effectiveness, and have a need to look good for their supervisors and/or peers, causing their assessments of client improvement to be more positive and optimistic than they are factual.

Thus, while some outcome effectiveness studies may include only staff assessments, it is clear that this source is not free from bias, and should be complemented with additional information. Clients are a logical choice for this information.

Regardless of how program staff rate service effectiveness, clients have their own views on this matter. The purpose of a program is to provide service that helps clients. One clue as to whether this has been accomplished is to ask the recipients whether they found specific aspects of the service helpful or effective. Not unlike the responses of service providers, however, the responses of clients may be influenced by a desire to give what they perceive to be the "right answers," answers that validate the time and effort they have given to participating in a program. Or they may want to please their service providers, regardless of assurances that their responses will be kept confidential. All of these are forms of social desirability biases that need to be considered. (See Cook & Campbell 1979; Sudman & Bradburn 1974, 1982.)

Another factor that may influence the validity or accuracy of client judgments is the crisis or great need that precipitated their receipt of service. It is often difficult to think clearly during a time of high stress, whether it is at intake or after service. Services with a mental health component present another difficulty. A worsening of problems or feelings may be interpreted as progress by the service provider, but seen as a step backward by the client. For example, moving past denial of a problem may be a necessary step in treatment, although it makes the client feel worse until the problem gets resolved satisfactorily.

Other Sources of Data

If despair is setting in at this point, take heart. There are other places to get information on outcome effectiveness. The organization's bookkeeping and client records may be important data sources. These sources may be computerized, and can provide objective information on the overall picture of service effectiveness. One example is how often appointments were kept. Documentation of observable changes, such as improvement in a parent's employment status, reunification of a biological family after a child has been placed outside the home, and maintenance of a placement at risk of disrupting, provide data that may be helpful in assessing outcome effectiveness. Yet another source of outcome information is people in ancillary or collateral roles, such as a teacher who can observe changes in the classroom or a program director for an adult client in a job training program. For some sources, client consent is a prerequisite to obtaining information.

Planning

Pulling all these pieces of information and varied perspectives together may be a major headache. Organizing or analyzing the information around the client, however, provides the most complete composite of the program's effectiveness or impact on clients' lives. So, for each client, there might be information provided by the service provider, the client, a collateral provider, and the agency's automated system. Some questions may have deliberately been asked of multiple sources. Consider the possibilities. At one extreme are results from different sources that may be in complete agreement about the effectiveness of a program for a particular client. On the other hand, there may be lots of disagreement. Points of divergence are of interest, as they can result in improved understanding of clients. Depending on where the discrepancies are, the differences may give encouragement and validation to service providers who rate their effectiveness lower than do their clients. Conversely, some staff may need to review long-standing assumptions and treatment strategies if their ratings are higher than their clients'.

Figure 5.2

Sample Data Collection Summary Table for a Treatment Foster Care Program

Research Question	Measure	Completion by Whom	How Often
1. Does child behavior at home change?	• Child Behavior Checklist (CBCL)[a] • Social Skills Checklist	• Primary Caretaker • Primary Caretaker	• Every six months • Every six months
2. Does school attendance improve?	• School records of attendance • Parent report	• Teacher • Parent	• Every report card period (e.g., 3 times per year) • Same schedule as above
3. Does school performance improve?	• Teacher Report Form (TRF)[b] • Report card	• Teacher • Teacher	• Every report card period (e.g., 3 times per year) • Same schedule as above
4. Do youth skills for independent living improve?	• Ansell-Casey Life Skills Assessment (ACLSA)[c] • Social Problem-Solving Inventory for Adolescents[d]	• Youth and Caregiver[c] • Youth[d]	• Once a year • Once a year

a. *Achenbach Child Behavior Checklist 4/18* [Achenbach 1991a]

b. *Achenbach Teacher Report Form* [Achenbach 1991b]

c. *Ansell-Casey Life Skills Assessment—ACLSA for Youth* [Nollan et al. 1996]

d. *Social Problem-Solving Inventory for Adolescents—SPSI-A* [Frauenkenecht & Black 1995]

Figure 5.3

Collection of Study Information Sample Timeline

Task   **Time Period**

I. Pilot and procedures
      A. Identify pilot participants
      B. Schedule pilot
      C. Review feedback from participants

II. Revise measures and procedures
      A. Identify new participants
      B. Schedule data collection for revised
         measures and procedures
      C. Review feedback from participants
      D. Finalize measures and procedures

III. Repeat Tasks I and II for any translated
     versions of the measure

IV. Notify potential participants that a study is
     being conducted

V. Conduct formal data collection:
      Collect information from all sources
      during a specified time period

A few words of caution: The team needs to balance its enthusiasm for including many information sources and measures in its study with realistic demands on its study participants, evaluators, and others, such as clerical staff, whose time will be needed to collect the information. It is often helpful to develop a table that lists the research question, the measures, who completes them, and when. (See Figure 5.2.) As noted earlier, when choosing measures, it is important to ask: How will the information collected be used? Do we really need it?

Scheduling of events is critical. (See Figure 5.3 for a partial example of an evaluation timeline.) Timelines may include the following tasks or phases:

- Develop consent forms to be completed by clients.

- Test newly developed measures or questions for surveys or interviews.

- Translate these measures and consent forms into various languages, "back-translate" for accuracy, and field test for client/worker understanding.

- Test information collection procedures and time needed for possible corrections.

- Develop a procedure for telling potential study participants (e.g., clients, referring workers) about the study before asking them to participate.

- Make any needed conversions, groupings, or coding of collected responses.

- Input data into a computer if necessary.

- Analyze the information collected.

- Review preliminary results.

- Further analyze issues suggested by the preliminary review.

- Review these additional analyses and implications as a team.

- Write the final report.

- Share findings with service providers, top management, and others involved in the study, including clients.

A way of informing potential participants about the study must be developed before their participation is requested. These human subjects procedures are very important. (See American Psychological Association [1982].) A notification period before beginning the actual collection of information allows clients time to decide whether they want to participate and to ask the program staff or evaluator any questions about the study. Depending on the study design, the client may or may not have already begun to receive services.

Also before formal data collection, issues regarding language fluency of clients must be addressed, leaving time for translations, if necessary. Measures should be field tested to be certain that the questions are clear and answerable by clients, staff, and others. Often changes are suggested and a second round of testing or piloting needs to occur before the instruments and the information collection protocol are finalized.

Sensitive Issues

An organization conducting an outcome effectiveness study must deal with several sensitive issues in order to get buy-in from participants. To the extent possible, the reasons for doing the outcome effectiveness study and the proposed ways in which the results will be used should be decided in advance and explained in a candid, open manner. One concern may be what happens if the findings are negative—that is, there is a lack of evidence on the efficacy of the service. Will it lead to the service's demise, or will the information be used to improve the program?

As mentioned earlier, service providers are often worried that program effectiveness data constitute a personal evaluation of their job performance. There is often concern that information collected during the study may be shared with supervisors or top management and used punitively. This fear has to be allayed by supervisors as early as possible. Supervisors need to be clear in advance, both with themselves and their staff, about *why* they are gathering information and *how* it will be used, especially if it is negative. Quality improvement or total quality management and its emphasis on process improvements and outcomes is a major cultural change for many child welfare organizations. Consequently, it requires the commitment of top leadership to create a learning environment that focuses on improvement and views problems as opportunities for improvement rather than reasons to assess blame. Participants must understand that the findings will be presented only in summary form—in the aggregate—and that individual responses will not be linked and presented in study reports.

It cannot be denied that effectiveness is influenced by the quality of the service provider, but without these assurances to providers, the study will fail. The study will lead to a defensive posture on the part of program staff, particularly among those who have had a less than active role in the study's development, and candid assessments of program effectiveness will be unattainable. If information providers do not feel free to respond fully and without fear of consequences, valid findings cannot be obtained. Executives and supervisors should bear in mind that if there actually is a performance problem, it will not take a study to uncover it. More than likely, the problem is already known to the manager and can be handled through individual employee supervision.

Linking service provider and client information has one strong selling point: the ability to report back confidentially to individual program staff members an *aggregate* or summary of the information their clients provided. This client feedback may enable the staff member interested in continuous improvement to make changes in his or her delivery of service.

Because the information is so sensitive, program staff must be assured that all information collected will be guarded carefully. All information must be kept in a locked file. No names should ever be entered into a computer file for general evaluation purposes. Only the evaluators should have access to any lists that match client evaluations with their service providers.

Just as program staff need to be assured of the confidentiality of their responses, clients must receive the same assurances. Accreditation standards require using some type of informed consent that includes assurances of confidentiality. To be as honest as possible in their answers, clients need to feel that their individual answers will not be shared with their service providers. Clients need to understand the overall purpose of the outcome effectiveness study and how information they provide will be protected. Clients participating should also be given the opportunity to receive a copy of the general findings at the end of the study.

Examples of Studies

In this fledgling era of outcome evaluations, a number of family service agencies are attempting to conduct their first studies. In contrast, other agencies have already completed outcome studies and have developed strategies for making assessment of effectiveness an inherent part of their programs. The next two sections describe two evaluation case studies.

A Day Care Study

The Village for Families and Children, Inc., of Hartford, Connecticut, has conducted five outcome effectiveness studies over the past few years, including an outcome effectiveness study of a family day care program that focused on several key aspects of service delivery [Mika et al. 1991]. This program offers affordable care for infants and children whose parents are out of the home due to employment, job training, or education. The program offers licensed family day care providers, social worker support, management collection of parent support payments, and parent support groups.

The study team of program staff and agency evaluators met over several months to come up with the following definition of service effectiveness for the Villages' family day care program:

> Family day care services are delivered effectively when children are placed in homes that provide consistent and interesting days that include the following elements:
>
> • *Appropriate physical care*, as measured by whether the day care provider had safety rules for the child to follow, the provider's ability to handle emergencies, and whether there was an opportunity for the child to nap each day;
>
> • *Nurturing emotional development,* as indicated by the frequency of day care provider praising, comforting, and listening to the child, and effective discipline techniques;
>
> • *Good communication among parent, provider, and social worker*, as indicated by the degree of respect the day care provider showed for the parent's beliefs about child-rearing and the frequency of discussions about the child's learning of new skills; and
>
> • *Planned activities that encourage social, physical, and cognitive growth,* as evidenced by frequency of activities that used arts and crafts, puzzles, and age-appropriate toys.

Questions were derived to measure each aspect of the four-part definition. Items were tested on day care providers, parents, and professional staff members—who constituted the three sources of information. Information was then obtained from all 37 day care providers in the program via telephone interviews conducted by agency evaluators. All 96 parents were reached by telephone and consented to an interview with the agency evaluator. The agency social workers assigned to these cases completed questionnaires on each child and his or her day care home.

After this information was gathered, coded, and entered into a computer, team members discussed their preliminary analyses and interpretations. Additional analyses were further discussed by the team. The findings were distributed in several ways: in brief reports sent to day care providers and parents, verbally at program and divisional meetings, at a meeting of the full board of directors, and at professional conferences.

This study did not employ a control group, comparison group, time-series design, or other rigorous research design. It is not a study of child outcomes per se, but an examination of key service delivery components. Yet the study findings offered preliminary evidence that services were effectively delivered, and also found areas for improvement. All four areas of the effectiveness definition were addressed—as supported by information collected from the parents, day care providers, and social workers. Highlights of the findings included the following:

- Day care providers offered warm and nurturing environments for the children, as exemplified by praising, showing affection, comforting a child when upset, and using consistent and appropriate discipline.

- The day care homes offered a wide range of activities that reinforced key developmental skills children need at those ages.

- The degree of variation of scheduled activities was not uniform across the day care homes, and some children may have missed stimulating experiences.

- Social workers rated the day care providers' physical care skills lower than did the parents and day care providers themselves, suggesting one potential area for improvement.

- Although parents indicated their satisfaction, the day care providers thought more communication was needed to heighten the quality of care.

Following the study, service delivery was changed to make it even more effective. For example, an article was published in the agency's newsletter for parents on how to talk to their day care providers about their child's day. Parent support groups were formed, and the CPR/first aid training that was routinely given to day care providers was extended to parents. Researchers and agency staff worked hard to implement the recommendations.

A Residential Group Care Study

The study described here is a pilot research study on residential group care, and is presented to the reader as an example of the role that preliminary research studies can play in preparation for ongoing outcome evaluation. It is also an example of a collaboration between a child-caring agency and an external consultant. The study paved the way for acceptance of an ongoing assessment (as opposed to a one-time assessment) of outcome effectiveness.

The Villages of Indiana, Inc., with Indiana University, conducted a two-state research study of its group home program [Alexander & Huberty 1993]. The group homes serve children ages six to 18 who have multiple emotional and behavioral problems, and are located in both rural and urban communities. Houseparents who are married couples live in the homes, and they and the children receive support from child care workers, social workers, and psychiatrists.

The Board of Directors authorized the study with the goal of determining how effective The Villages was in meeting the needs of the children it served in group home care. The study team consisted of agency board members, staff members, and a university-based research consultant. After numerous meetings and input from many levels of agency personnel, the following research questions were developed to guide the course of the study:

- What factors led the former Villages youths to be in care?

- What relationship, if any, exists between these factors and their in-care behavior, discharge adjustment, and adult functioning?

- How did former residents function while in care, as reflected in their discharge adjustment?

- How are former residents faring as adults?

- What are the magnitudes of the relationships of historical factors to the adult functioning of the former residents?

The study was conducted in two phases. In the first phase, the closed case records of 390 youths who had lived in a Villages group home from 1970 to 1989 were analyzed. These data cover family history, placement history, certain risk factors such as the experience of abuse and neglect, psychiatric and behavioral disorders, and educational needs. Indicators of outcome were developed based on the agency's established goals for each child in care:

- To be provided permanency;

- To become educated;

- To become capable of making and maintaining nurturing relationships; and

- To become self-sufficient as adults.

Outcome measures specifically developed for the study assessed adjustment to placement, reasons for discharge from the program, and where children went at discharge.

The second phase involved looking at the adult lives of former group home youths. Personal interviews were conducted with alumni from Indiana who were 18 or older. In Indiana, of the 134 former youths who were adults at the time of the study, 86 were located and interviewed. The interview was designed to assess their functioning in important aspects of their lives, including family, income and employment, education and training, conflicts with the law, social supports, and experiences in the group homes. Personality functioning was assessed through the use of a standardized measure, the Sixteen Personality Factor Questionnaire [Cattell et al. 1970].

Analyses of the data occurred during and between phases, and interim reports were presented to the board and staff. While the Indiana portion of the study is complete, interviews of former youths from the sister agency in Kansas continue. The final report of the Indiana study was presented to board and staff in meetings, presentations, the agency newsletter, and a printed summary. It was also distributed to a variety of consumers and child caring agencies.

The profile of former residents presents a picture of children at risk. Most came into care due to abuse or neglect. The youths had experienced multiple placements away from their families. Educational deficits were common. Maladaptive behaviors such as stealing, self-destructiveness, and aggression were the most common reasons for needing group home care. Research findings included the following:

- Length of stay was positively associated with good adjustment (i.e., the longer the youths were with Villages, the better their functioning at follow-up).

- The majority of children returned to their families or went into family foster care. About 17% were emancipated and went on to live independently.

- Being emancipated or going to a family setting was significantly related to good adjustment.

- The degree to which the youths adapted and functioned while in care had some predictive relation to adult functioning. Stealing and aggressiveness while in care had a positive correlation to lawbreaking as an adult.

- Despite painful childhood experiences, most alumni are doing well as adults and are like other young adults in the general population with respect to education, income, marriage, and child bearing.

- The majority (85.8%) are not dependent upon welfare or other forms of public assistance.

- Seventy-one percent are high school graduates, and over a quarter have completed some college or vocational training.

- Almost all alumni maintain relationships with their families, as measured by frequency of contact.

- The former residents cited the need for the agency to provide more comprehensive independent living training and increased services to families.

- Most alumni (78%) view the agency positively and feel they would be worse off today if not for their experience in the program.

As a result of the study, a number of programmatic changes were made, including the development of increased independent living skills training, a transitional apartment living program for newly emancipated youths, and the addition of intensive family preservation and reunification services. The agency has also developed a systematic and comprehensive method to monitor intake, program, and outcome data for use in future planning and decision-making. This has been accomplished through the regular use of measures developed for this study, as well as the routine use of standardized measures to assess youth progress over time and assess outcomes at the time of discharge. The measures have been adapted for use in each of the agency's services, including group homes, therapeutic foster care, and family services. Future outcome effectiveness studies will examine therapeutic foster care, family preservation, and reunification services.

Using Your Evaluation Results for Quality Improvement

Now that you have completed an outcome study, how can you use your results as part of a process of quality improvement? The case studies illustrate some possible uses. But a word of caution is in order. Throughout this handbook, you will see that creating an organizational culture of quality requires a commitment from the top, from your agency board of directors and executives. There is no perfect program or service. Your findings will bring both good and bad news. We need to acknowledge that people may be afraid to expose weaknesses given the current political or agency climate. An organization that is solution focused and learning oriented [Senge 1990], however, is in a better position to use findings to its advantage than one that focuses on assessing blame or "killing the messenger." The good news for the study team is that the latter type of organization probably will not be involved in much outcome evaluation.

There are many ways to use outcome evaluation results, including improving services, informing policy and funding decisions, promoting the agency to consumers and other stakeholders, and building a database for program monitoring.

Improving Services

Agencies may choose to use their findings in a variety of ways. The most common way of using results is to improve a specific program or service. It is important to remember that staff participation in a study does not necessarily mean staff members know how to use the results for program improvement. Once an agency has invested a great deal of time and money in an outcome evaluation, it may want to read more into the findings than is actually there. It is the role of the study team, with the participation and support of key management, to discuss and review the findings and to interpret the results in meetings with staff. This is especially true when the findings of an evaluation are mixed—some findings support a service and some do not. The study team must assist the agency leadership and staff in drawing interpretations and making clear recommendations about program improvements.

Staff ownership of program change is crucial for success. Consequently, staff members need time to see the relationship between the study's findings and any necessary actions, and they must be given the opportunity for input in any changes that are made.

Clients can also be involved in determining how results are used to modify and improve services. One way of doing this is through client meetings with the study team in which the findings are presented and discussed. It is empowering for clients to know that their opinions and suggestions are valued and used in decision-making.

Leadership must be willing to provide the resources necessary to maintain improvements. While many improvements center on policy, program design, or supervisory support, additional or more specific staff training may be needed. Learning is a key component of quality improvement efforts. Management must provide the leadership to treat training and learning as a required investment in human resources to achieve desired outcomes, rather than as merely an added time burden or an expense that can easily be cut.

The findings of your outcome study will help management decide where to direct training efforts for the greatest effect. For example, in the group care study cited earlier, the findings identified a need for more independent living skills training. As a result, a more comprehensive independent living skills program was developed and intensive training in implementation of the service was given to all relevant staff over an extended period of time.

Related to training are staffing issues, which are often highlighted in the findings of an outcome study. Are more staff needed? Are different staff needed? Do staff duties need to be realigned to focus on different or unmet needs? In the preceding example, more staff were required to prepare young people for independence in a systematic and developmentally appropriate way, and an additional staff person was hired to support the program. But again, whatever recommendations and actions for service improvement are decided upon through the review of the study findings, leadership must be supportive in providing the resources to sustain them.

Informing Agency Policy Decisions

While program directors and practitioners typically use the findings of an outcome study to refine services, an organization's leadership uses findings to inform its decision-making about policy and funding issues. Outcome data can provide an objective approach to planning and decision-making. It allows agency leadership to make decisions based on known results, rather than relying on impressions, anecdotal evidence, or the popularity of a service.

Information about program efficacy is also an important tool in establishing long-range organizational goals and objectives. Chapter 1 discussed the concept of strategic planning and how it incorporates the principles of quality improvement. Clearly, the results of an outcome study are a natural fit for an agency's strategic planning process. They provide valuable information about which of the agency's programs are most successful and where changes are needed that can help determine future directions for the agency.

We are making a distinction here between agency policy and large scale social policy. The evidence base is less compelling regarding the use of research to change social policy on the state or national level. But even in those areas, there have been some successes, such as the permanency planning movement and, to some degree, the Adoption Assistance and Child Welfare Act of 1980 (P.L. 96-272).

With the advent of managed care, many child welfare organizations are being called upon to justify their costs. Funders expect a return on their investment. They want to see positive outcomes. Knowing which services are most effective in achieving desired outcomes is an invaluable aid to the director and board in determining where to direct resources and in establishing and defending reasonable rates for services. A demonstrably effective program also brings credibility to fundraising efforts, making it easier for directors and boards to attract public and private dollars.

Agency directors often receive requests to expand or add programs. The results of outcome evaluations can be used to determine where and in what areas a program should or should not be expanded. As discussed earlier, additional allocation or reallocation of resources is often needed to make program changes. Certainly, any expansion of services needs additional resources, and directors and boards can use their findings to justify or find funding for those resources.

Promoting the Agency

There are many ways of using the findings of an outcome study to promote the agency and its staff. Findings can be incorporated in marketing and public rela-tions materials to show that consumers are receiving the services they expect. Staff and clients who are willing can be recognized for their good work internally by management and the board, and externally through the media and commu-nity groups. As seen earlier in both the day care and residential care examples of outcome studies, agency newsletters are an effective means of promoting positive findings. Demonstrating positive outcomes also aids in meeting licensing and ac-creditation requirements, as credentialing bodies increasingly focus on outcome-based services. Chapter 8 provides a comprehensive discussion of two major child welfare and mental health accrediting bodies and their quality assurance require-ments.

Building a Database

Building a database to monitor programs and services is another way to use out-come study results. Through your study, you will have measured and quantified client outcomes for a specific program and service. As we have seen, making measurable and "provable" the changes that occur in the clients you serve is mandatory for many agencies. With this in mind, you can use the outcome study to decide what information needs to be kept routinely and what can be collected periodically. Your study may also guide you in determining how the data will be evaluated, how often, and by whom. For example, can any of the measures used in the study be incorporated into the daily work of practitioners to help them assess client changes or improvement? If so, you have added to your tools for building continuous quality improvement into your programs. (Chapter 9 deals more in depth with creating a management information system and the multiple data elements that can be included.) Finally, the study findings may move your agency to conduct a comprehensive program evaluation or research study, and your database will be helpful in making decisions about the study design.

Conclusion

This chapter described the fundamental importance and major phases of an out-come study. It highlighted the reasons for conducting an outcome study, outlined the critical steps, and reviewed the essential role of agency leadership in support-ing and using evaluation efforts. Conducting outcome studies is not easy. It re-quires a significant commitment of time and resources. But the payoff is the abil-ity to answer the question that began this chapter: Are your services really mak-ing a difference? Accountability is at the heart of any outcome study—account-ability to consumers and to funders. Chapter 6 presents ways to make account-ability and service refinement an integral part of your programs by incorporating quality improvement practices in your agency.

References

Achenbach, T. M. (1991a). *Manual for the Child Behavior Checklist 4-18 and 1991 profile*. Burlington, VT: University of Vermont, Department of Psychiatry.

Achenbach, T. M. (1991b). *Manual for the Teacher's Report Form and 1991 profile*. Burlington, VT: University of Vermont, Department of Psychiatry.

Alexander, G. M., & Huberty, T. J. (1993, October). *Caring for troubled children.* Bloomington, IN: The Villages of Indiana, Inc.

American Psychological Association. (1982). *Ethical principles in the conduct of research with human participants.* Washington, DC: Author.

Bingham, R. D., & Felbinger, C. L. (1989). *Evaluation in practice —A methodological approach.* White Plains, NY: Longman Inc.

Campbell, D. T., & Stanley, J. (1963). *Experimental and quasi-experimental designs for research.* Chicago: Rand McNally.

Cattell, R. B., Eber, H. W., & Tatsuoka, M. M. (1970). *Handbook for the 16PF (6th ed.).* Champaign, IL: Institute for Personality and Ability Testing, Inc.

Frauenknecht, M., & Black, D. R. (1995). Social Problem-Solving Inventory for Adolescents (SPSI-A): Development and preliminary psychometric evaluation. *Journal of Personality Assessment, 64,* 522-539.

Cook, T. D., & Campbell, D. T. (1979). *Quasi-experimentation: Design and analysis issues for field settings.* Boston: Houghton Mifflin.

Grinnell, R. Jr. (Ed.). (1993). *Social Work research and evaluation.* Itasca, IL: Peacock.

Magura, S., & Moses, B. S. (1986). *Outcome measures for child welfare services: Theory and application.* Washington, DC: Child Welfare League of America.

Mika, K. L., Kluger, M. P., & Aprea, D. M. (1991, September). *Outcome effectiveness study of family day care services.* Child and Family Services, Inc., Hartford, CT.

Nollan, K. A., Downs, A. C., Pecora, P. J., Ansell, D. A., & Wolf, M. (1996). *Ansell-Casey life skills assessment manual (Field Test Version 1.1).* Seattle, WA: The Casey Family Program.

Rossi, P. H., & Freeman, H. E. (1993). *Evaluation: A systematic approach (5th ed.).* Newbury Park, CA: Sage Publications, Inc.

Rubin, A., & Babbie, E. (1993). *Research methods for social work.* Belmont, CA: Wadsworth Publishing Company.

Senge, P. (1990) *The fifth discipline: The art and practice of the learning organization.* New York: Doubleday.

Sudman, S., & Bradburn, N. M. (1974) *Response effects in surveys.* Chicago: Aldine Publishing Co.

Sudman, S., & Bradburn, N. M. (1982) *Asking questions.* Chicago: Jossey-Bass (now Macmillan).

For Further Information

Berk, R. A., & Rossi, P. H. (1993). *Thinking about program evaluation* (5th ed.). Newbury Park, CA: Sage Publications, Inc. Provides solid coverage of the major program evaluation concepts, including benefit cost analysis.

Bickman, L., & Rog, D.J. (Eds.) (1992). Evaluating mental health services for children. In *New Directions for Program Evaluation, 54.* San Francisco: Jossey-Bass. Provides useful methodological approaches to evaluating agency effectiveness.

Finch, S. J., Fanshel, D., & Grundy, J. F. (1991). *Data collection in adoption and foster care.* Washington, DC: Child Welfare League of America. Provides a concrete overview of key data elements in two child welfare program areas.

Grinnell, R. Jr. (Ed.). (1993). *Social Work research and evaluation.* Itasca, IL: Peacock. Presents an understandable overview of major concepts in research.

Weiss, H. B., & Jacobs, F. H. (Eds.) (1988). *Evaluating family programs.* New York: Aldine de Gruyter. Provides an excellent set of "evaluation exemplars" and some essential principles for evaluation, with a focus on family support programs.

Appendix B

Evaluation Designs

Mark W. Fraser

Overview

This appendix describes common evaluation designs for assessing program outcomes. We will not review needs assessment, process evaluation, or cost analysis methods because these approaches are used to address different data needs and often involve different evaluation strategies [see, e.g., Rubin & Babbie 1993]. Here, we focus on strategies for assessing the impact of service.[1] Starting with simple single-system designs and working up to more complex group designs, these are approaches that may be used to answer questions such as: Is a particular program having an impact on family functioning? Are out-of-home placements prevented?

Single-System Designs

Single-System Studies

A single-family or single-system study provides data over time on a particular case. Although there are some exceptions, single-system designs (SSDs) often require that data be collected on a daily or weekly basis well before the start of service and well after the conclusion of service [Bloom & Fischer 1982]. There are many different kinds of single-systems designs. Some involve the collection of data on multiple aspects of family functioning (multiple baseline studies); others focus on the responses of individual parents or children to different kinds of treatment techniques (multiple element studies); and others focus on responses to the termination and re-introduction of services (withdrawal studies).

To show that changes occur, most SSDs require that families demonstrate a stable baseline of functioning before the introduction of service. This limits the utility of

---

1. Adapted and modified from Pecora et al. (1995), *Evaluating family-based services* (New York: Aldine de Gruyter).

SSD in evaluation, because referral criteria for many service agencies, such as those involved in crisis intervention or family-based services (FBS), require that a family be "at risk of imminent placement." If a family is at risk for placement of a child, behaviors that one might wish to target in intervention are probably not stable. Lack of stability is, in a sense, a reason for referral to child protective services or FBS, so evaluation designs that require stability are compromised. Moreover, the mere requirement that baseline data be collected *prior to* the delivery of service renders many SSDs ill fitted to many practice areas, where emphasis is placed on immediate responses to family problems.

Single-System Time-Series Studies

One important extension of single-system studies is the single-system time-series design. In this design, data are collected daily or weekly on a small number of variables for as long as a client is in the program. The evaluation design does not affect the course of treatment, and findings are based on observation of changes over many months [Corcoran 1993]. The Alaska Youth Initiative used such a design, selecting nine daily performance indicators to track children on placement, medications compliance, school attendance, drug/alcohol use, and various behavioral problems [Burchard & Clarke 1990]. Over time, such data provide a record of improvement or lack of improvement in various settings and programs. Even when a small number of variables are selected, these designs require careful data collection and analysis efforts. But when children or parents can be tracked over long periods of time, single-system time-series designs provide rich information.

Group Designs: The Basics

Group evaluation designs are more common than single-case designs for a reason. Single-case methods are vulnerable to two kinds of criticism. First, with the less complex SSDs, observed changes may be due to factors other than the program. Critics may argue, for example, that observed changes are due to the inherent creativity of families in crisis; that families in crisis often make adjustments on their own that lead them out of crisis. Thus the skeptic would say that service had no effect and that, if left alone, most families would recover to a stable state. To counter such arguments, some sort of comparison to families who were similar at the point of referral but did not receive the service is necessary.

Second, critics can argue that a single family is unique; that the case observed was not representative of the target population, and, thus, that the findings cannot be generalized to the broad population of families who are served. While the argument that a group of families may also be unrepresentative of the target population is heard occasionally, it is not convincing when some form of probability sampling is used. This criticism leads, then, to the use of more than one case, and to some method of selecting cases so that they are representative of a target population.

The essential elements of group designs include:

- systematic sampling of families or cases,

- assignment to experimental and control or comparison groups,

- measurement after treatment,

- comparison of differences between experimental and control groups, and

- follow-up.

Selecting Cases

A group design is only as good as the sample. If a study involves only those families that are court referred or only those families that have young children, it is not possible to generalize findings to a broader population of program participants. (Of course this is fine if that client group is the population of interest.) Some form of probability sampling is always necessary in group designs.

Random sampling is one type of probability sampling. There are many sampling approaches that produce representative samples. The class of sampling procedures known as probability sampling procedures have a unique and important characteristic. When probability sampling is used, the likelihood that a case in the target population will be selected is known. In a purely mathematical sense, then, it is possible to generalize the findings from a small group to the population of interest. No matter what design is chosen, the sampling procedure should be specified as a part of the larger research design. (See Grinnell [1993, p. 125] for information on sampling and random assignment to experimental and control groups.)

Types of Group Designs

There are many types of group research designs, each of which employs different design elements. The most common designs useful for child and family services are described below. The following symbols are used to represent service provision, data collection, random assignment, and other aspects of a research design:

X: provision of the service,

A: provision of alternative or routine services,

O: data collection or observation,

R: random assignment, and

M: matching.

Pretest-Posttest Single Group Design

The pretest-posttest single-group design is the most commonly used and weakest group design. As shown in Figure B.1, it compares a group of families at two points in time, once before treatment and once afterwards. It does not control for changes in the environment, such as new laws that might affect placement resources and rates. Nor does it control for naturally occurring changes in family functioning over time. Many families enter treatment in a state of crisis, and soon make some sort of accommodation on their own. Their accommodation may be

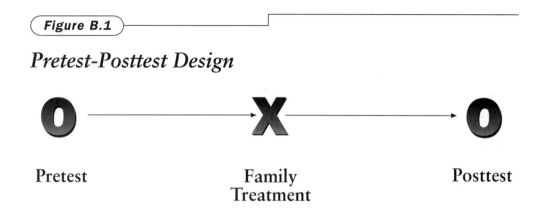

Figure B.1

Pretest-Posttest Design

Pretest   Family   Posttest
                               Treatment

poor or it may be good, but it is likely to reduce the stress that family members feel. From a systems perspective, families tend to recover from instability and move towards a less stressful, stable state; they move out of crisis even in the absence of treatment. In this design, there is no way to distinguish such natural changes from the effects of treatment.

This design is not strong for a variety of other reasons. Figure B.2 shows seven alternative explanations for an observed treatment effect. Each represents an explanation other than service effectiveness for findings from pretest-posttest designs. The forces of history (environmental effects), regression, maturation, testing, instrumentation, selection, and attrition can produce significant pretest to posttest differences, even when there are no differences resulting from the program's intervention. With the pretest-posttest design, one never knows whether treatment was effective or whether one of these other factors was at play.

Time Series Single Group Design

Like the pretest-posttest design, the time-series single-group design uses a reflexive control: group members' behavior and attitudes before treatment are compared to group members' behavior and attitudes after treatment [Rossi & Freeman 1993]. Although it has this reflexive character, the time-series design is stronger than the pretest-posttest design because trends over time are portrayed. Figure B.3 shows the use of multiple pretests and posttests.

Sometimes this design is called the interrupted time-series design because treatment interrupts the measurement of a particular behavior over time. Changes in behavior (or other outcomes) are interpreted as resulting from family-based treatment. Time-series designs can be used when daily or weekly measures of an outcome are available before and after the intervention. Like single-subject designs, this design can be interpreted only when baseline data are stable.

Pretest-Posttest Control Group Design with Random Assignment

The pretest-posttest control group design with random assignment is the classic experimental design. It controls all of the alternative explanations in Figure B.2,

Figure B.2

Seven Alternative Explanations

History

History refers to specific events other than FBS treatment that occur between the first measurement at pretest and the second measurement at posttest. These events occur during the course of treatment and pose rival explanations for an observed pre-post difference. The longer the time between the start and termination of service, the greater the likelihood that historical events will covary with treatment and confound the effects of treatment.

Regression

Regression refers to the statistical artifact that with repeated testing, extreme scores tend to become less extreme. Groups of scores that fall into extreme ranges tend to have more measurement error in them. Because they contain a larger amount of error than more moderate scores, extreme score "regress" toward the mean upon repeated application of the same test. They tend to become less extreme because the repeated occurrence of large random errors in measure decreases over time.

Maturation

Maturation refers to changes that occur in organizations, families, parents, and children as a result of the mere passage of time. When a treatment program is long, some subjects—especially children—tend to change as a result of social, cognitive, and physical development. Programs also mature. They go through stages of development. Pretest-posttest differences in studies of children exposed to a brand new FBS program could be due to developmental changes in the children or program, rather than to effect of treatment per se.

Selection

Selection refers to the use of a group assignment procedure that results in experimental and control conditions that are not equivalent. Random assignment usually eliminates selection biases.

Testing

Testing refers to the effect of taking the pretest. Pretest-posttest differences may be due to the effects of subjects remembering pretest items and being sensitive to them. Suppose, for example, parents were asked to score their children's temper tantrums at pretest. During the treatment period, parents might have heightened concern for tantrums. They might read and be influenced by material on tantrums that is not associated with FBS treatment. (Note: Fortunately, research indicates that the effect of a pretest on posttest scores is usually insignificant. See Bingham and Felbinger [1990].)

Figure B.2, cont'd.

Instrumentation

Instrumentation refers to changes in the data collection instrument or data collection procedures over time. Sometimes interviewers become jaded and their effectiveness wanes across the course of study. Occasionally, instruments are actually changed in the middle of a study. Instrumentation effects can be controlled by careful, ongoing training of interviewers and by avoiding changes in data collection procedures during the course of a study.

Experimental Attrition

Attrition, also known as "mortality," refers to dropout rates that differ between experimental and control conditions. Differential dropout can produce incommensurability, even when random assignment has been used to create groups. Whenever attrition occurs, subjects who drop out must be compared against subjects who remain. When significant differences are found, attrition is called *biased*. When it differs between experimental and control groups, it is called *biased experimental attrition*.

---

so long as attrition in the treatment group is equivalent to attrition in the control group. This can be tested post hoc, and, if attrition is found to be biased, statistical adjustments usually can be employed to make the groups equivalent for comparison on posttest measures.

The classic experiment shown in Figure B.4 relies on random assignment of individuals or families to treatment and control groups. In theory, the control group is not supposed to receive services. But in most child and family social services research, this is unethical, so control group families receive routine services while experimental families receive innovative family-based services. Technically, there are no limits on the number of control and experimental conditions that can be used. For practical reasons, however, most experimental research uses just one experimental group and one control group.

Random assignment is done in a variety of different ways. Often a table of random numbers is used to assign families to experimental and control groups. As long as the group sizes are large, random assignment is assumed to produce equivalent groups. However, it is a probabilistic procedure, so there is always a chance that random assignment will not result in comparable conditions. It is good practice to double-check the equivalence of groups by comparing group means on pretest variables.

After randomization in the pretest-posttest experiment, difference scores are used to compare subjects. For each group, pretest scores are subtracted from posttest scores. This produces a mean difference for each group. If the treatment was effective, the difference score of the treatment group should be significantly larger (or smaller) than the difference score of the control group.

(**Figure B.3**)

Time-Series Single-Group Design

| Pretest | Family Treatment | Posttest |

Posttest-Only Control Group Design with Random Assignment

The posttest-only control group design is a twist on the classic experiment. This design, shown in Figure B.5, is exactly the same as the pretest-posttest design with randomization except that no pretest is used. Families are randomly assigned to experimental and control groups. The impact of treatment is estimated by comparing posttest scores only.

This design relies upon random assignment to create equivalent and comparable groups. Again, random assignment is usually reliable, but it is a probabilistic procedure, and there is always the chance—a fairly large chance when the sample size is small—that it will not work. When that happens, the evaluator who uses a posttest-only design has little recourse for salvaging the study.[2]

Notice that in this design an alternative treatment, A, is introduced by assigning control families to routine services. In evaluation, this is nearly always a desirable practice. The classic experiment with a no-treatment control group is practically, ethically, and legally objectionable. Families referred for child welfare, mental health, and court services are entitled to professional services. There can rarely be such a thing as a no-treatment control group.

When no-treatment control groups are replaced with alternative treatment control groups, the treatment effect is usually smaller. In most cases, the effect of an alternative treatment will be larger than the effect of no treatment. Thus the differences between experimental and alternative (routine) treatment conditions will be smaller than if the control group received no services at all. Although there are several ways to compensate for this problem (e.g., employing measures of outcome that are more precise), with this design there is a real risk of finding no significant difference. In the view of many, however, this risk is counterbalanced by the fact that all participants receive an ethically acceptable service.

---

2. Sometimes it is possible to rescue posttest-only studies where random assignment has failed by increasing the sample sizes; by adjusting groups, using covariance analysis; or by matching families on known variables. The latter two approaches will produce tacit equivalence, but the evaluator can never have confidence that the groups are equivalent on unknown variables. Only random assignment does this, and no amount of statistical adjustment or matching can produce the equivalence that comes from randomization.

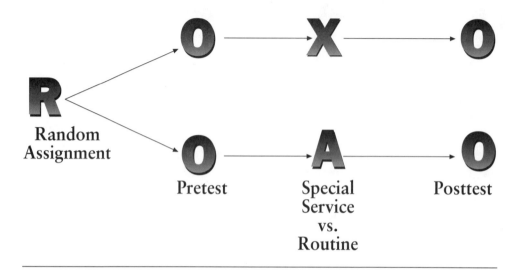

Figure B.4

Classic Experiment with Routine Services Control Group

Matched-Pairs Comparison Group Design

The term *experiment* is usually reserved for designs that employ random assignment, whereas the term *quasi-experiment* is usually applied to designs that do not employ random assignment. Quasi-experiments rely on comparison groups rather than control groups. The distinction is an important one. Control groups are created by random assignment; comparison groups are created by matching or some other procedure. While random assignment is broadly recognized as creating equivalence in all areas between treatment and control conditions, matching designs create equivalence only on the matched variables.

A common matching design, pictured in Figure B.6, involves pairing individuals who are similar on several variables. In matched pairs designs, the evaluator chooses variables that are likely to influence the outcome measure. Then cases are matched on these variables. In a program for ungovernable children, for example, you might match children on truancy, drug use, gender, ethnicity, and age. After matching, one member of a pair is assigned to the comparison group and the other to the treatment group. Matching is usually done prospectively, but occasionally, when a large number of families who receive the service or an alternative treatment are available, it may be done after the fact (see, e.g., Fraser et al. [1991]. In principle, matching produces equivalence between the treatment and comparison groups on key variables—those variables that are conceptually important.

Matched pairs designs are analyzed by computing and summing the differences across pairs. If a family-based intervention were successful in reducing ungovernable behavior, the results of a study where matching was based on truancy and drug use might be reported as follows:

Matched for truancy and drug use at the start of service, children in the

Figure B.5

Posttest-Only Experiment with a Routine Treatment Control Group

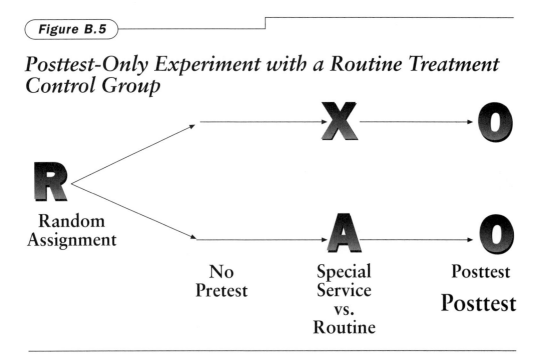

Random
Assignment

No
Pretest

Special
Service
vs.
Routine

Posttest

Posttest

experimental family-based treatment condition were significantly more compliant in home, school, and...

Matching designs can provide persuasive findings that all but eliminate the seven alternative explanations in Figure B.2. To pair subjects so that they are truly equivalent, however, requires matching on a number of variables, and therein lies a problem. People are different, and it is hard to match subjects on more than a few variables. Some children or families may simply not be "matchable," and must be eliminated from the study. Aside from reducing the representativeness of the sample, this tends to reduce variability. In the hands-on world of pair-making, there is a practical upper limit to the number of variables on which subjects can be matched. Moreover, the evaluator is faced with a conundrum: The more variables on which one tries to match, the more likely matching will fail. The fewer the variables on which matching is successful, the weaker the design.

Case-Overflow Comparison Group Design without Random Assignment

Sometimes naturally occurring events produce opportunities to conduct evaluations that approximate the strength of the classic experiment. One such evaluation is called the *case overflow design*. This design is based on the idea that caseload openings occur randomly. That is, when a particular program is small and cannot take every referral, families who are referred but turned away (and usually referred to other programs) constitute an equivalent control group that does not receive the service. By tracking what happens to these referred-but-not-served cases, an evaluator can generate information on what should be an equivalent comparison condition.

The linchpin of case overflow designs is the referral and case screening process. If referrals are similar throughout the study period, and if it is possible to identify families that would be eligible for the program but were turned away for admin-

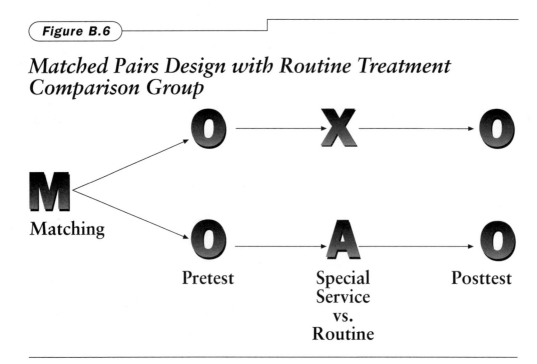

Figure B.6

Matched Pairs Design with Routine Treatment Comparison Group

istrative reasons, then the referred-but-not-served families should be quite similar to the referred-and-served families.

Case overflow designs may be compromised when there is a systematic bias in the referring process, so that families who are referred but not served are different from those that are referred and served. This can happen, for example, when referring agencies become aware that caseloads are full. They may refer only extreme cases, in the hope that the urgency of the case will compel the agency to serve a family in dire circumstances. Or, alternatively, they may refer families with relatively minor needs, preferring to divert families in crisis to agencies that they know will be able to respond immediately. Either way, this can bias the findings from case overflow designs.

Dismantling or Factorial Designs

In long-standing programs, resources may be such that caseloads are rarely full, and therefore, an agency cannot consider a case overflow design. But agencies can still do rigorous research by testing innovative aspects of programs against the basic program. "Dismantling" or factorial designs are used for this purpose.

Dismantling designs get their name from the idea that service can be dismantled or partitioned into discrete components. Many child welfare programs make use of different kinds of skills training in combination with concrete services. If one wanted to test a new kind of skills training, for example, some families might be randomly assigned to a special unit using the new skills training component, while others would receive the standard treatment.

Dismantling designs have an important limitation. They do not tell you whether the service is effective compared to other kinds of programs. They are more useful in developing new elements of service that respond to specific client problems or developments in interventive technology. Because dismantling designs lack a no-treatment or routine treatment control, the differences between groups are apt to be small. And when differences are small, it is hard to detect them. Thus the expected effects of the aspect of treatment that is partitioned should be precisely measured, and all stakeholders should understand that no-effect findings do not imply that a program is ineffective. They show only that the particular service being tested does not, by itself, have a significant impact on outcomes.

Guidelines for Selecting a Design

Whether simple or complex, evaluations are often based on a common set of strategies. These strategies may help you to tailor a design to regional or local needs.

1. Think in terms of a series of evaluation studies.

As services become more refined, work from small studies to larger ones. Resist pressure to conduct an impact assessment on a new program.

2. Match the evaluation design to the problem, treatment model, level of program development, and stakeholders' needs.

Knowledge about the effectiveness of a program tends to spiral upward as a result of a variety of evaluation activities. One's own introspection, observations from workers, and the sometimes stinging words of skeptics can help to formulate program theory, which should be tested by multiple evaluation methods.

3. Use the literature.

You are not alone. Often your concerns will be shared by others who have written about the program you are evaluating. The literature on most source areas in child and family services is easily accessed through PsychLit and Social Work CD/ROMs.

4. When assessing the impact of service, minimize the alternative explanations by using as strong a design as possible.

Include follow-up in all evaluation designs wherever possible. Although our figures do not show follow-up observation, post-treatment measurement should occur multiple times. It is a common evaluation practice to examine outcome measures at the close of service and again six and 12 months after service.

5. Reduce attrition.

Attrition occurs when families or family members discontinue participation in a study. When this happens, the study's sample size and statistical power are reduced. Because attrition can produce bias, many evaluators use incentives to maintain high levels of participation. In budgets for evaluation, they allocate resources to pay family members for participating in data collection. Some evaluators also recommend that permission be obtained from participants to contact neighbors and relatives in the event that subjects cannot be located during the study period.

6. Use multiple sources of information

If a variable is important for pairing subjects in a matched pairs design, measure it several different ways. Take advantage of existing tests and instruments. (For reviews of instruments, see the references section of Chapter 3.) Make use of parent, child, worker, and teacher reports.

Conclusion: Control and Variation

In the evaluation of child and family social services, control and variation counterbalance one another. *Control* is important in several different ways. A service must be controlled, or stable, during an evaluation. If it is fluctuating (because of worker turnover, because of inadequate in-service training, because of poor leadership, etc.), a mix of qualitative and quantitative approaches might be used to identify the sources of variation and to develop a knowledge base from which to stabilize the program. Control is important because there are many alternative explanations for an observed difference between pretest and posttest scores. Lacking a comparison or control group, one cannot argue that a program is effective on the basis of pre-post changes in the behaviors of children or parents who received the intervention. Used this way, the word *control* denotes an element of the design that reduces variability due to alternative explanations. No design does this perfectly, but some designs are better than others.

Variation is important in several different ways. On balance, evaluators like big differences. The intervention should be genuinely different from the routine treatment offered to a control or comparison group. Big differences in the nature of services provided to the experimental and control groups are likely to produce large posttest differences. It makes little sense to spend a great deal of time testing a weak intervention.

The experimental intervention should be potent. It should be significantly different from the control or comparison intervention. In a similar sense, differences across important variables should be maximized. Say, for instance, that young children and teens are expected to have different outcomes. There should be enough variation in the sample to conduct separate analyses of differences by age groupings. That is, the subsamples of young children and teens should be large enough to detect differences if the treatment is effective. This involves the estimation of expected treatment effects and statistical power for different sample sizes.

Variation and control are sought simultaneously. While seeking variation, evaluators also want control. It is this fact that makes evaluation design exhausting. Large samples produce greater variation than small ones, but they often introduce control problems. Only with a rigorous sampling strategy, a rigorous group assignment mechanism, and careful implementation of service is it possible to have variation without sacrificing control.

References

Bingham, R. D., & Felbinger, C. L. (1989). *Evaluation in practice—A methodological approach.* White Plains, NY: Longman Inc.

Bloom, M., & Fischer, J. (1982). *Evaluating practice. Guidelines for the accountable professional.* Englewood Cliffs, NJ: Prentice-Hall.

Buchard, J. D., & Clarke, R. (1990). The role of individualized care in a service delivery system for children and adolescents with severely maladjusted behavior. *Journal of Health Administration,* 17(1), 48–60.

Corcoran, K. J. (1993). Practice evaluation: Problems and promises of single-system designs in clinical practice. *Journal of Social Service Research,* 18(1/2), 147-159.

Fraser, M. W., Pecora, P. J., & Haapala, D. A. (1991). *Families in crisis: The impact of intensive family preservation services.* Hawthorne, NY: Aldine de Gruyter.

Grinnell, R. M. (1993). *Social work research and evaluation.* (4th ed.) Itasca, IL: F. E. Peacock.

Pecora, P. J., Fraser, M. W., Nelson, K., McCroskey, J., & Meezan, W. (1995). *Evaluating family-based services.* New York: Aldine de Gruyter.

Rubin, A., & Babbie, E. (1989). *Research methods for social work.* Belmont, CA: Wadsworth Publishing.

For further information

Jacobs, F. (1996). *Evaluating family preservation services: A guide for state administrators.* Boston: Tufts University.

Section IV: Improving Your Services

Chapter 6

Quality Improvement in the Agency: What Does It Take?

Fotena A. Zirps and David J. Cassafer

Introduction

You have specified your programs. You are conducting process and outcome evaluation. You and your staff are buried in data and information. What now?! Chapter 6 is your reward—your stairway to paradise. In this chapter, tools will be provided for using your data to make programs and ideas work even better.

Why Implement Quality?

You are a busy leader. Your agency is refining the process of using evaluation and possibly a few quality improvement (QI) techniques. You have seen that these approaches generate solutions for pressing problems and techniques for seeking out root causes, as well as ways of conducting solid research and engaging in substantive improvement. You are ready to start climbing further by exploring the use of additional QI approaches. But where do you start? What steps must you follow? This chapter will tell you how to:

- Select areas for improvement;

- Organize information that you are already collecting and use it in the most economical and productive ways; and

- Employ easily learned and implemented tools for making positive change as painlessly as possible.

Quality Takes Leadership

The first step to quality is a commitment on the part of agency leaders to ensure quality throughout the agency. Obviously you as a leader have made this commitment, or you wouldn't be reading this handbook. Chapters 1 and 10 offer greater detail on the difficulty of leadership in this area and the energy that must be devoted to organizational change.

Figure 6.1

The Stairway to Quality

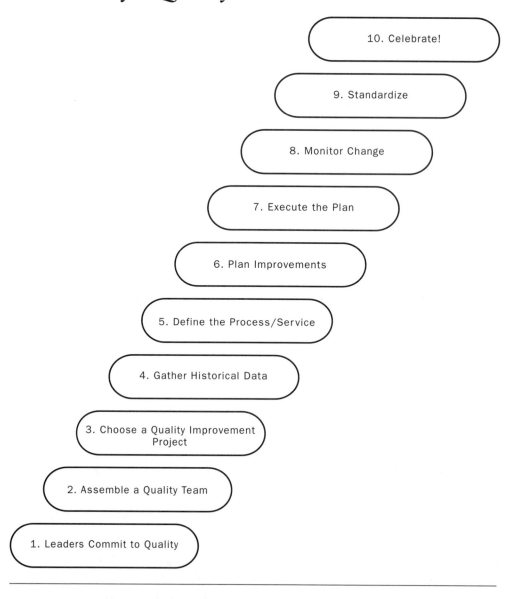

10. Celebrate!

9. Standardize

8. Monitor Change

7. Execute the Plan

6. Plan Improvements

5. Define the Process/Service

4. Gather Historical Data

3. Choose a Quality Improvement Project

2. Assemble a Quality Team

1. Leaders Commit to Quality

Assemble a Quality Team

Your next step is to put together a team to work on improvement. The first team may be composed of agency management personnel or a mixture of line staff and administrators. If the people in the organization can see management team members personally working on a quality improvement project, they will be ready to buy into the quality culture that you are trying to create. This initial team will likely be followed by other teams—some of which may be time-limited in nature. Subsequent teams should include staff at all levels, especially those closest to the issues selected for improvement.

Here are a few things to keep in mind when assembling a quality improvement team.

- The team members need to have experience with, and understanding of, the process to be improved. You cannot simply assign anyone who has some free time. (This may sound obvious, but many people have tried to break this rule, without success.)

- The team members need to own the whole process. Watch out for the situation in which you are trying to improve a piece of a large process, but you can't really make any improvements unless the other parts of the process (or organization) make changes too. In this case, either get them involved, by expanding your scope, or tackle something else.

- The team members need the authority to make changes. Beware of a quality improvement team that is chartered only to investigate a situation and then present recommendations to the decision makers. If, for whatever reason, the team can't be given real authority, perhaps the solution is to have one or more of the decision makers on the team. The information and understanding that come from being an active member of the team will help that person to make the right decision. It's tough for anyone outside to have that level of understanding after merely listening to a presentation from the quality team. It's also very demoralizing for the team to be second-guessed by a group of people who truly don't have the information and the grasp of the situation that the members of the team have.

Team Roles and Responsibilities

A few key roles should be identified immediately.

Team Leader

This is the person who is responsible for the expected results. The leader makes sure that the team has the right members, that those members have enough time to devote to the project, and that they meet their responsibilities to the team. The leader also represents the team in presentations to the rest of the organization.

Team Facilitator

The facilitator is responsible for seeing that the team follows the quality improvement process. This includes keeping the team from rushing to closure before they've gathered sufficient data to make informed decisions, and reviewing which quality tools to use at different points in the project. The facilitator also sees to it that the team meetings go smoothly, drawing input from all the members and making sure that the most vocal people do not overwhelm their quieter teammates.

The facilitator and the team leader should work very closely together. In fact, it's a good idea for the two of them to draw up a contract stating what they expect from each other. For example, one team leader may want the facilitator to run the team meetings and another may want to keep that responsibility. The facilitator and the team leader will often spend a few minutes together at the end of the team meeting to review the team's progress and discuss any issues they need to deal with.

Team Scribe

The scribe may be the most important person on the team. He or she is responsible for taking and distributing the minutes of each meeting. This includes recording decisions, actions that people have committed to, and a general recap of the discussion. If the scribe takes good minutes, and the team members each spend five or 10 minutes reviewing them before the start of the next meeting, very little continuity will be lost from one meeting to the next. On the other hand, without good minutes, people can waste precious time arguing about past decisions, rehashing discussion from last time, or bickering about who committed to do what.

Team Members

The rest of the team should consist of people who have relevant perspectives on the subject at hand. They should be committed to attend regular team meetings and to spend an appropriate amount of time outside of the meeting (usually a few hours a week) collecting data and doing other tasks for the team.

Which Comes First, the Project or the Team?

This is a good question! Sometimes the team is picked before the specific project is decided. For example, the leadership team may decide that they want to set an example by being first to tackle a quality improvement project. Or, perhaps a department may decide that they want to try QI. In these two cases, they would select a project based on the knowledge and experience of the team members. Other times you may select the project first, and once it is decided, look for the people who can best contribute to the project. Either way works!

As the team goes through the phases of the quality improvement project, it is helpful to track their progress on a worksheet called the Quality Improvement Storyboard. Many organizations use this convenient tool to present information about their projects in a consistent and easy to understand format. In a later section of this chapter, in Figure 6.15, you'll find an example of a storyboard, with information on how to use it.

Choose a Quality Improvement Project

Overview

There are a number of good ways to select an area for improvement. The next several pages describe seven of them:

- Program evaluation results,

- Customer feedback,

- Weighted gap analysis,

- Employee suggestions,

- Brainstorming,

- Nominal group technique, and

- The JCAHO chart.

One of the most common mistakes is for a team to take on too much for its first quality improvement project. Take it easy the first time, gain some experience, and have fun. Tackle a big, complex subject for your second project. Choose a first project that has the potential for relatively quick results. If the process you select has a cycle time of one week, you could go through several cycles in just a few months. Any improvements would be quickly visible.

Program Evaluation Results

Program evaluation results are an excellent tool for selecting areas of programs that need improvement. In Chapters 2, 3, 4, and 5, you learned about some of the essential steps of program evaluation, both process and outcome. Good evaluation data should not only point to a program's successes, but highlight its weaknesses as well [Hoefer 1994]. The program's weaknesses can serve as a starting point.

If you are working with evaluation data, consider the following steps: (1) the evaluator and the team summarize and list areas of weakness uncovered in the evaluation report; then, (2) through team judgment or a more formal process such as nominal group technique, select an area for further definition and study; (3) assign roles; and (4) set a timeline for task completion.

Customer Feedback

Customer feedback is another good source of ideas for improvement. Most agencies have some means for gathering client feedback data. The feedback can take many forms, the most common being client satisfaction surveys, focus groups, and exit interviews. The Child Welfare League of America (CWLA), for example, has developed a four-item client satisfaction assessment measure that is easy to implement and analyze (adapted from Magura and Moses [1986]). The CWLA survey asks clients to rate the following items on a scale of strongly disagree, slightly disagree, neutral, slightly agree, and strongly agree:

1. I was completely satisfied with the service I received.

2. My caseworker was attentive to my (my family's) needs.

3. I would recommend this agency to my friends or family.

4. The agency required too much paperwork during the intake process.

The survey then asks for two ways the agency could improve the services it provides. While this is a simple instrument to use, it may lack the specificity to suggest problem areas for program improvement. Other surveys ask clients to check areas that they found problematic, and include such things as office location, waiting time, changing counselors, appointment hours, fees, and "other" (asking them to specify what the other is). This helps identify an area for improvement activities. (For other approaches see Fraser et al. [1991], and Reid & Gundlach [1983]).

An agency may decide to conduct focus groups as well. A focus group is a meeting at which customers (internal or external) are brought together in a small group and asked to discuss a specific set of topics in depth. Ideally, a single focus group has eight to 10 members. An agency will likely choose to conduct a number of such groups, and will need to consider the following issues: group configuration (number of groups, number of respondents per group, types and representativeness of respondents, composition of each group), location for meetings, moderators (one is preferable if conducting fewer than six groups), incentives, refreshments, and the recording of information. For helpful resource books on focus groups see Goldman and McDonald [1987] and Morgan [1988].

Weighted Gap Analysis

Weighted gap analysis is also based on customer input. It is useful in prioritizing which areas to focus on when you have limited resources. (If you don't have limited resources, please give us a call. We'd like to talk to you!)

Since we know how difficult it is to implement change in an organization, we want to make sure we are addressing the areas of greatest need. Here we have a powerful tool to identify those key areas. The term *weighted gap analysis* may sound intimidating, but it is really quite straightforward. The *gap* we're talking about is the gap between the importance your customers place on a service that you provide and their satisfaction with what is actually provided. An importance level of five and a satisfaction level of two reveal a gap of three. If the importance level is two and the satisfaction level is two, the gap is zero. We don't want to imply that it's ever a good idea to have customers dissatisfied with one of your services. We are, however, most concerned when satisfaction is low and importance is high.

The *weighted* part of weighted gap analysis simply means that the formula is set up to give additional weighting (i.e., a higher score) for higher levels of importance. For example, if you had two services with a gap of two, but for one the importance was five and the satisfaction three, while the other had an importance of three and a satisfaction of one, you would give priority to the one with higher importance.

Figure 6.2 is an example of a survey to collect information on customer satisfaction and importance for several services an agency might provide. Figure 6.3 shows some hypothetical results from that survey.

A Pareto diagram is an effective way to look at the data and decide where to focus attention. The diagram is simply a vertical bar chart, sorted by the height of the bars (See Figure 6.4). The Pareto principle (also known as the 80/20 rule), discussed in more detail later in this chapter, tells us that about 80% of our potential benefit comes from addressing a few key areas (the 20%). In the diagram given we can see that the greatest opportunity for improvement lies with services 3 (providing snacks) and 4 (parental discipline training).

Another way of looking at the data is by plotting it as a Scatter Diagram, with satisfaction on the y (vertical) axis and importance on the x (horizontal) axis.

(**Figure 6.2**)

Consumer Satisfaction Survey

*Please help us improve the services we provide by filling out this short
survey. Your honest input is important to us. Thank you!*

*Please answer the questions below using this five-point scale:
1=not at all important, 2=unimportant, 3=neutral, 4=important, 5=very important*

How important to you are each of the following services we provide?
(Please circle the appropriate number.)

	Not at all important	Unimportant	Neutral	Important	Very important
1. Parenting materials notebook	1	2	3	4	5
2. Child care while you're in class	1	2	3	4	5
3. Nutritious snack for you and baby	1	2	3	4	5
4. Class instruction in discipline	1	2	3	4	5
5. Class instruction in play activities	1	2	3	4	5
6. Structured mother-baby time	1	2	3	4	5

Now please tell us how well we are delivering these services.

*Please answer the questions below using this five-point scale:
1=very dissatisfied, 2=dissatisfied, 3=neutral, 4=satisfied, 5=very satisfied*

How satisfied are you with each of the services we provide?
(Please circle the appropriate number.)

	Very dissatisfied	Dissatisfied	Neutral	Satisfied	Very satisfied
1. Parenting materials notebook	1	2	3	4	5
2. Child care while you're in class	1	2	3	4	5
3. Nutritious snack for you and baby	1	2	3	4	5
4. Class instruction in discipline	1	2	3	4	5
5. Class instruction in play activities	1	2	3	4	5
6. Structured mother-baby time	1	2	3	4	5

Figure 6.3

Mean Ratings of Consumer Satisfaction and Gaps

	Importance	Satisfaction	Gap	Weighted Gap
1. Parenting materials notebook	3.7	3.1	0.6	2.22
2. Child care while you're in class	2.3	2.9	-0.6	-1.38
3. Nutritious snack for you and baby	4.5	2.8	1.7	7.65
4. Class instruction in discipline	4.8	3.7	1.1	5.28
5. Class instruction in play activities	2.2	2.0	0.2	0.44
6. Structured mother-baby time	3.1	2.9	0.2	0.62

Multiply gap by importance to get weighted gap.

This method shows the data a little more completely, but takes more experience to interpret. An example is provided in Figure 6.5.

In the diagram you see a line that goes up and to the right. If a point lies above that line, it means that for that service, the customer's satisfaction level is greater than the perceived importance of the service. Please don't assume that you shouldn't care about customer satisfaction for "less important" services. But this is a tool for prioritizing, and, in general, it is better to focus your resources where the importance is high and the satisfaction is low.

Employee Suggestions

Employee suggestions are another easy and inexpensive way to obtain improvement ideas. One of the basic tenets of the quality movement in the business world is that workers know their jobs best and should be consulted first about how to make improvements. Employees deal with customers on a daily basis, are very aware of problem areas, and often have practical ideas on how to address these areas.

Child welfare agencies have found a number of creative ways to gain input from employee suggestions. These include formal systems, such as those in which employees drop written ideas into a suggestion box, exit interviews when an employee leaves the agency, and regular evaluation meetings where employees have a chance to offer suggestions. Ohel/Bais Ezra in New York uses a new employee review procedure as an additional strategy. Each employee meets with supervisory staff at the end of probation to discuss suggestions and assure that the worker is clear regarding job tasks and responsibilities.

Suggestion systems have not been without problems. If management is not committed to making it easy and productive for employees to make suggestions, they will quickly cease to do so. Heath [1994, p. 37] suggested five ground rules for making suggestion programs work:

1. *Be progressive.* Regularly ask employees for suggestions.

2. *Remove fear.* Don't shoot the messenger.

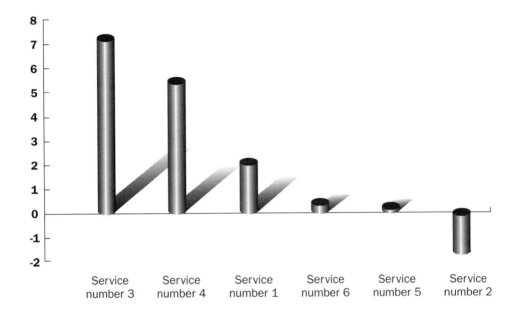

Figure 6.4

Pareto Diagram of Weighted Gap Results

3. *Make it easy to participate.* Stamp out the superfluous paperwork, review, and procedures.

4. *Respond quickly.* Commit to respond to suggestions within some specific period of time.

5. *Reward with recognition.* Let everyone know the value of suggestions that make a difference.

Brainstorming Methods

Brainstorming is used to help a group generate as many ideas as possible in a short amount of time. There are two general methods: structured—where every person must give an idea as their turn arises in rotation or pass until the next round—and unstructured—where group members simply give ideas as they come to mind. GOAL/QPC [1994] offer the following rules for effective brainstorming:

1. Never criticize ideas;

2. Write every idea on a board or chart;

3. Be sure everyone agrees on the issue being brainstormed—write it on the top of the page;

4. Record verbatim—don't interpret; and

5. Do it quickly—5 to 10 minutes.

Figure 6.5

Importance vs. Satisfaction: Scatter Diagram

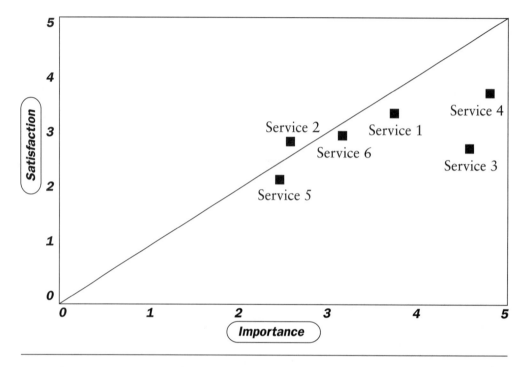

Once the items are recorded, judgment or a voting system of some kind (e.g., the nominal group technique) can be used to select the most important ideas.

Nominal Group Technique is a structured brainstorming and group process decision-making method for selecting areas for improvement [Delbecq et al. 1975, GOAL/QPC 1994]. In this technique each group member is asked to list what they see as the most important problems, generally after a silent brainstorming session. These are written on a board or flip chart so everyone can see them. There is no discussion at this point, except to clarify what a particular item means or combine similar items. Each problem should only appear once. The team members list the problems on a sheet of paper and give each a letter. After group discussion of the items, the members rank them—most important to least important. Each person's ranking is put next to the list and then the totals are added for each item. The highest scoring items are those most important to the total team. Figure 6.6 presents an example from an employee quality group on working conditions. In this example, the item of most importance to the team was health benefits, followed by both flexible hours and extra vacation. The team could vote to break the tie if members wanted to work on more than one item.

The JCAHO Chart

Finally, we have the Joint Commission on Accreditation of Healthcare Organizations (JCAHO) chart, Measurable Components of Quality of Services (see Figure 6.7). Aspects of performance such as client access, appropriateness of services,

---

Figure 6.6

Nominal Group Technique for Employee Compensation

Items

a. salary
b. health benefits
c. flexible hours
d. opportunities for paid training
e. extra 1/2 day vacation time per month

Scores of 5 members

a. 2, 5, 2, 4, 1 (total=14)
b. 1, 4, 5, 5, 5 (total=20)
c. 4, 1, 3, 3, 4 (total=15)
d. 5, 2, 1, 1, 2 (total=11)
e. 3, 3, 4, 2, 3 (total=15)

---

and coordination of providers represent some of the core aspects of quality. Any one of these topics would be a good first project for staff.

Problem Statement

At this point your quality team should have selected an important area for quality improvement efforts. The last action in this phase is to write up a short problem statement and a paragraph or so summarizing why this problem was selected. Having this written down will cement the team's understanding of what they are doing and why. We can almost guarantee that at some point in the quality improvement project the team will start to wander off course. At this point one of the members can read the problem statement and the rationale back to the team to get them on track again. One very effective format for the problem statement includes the following three elements:

- The name of the process

- The main measure of the process

- The intended direction of change

For example, we might say: Reduce (the direction) the number of errors (the measure) in billing (the process).

Gather Historical Data

We need to gather historical data for two reasons. First, we need to have a baseline from which to measure progress. This should at least include data about the main

Figure 6.7

Measurable Components of Quality of Service

(Accessibility) *How easy is it for clients to get service when they need it?*

Is there a waiting list?
How long do clients wait?
What is the time lag between calling the agency and getting help?
Do clients feel it is easy to access service (perception)?

(Appropriateness) *Is the correct service provided, given state-of-the-art knowledge?*

Do post-service analyses of program completers and noncompleters
  suggest that the correct services were offered?
Are staff up-to-date?
What continuing education opportunities have they been offered and
  participated in?

(Continuity) *Is the service coordinated with other services?*

How many agency services do clients receive?
What links are made to other services in the community?
How do staff know what else is available in the community?

(Effectiveness) *Is service provided in such a manner that individuals and families
benefit?*

Do pre- and post-service measures show beneficial change?
Are client goals met?
Do clients report that the service was beneficial to them?
Would clients recommend the service to a friend?

(Efficacy) *Does the service have the potential to meet the need for which it is used?*

What services did clients need that they did not receive?
Are clients coming to the agency looking for the service?

(Efficiency) *Does the service have the desired effect with minimum effort, expense, and
waste?*

What would it cost if clients didn't get the service?
What parts of the service can be eliminated or streamlined?

(Customer Perspectives) *Does the agency involve the consumers it serves and evaluate
their level of satisfaction?*

Who are the agency's customers?
In what ways are they satisfied?
What else do they need?
Are clients involved in planning?

(Safety) *Is the program environment free from hazards or dangers?*

Do clients have to take risks to receive the service?
Is there a safe place for client children while parents receive service—
  or vice versa?

(Timeliness) *Were individuals served when they needed to be served?*

Does assessment occur in a timely manner?
What happens to individuals on the waiting list?

Source: Joint Commission for the Accreditation of Healthcare Programs. (1991). *An introduction to quality improvement in healthcare.* Oakbrook Terrace, IL: Author. Reprinted with permission.

measure of the process (in the example above, the number of errors in the billing process). If the data do not already exist, our first step is to collect them. We *must* know the state of the process before we make changes. It is always possible that our changes could actually make things worse. If we have a known baseline, we can quickly see the data moving in the wrong direction and undo our changes. Second we need these data to understand the process. The data will be analyzed in the next phase as we try to develop solutions and process improvements.

Data You Already Have

Evaluation results and recommendations are data that you may have in hand already. If your staff is completing program evaluation activities, or is tied into a funder that uses data from your agency for program evaluation, you can use these data for defining the services to the quality team. In good evaluations, as you saw in Chapters 2, 3, 4, and 5, processes and services are defined thoroughly and analyzed statistically in program evaluation reports.

Good evaluation data generally answer all of the definitional questions—what the program is about and what services are provided, when are services provided, extent of intervention and change, possible causes of client change, and some information about under what conditions similar change might occur for other clients. These data should also highlight areas of weakness in the program, such as services that were needed but not provided. The leadership team will have to find out what program changes are necessary to address these identified weaknesses, and what is possible and reasonable under the current conditions.

Retrospectives

Retrospectives are a structured way of looking backward at a recently completed project to learn from our mistakes and reinforce our successes. A retrospective can be as simple as a brief description of the project, followed by a four- to five-sentence analysis of each of its major strengths and shortcomings. Retrospectives can be applied to many things: implementation of a new service, a major change to agency policy, incidents and accidents, or a review of a failed audit.

In the past, retrospectives have usually been referred to as *postmortems*, but that word has an unpleasant connotation and isn't entirely accurate. *Postmortem* implies that the project being reviewed is complete and that it was probably unsuccessful. In fact, retrospectives are very useful between phases of a multistage project, to help make the remainder of the project go more smoothly.

Retrospectives are also valuable in reviewing successful projects. We tend to pay attention to problems and forget about things that went well. We may have some sort of celebration, but that's about it. It is vital to the accomplishment of our future goals that we invest in learning why a project was successful. We need to identify the behaviors responsible and reinforce them in the organization. One particularly good example of a continuous retrospective practice is the Professional Review Action Group (PRAG). PRAG was set up in Indiana for the purpose of determining circumstances leading a child to be placed in foster care. The PRAG teams read case reviews and interviewed significant persons surrounding placed children and, whenever possible, the children themselves. Through this review, services to individuals and families became better, but there were systemic benefits as well. Quarterly summaries of these reviews were compiled, and over time the teams gathered information on the impact of caseload size, the process for decision making and its pitfalls, service gaps and program design issues, and recommendations for resources and funding. A number of these recommendations were put into place statewide as a result (Hess & Folaron 1992, p. 6).

After your agency gains experience doing retrospectives on your projects, you will be able to analyze a group of them to see if there are any problems that keep coming up. Once the process or service has been fully analyzed and improved, you will want to spread the good news throughout the agency, and implement the improvements across programs.

Check Sheets

A check sheet is a simple tool for gathering data. Like a tally sheet, it records how often certain events occur. Quality team members design the check sheet for staff to use. The process should be efficient, so staff members can easily understand how and when to tally an event, and the event must be clearly described.

For example, staff might keep track of each time they handle an information and referral phone call. Often these calls take up a good bit of staff time, but are not credited to staff productivity. The quality team would provide counseling staff with a form to record such things as date, time of call, number of minutes, and a brief description of the client need. The team might also provide participating staff with small desk clocks to make accurate time recordings.

One other consideration is whether all participating staff are in comparable circumstances. If this is not the case, a separate tally should be completed for each type of circumstance—for example, staff who provide employee assistance counseling versus staff who provide counseling for regular clients.

At the end of some specified period (perhaps each week), the times are tallied for the whole group and the quality team sees a clear picture of time spent in information and referral. This process could be repeated for a month, or carried out one week each month for a quarter. A bar graph or pie chart would be a clear way to visually represent the data. The information will also be helpful when assembling fishbone charts (to be explained later). GOAL/QPC [1994] recommend the following steps for check sheets:

1. Agree on the event being observed: everyone needs to be looking at the same thing;

2. Choose the time period to collect data: this can range from hours to weeks;

3. Design a form for data collection that is easy to use, with the columns clearly labeled and adequate space for entering data; and

4. Collect the data consistently and honestly: Make sure there is time for this data gathering task.

Define the Process or Service

The next step is to define your process for service or the organizational actions you are analyzing. This is usually done by using a flowchart.

Flowcharts

This tool is simply a pictorial representation of a service or support function, showing all the steps of the process. Flowcharts are useful tools for the documenting a process and for examining how the various steps of a process are related to each other.

One of the biggest benefits of doing a flowchart is that team members realize they each had a different understanding of how the process worked. Many of the accomplishments of a quality team come from simply having everyone see things the same way.

Drawing a flowchart can help you find areas of unnecessary work, missing steps, areas of complexity and confusion, and process disconnects. In the example in Figure 6.8, we see a possible disconnect in the process at the point when a family is put on the waiting list. It looks like this is a point where people could fall through the cracks. Maybe we need to set up some mechanism to make sure they are periodically contacted and that an appointment is eventually scheduled. We also see in this example that no work is done to identify why people are missing their appointments. Perhaps this step should be added.

Improve the Process

Now that you have clearly defined the process and have assembled data about it, you need to analyze the data and propose process improvements. Several tools can help in this phase.

Pareto Diagrams

We've already seen the use of the Pareto diagram to display the data from the weighted gap analysis. Pareto diagrams help us understand how to use something called the law of unequal distribution. An economist named Vilfredo Pareto once noticed that the rich people have more money than all the rest of us put together. Well, he wasn't the first to notice it, but he was the first to realize that there was a generalized principle at work here. The Pareto principle is also known as the 80/20 rule.

In a complicated manufacturing process you could find a few steps in the process that account for 80% of the defects in the completed product. But let's say that you were trying to address the following problem: Clients are not keeping their appointments. You could investigate why each appointment was missed, and record the reason on a check sheet. The next step would be to tally up the number of times that an appointment was missed for each of the reasons on the check sheet. If you present the data in a Pareto diagram you will undoubtedly see a small number of reasons that kept showing up again and again. You could try to address every reason why clients are missing appointments, but you would get far better return on your effort if you focused on the top two or three reasons.

Run, Process Specification, and Control Charts

Run, process specification, and control charts are other types of specialized graphs used to analyze and visually present data. *Run charts* (Figure 6.9) are simply

Figure 6.8

Flowchart of the Intake Process

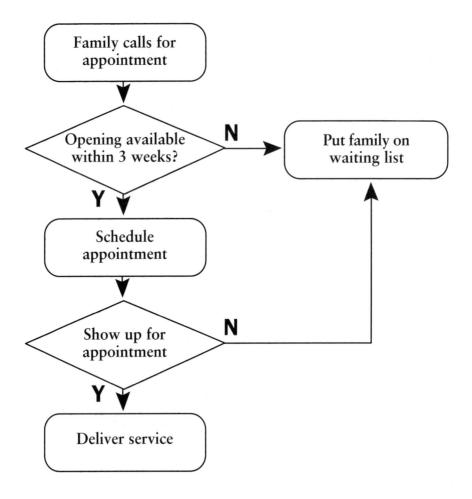

visual representations of what is occurring, such as the number of days that it takes to complete a family assessment. *Process specification charts* (Figure 6.10) show your process results as they relate to customer needs or other externally imposed requirements. These would be the specification limits. For example, the quality team may determine, based on funder requirements, that the family of every child entering the residential treatment setting must have an assessment within seven days of entrance. *Control charts* (Figure 6.11) are used to show what your process is capable of, and they help identify anomalies in process output within certain lower and upper limits. As we will see below, the upper and lower limits on a control chart are derived from actual service delivery process data, and represent the normal range of process operations.

These charts are helpful in understanding problems and monitoring improvements to see whether or not the long-range average performance is changing because of intervention.

Control Limits vs. Specification Limits

Control limits are statistically derived from the actual process output. If the data points are all very close together, then the control limits will be relatively close to the average. However, if the data points are spread out, we can expect the control limits to be spread out as well. The upper and lower control limits show the range of process results that can be expected. In the language of quality, when we say a process is *in control* we mean that the variation in process output is solely due to random variations inherent in the process.

Specification limits, on the other hand, are externally generated by people who know nothing about how your process operates or what it is capable of. If the quality team determines that the family of every child entering the residential treatment setting must have an assessment within seven days of entrance, we might create a run chart showing how many days it is taking for that assessment to occur and track it over time (see Figure 6.9). We would then add an upper specification limit, in this case seven days (see Figure 6.10). In this example there would be no lower limit, since anything faster than seven days is OK.

Now we get to the exciting part. We calculate the control limits and add them to the chart (see Figure 6.11). For the actual method of calculating control limits see GOAL/QPC [1994]. When we can see the actual results along with the control limits and the specification limits, we can start thinking about how to address the problem.

For example, let's suppose that we see several data points above the specification limit, but that all the points are inside the control limits. What does this tell us? As we stated before, the control limits show the range of expected results. If the upper control limit turns out to be above the specification limit (as it is in this example), then we must expect that the process will continue to produce results above that specification limit. In other words, the current process is fundamentally unable to meet the requirements that have been specified. Any attempt to improve the situation should examine the entire process.

On the other hand, if the data points that were above the specification limit were also outside the control limits, what would this tell us? In this case we should take a look at the specific data points that were outside the control limits to see if we can understand what happened. In the language of quality, these points are due to *special cause,* not *common cause.* As the term implies, there will probably be an unusual reason for the data point. There could be a new employee who was improperly trained and misfiled the paperwork, or perhaps a key person could have been out sick for a long time.

One of the most common mistakes in problem solving is to examine every data point that is outside the specification limit to find the reason why that point is where it is. If it is inside the control limit, there is no reason why that point is where it is. However, if you look hard enough, you'll find something that you think is the cause, and you'll waste a lot of time addressing it without making a real difference. The bottom line is that when points are outside specification limits, but inside control limits, you must look at the entire process and not just the specific, offending data points.

In our specific example we see three points above the specification limit, and one of those points is also above the upper control limit. It may be valuable to find out why it took 13 days on one occasion for the assessment to be performed.

Figure 6.9

Run Chart of Time until Family Assessment Is Done

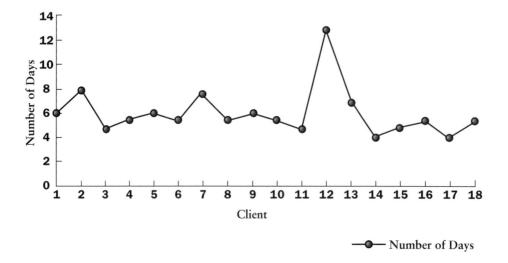

However, since the upper control limit was calculated to be 12, we must understand that this process is fundamentally unable to ensure that the seven-day specification limit will be consistently met.

Leadership might ask a number of questions when a program or service seems to be out of control. These questions, which can be answered from data collected on control and run charts, include:

- Are there any differences in the measurement accuracy of instruments used?

- Are there differences in the methods different workers use?

- Is the service affected by the environment?

- Has there been any significant change in the environment?

- Were any untrained workers involved in the process at the time?

- Has there been a change in the client population?

- Is the process affected by worker fatigue?

- Are workers afraid to report bad news?

Fishbone Diagrams

Fishbones (or cause and effect diagrams—a much less colorful name) are de-

(**Figure 6.10**)

Specification Chart

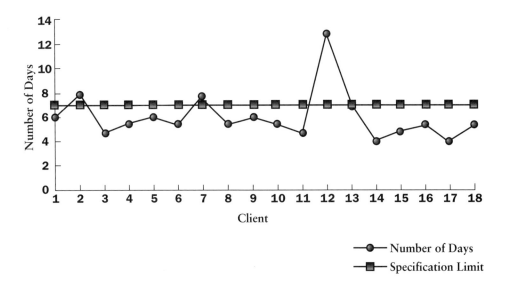

signed to represent the relationship between some effect and all the possible causes influencing it. The effect or problem is placed on the right side of the chart and the major influences or causes are listed to the left. As you can see in Figure 6.12, the resulting table looks like a fish skeleton. The ribs of the fish are made up of the causes of the problem, and the head is the problem.

For every effect there are likely to be several major categories of causes. The major causes that might be used in business are: people, machines, methods, and materials. In administrative areas and social services they might be: policies, procedures, people, and plant (facility). The example in 6.12 was completed with Michael Holt, a family preservation social worker, regarding why a teen had run away.

From this well-defined list of possible causes, the most likely possibilities for improvement are identified and targeted for improvement activities. The point of the analysis is to find a cure for the cause, and not the symptoms, of the problem.

The first step for constructing a fishbone is selecting an effect and generating the causes (perhaps through brainstorming). Using an empty "skeleton," the team writes in the problem or effect (teen ran away) on the right-hand side. Next the team writes in the major cause categories, such as school, parent-child relationship, mental health, friends, and community or societal issues. Place the brainstormed ideas into the proper categories. For each cause, ask why it happens and list the responses as branches from the major causes. (Be brief.) The next steps involve interpreting the chart to look for the most basic causes. Keep an eye out for those causes that appear repeatedly.

From this chart, problems that can be addressed are selected for improvement. One fishbone chart can offer a quality team many possible areas to address. You

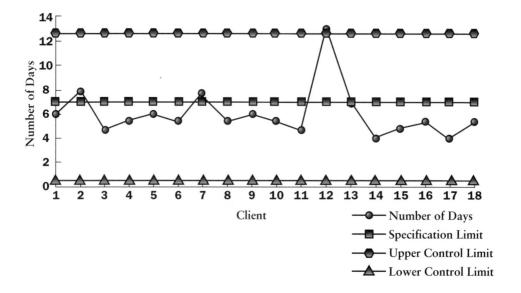

Figure 6.11

Control Chart (including specification limit)

could collect data to see which root causes contribute most frequently to the problem. Or, you might rely on the experience and judgment of the team (perhaps using the nominal group technique) to decide which areas to address first.

Review of Efforts to This Point

Let's recap where we are and how we got here. We've selected a team. Based on a combination of data and judgment, we've picked a problem area to address. We've documented how the process works. We've collected data about the results that the process is currently producing. We've used tools to help us identify possible contributing factors (fishbone charts), which factors contribute most to the problem (Pareto charts), and whether we should be looking at special causes, or the entire process (control charts).

Planning the Changes

At this point you begin to brainstorm solutions to the problems. It's very important to listen to everyone on the team. There is a great deal of benefit to be gained from diversity of opinions. The team needs to break free of conventional thinking and not be constrained by "this is the way it's always been."

If the project you are taking on is large enough, you may want to use a formal planning process, such as the one described in the next chapter, to implement your proposed solutions. At the very least, you should use a Gantt or similar planning chart to track who is doing what, and when.

Figure 6.12

Fishbone Diagram

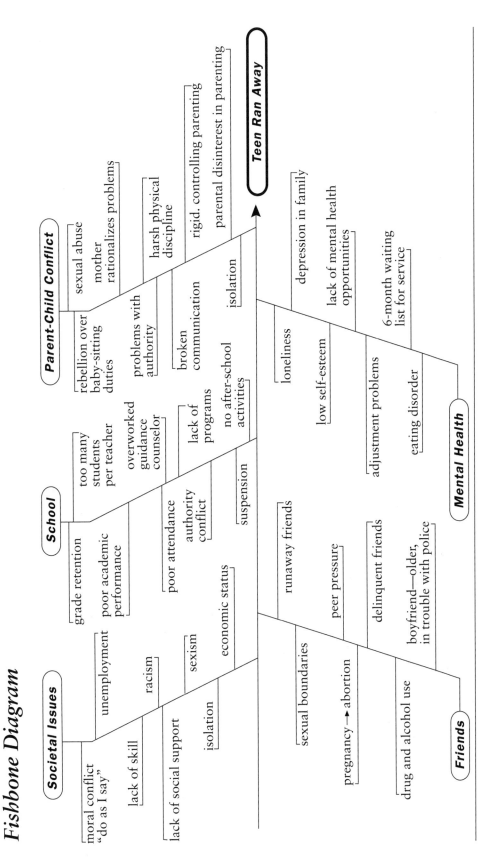

Execute the Plan

Here are a few things to watch out for during the implementation phase:

Time Constraints

At this point, teams usually find that the improvement project starts demanding more of their time. The team members need to make sure they do not overcommit and find their new roles in conflict with their primary job responsibilities. In such a conflict, primary job responsibilities almost always win. This can lead to delays in the project and demotivation for the team.

Doing Everything All at Once

You will probably come up with several possible solutions to the problem you are addressing. There will be a temptation to implement them all at once. *Don't do this.* If you try to do too much at one time you will aggravate the problem described in the previous paragraph. Perhaps more importantly, though, one change could mask the effect of another. Let's assume that one change makes the problem worse and another makes it better. If they were both implemented at once you might see no change, and dismiss both as being ineffective.

A Lack of Support for the Team's Actions

As noted earlier, it is important that the team be empowered to make changes. While there may be legitimate reasons why some proposed changes can not be allowed, if this is not a rare exception the team will be demoralized and other improvement teams may never start at all.

Monitor Change

It's vital to continue collecting data during the implementation process. We need to verify that our solutions are, in fact, working. We need to find out if any other problems are occurring. Run charts and control charts are good tools to monitor ongoing results. If check sheets were used to gather data about components of the process, it would be a good idea to continue collecting that data as well. The Pareto chart can be used to see if the major causes of the problem are still contributing at the same rate, or if the height of the bars is being driven down.

Standardize

Consolidate Your Gains!

The second to last step in a quality improvement project is to make sure that you do not lose what you have just won. It is unfortunately all too common for improvements to be made and then lost. To prevent this from happening, consider the following steps:

- Make sure that all documentation from the project is saved. If further work on the original problem is needed, being able to review the documentation from this project can help avoid unnecessary rework and other problems.

- Create training materials for the revised process. It is likely that there will be people involved in the process who weren't part of the quality improvement team. If they don't understand the new process, how can they do it right? Don't be frightened by a vision of a massive training program. Just put an appropriate amount of work into providing the materials people need to understand what they have to do.

- Schedule review meetings. Have a review meeting once a month or so for the next few months to see how the process is working. Are people following the process correctly? Are the improvements being sustained? Have any new problems come up? A little work here can protect the investment you've made with the original quality improvement project.

Standardization vs. Improvement Projects

Sometimes you find that a process is so poorly understood and inconsistently executed that it is not practical to do an improvement project on it. In this situation it is better to try a standardization project. This is especially helpful when a service or process is in such a condition that it can't be clearly conceptualized or understood by program staff and leadership. Such a project is focused not on improving results but on gaining consistency. It may involve the development of new agency policies, operational procedures, or practice guidelines. (For an example of practice guilines, see The Casey Family Program [1994].)

The desired result is that everyone understands the process, does it the same way, and gets reasonably stabilized outputs. Having said that the main purpose is not to improve results, we need to note that standardization projects inevitably have the side effect of doing just that. However, we must remember that improving results is just a side effect. Once the process is stabilized, if the results are not adequate, an improvement project may be needed. Figure 6.13 provides an example of a standardization project involving a client survey, used at one author's agency. A template with instructions on how to fill it in is included as Figure 6.14. You may want to compare this with the Quality Improvement Project Storyboard (Figure 6.15).

Celebrate!

Don't forget one of the most important steps—enjoy your success. Retrospectively look at what went right, then appreciate your team and bask in the sun. This important, but often overlooked step will keep you and the quality team fresh and excited about continuing quality efforts.

Figure 6.13

Standardization Project Example: Client Survey

Theme

- Client satisfaction survey process

Why Selected

- Each site is doing the survey differently. Application is inconsistent.
- The benefits are more surveys completed, correct completion, survey reliability, and staff comfort

Customer Requirements

- *Customers* = Director of Program Evaluation (DPE), Agency management (results)
- *Outputs* = completed surveys from all clients, completion on both sides
- *Important Characteristics* = all clients understand items, complete both sides of the survey; all
  clients complete a survey; survey is not given to EAP clients
- *Judgment of Client Importance* = primary client (DPE) is leading the process
- *Metrics for Measurement* = check log-in # with survey number, check to see that both sides are
  completed, check name against EAP list

Process Definition

- Inputs identified with a fishbone chart
- Flowchart of process shows as is and as should be
- Method of confirmation = run sheets and process specification sheets

Control Plan

- Train all intake representatives and unit directors
- Receptionist must sign initials on each survey after checking
- Use tape player to ensure consistent instructions for the clients
- Use control sheets regarding completion
- Unit director will check once a day. Use checklist

Standardization Plan

- Documents = job instruction sheet, check sheet — receptionist, unit director evaluation form,
  and taped instructions for clients
- Training = training list for receptionists and for unit directors
- DCA = unit manager checks once per day — client given pencil, survey, and tape player,
  receptionist watched client start, receptionist checked survey for completion and
  initialed it, receptionist sealed survey in envelope after checking EAP list, and then
  rewound tape

Results

- An average of 85% of all clients completed a survey at each site
- 98% of these persons completed both sides
- 99% of these persons were not EAP clients

Remaining Challenges

- 100% completion of client surveys

Moving to a Full Quality Program

So now you're really ready. You've moved to the top step. It's paradise! You're excited about quality and ready to build it into every area of your agency. You want to know exactly where you are in the process. Use the checklist presented in Figure 6.16 to find out where your agency or its specific programs are globally in terms of program evaluation and quality improvement.

Scoring. Give yourself a 0 for each No answer, a 1 for each In Process answer, and a 2 for each Yes answer. Items that receive 0 need attention first. All but two of these items (items 20 and 25) are taken directly from COA standards. Any item that receives a 1 should have a set of timelines and a strategy for moving to a Yes response. The grid easily tells what items need to be accomplished by agency staff.

Timelines

The concept of moving to a full quality program will be discussed at length in Chapters 7 and 10, but for here we will include JCAHO's guidelines for moving into a quality model (Figure 6.17). As you can see, the time frames are liberal and allow for easing your way. It will take time to learn about these concepts, customize an approach for your organization, and then jointly implement it.

We believe that every agency leader is fully aware of how important it is to evaluate programs and provide service of proven quality with a focus on constant improvement. We also know that most agencies are just beginning the process. It takes patience, time, and support. As the leader, you are in a key position to bring about change. Start with your own commitment to apply quality models in your areas of work, then train and encourage staff to do so. The rewards of ease in accreditation, funding, and excellence in the agency are worth it!

Conclusion

This chapter has exposed you to a lot of tools and ideas for continuous quality improvement. Experiment with fishbones, retrospectives, standardization sheets, and the other tools until you find those that work for your team. In our consulting, we have found that most child welfare agencies are just at the beginning of this process. As we move into the next century, we see that this is an exciting time, and truly the era of Peter Senge's "learning organization" [1990].

As you undertake a quality improvement effort it's helpful to remember these basic steps:

- Using a combination of customer data, quality tools, your experience, and collective good judgment, pick an area that needs improvement;

- Collect data on the current state of the process, both so you have a baseline and so you can understand the process well enough to make effective changes later;

- Use the quality tools along with your experience and judgment to analyze the data and propose improvements;

Figure 6.14

Standardization Project Storyboard

(1) Why Selected	(2) Customer Requirements
• What is the process that needs to be stabilized? • Describe the method used to choose this problem. • Show any customer data that was considered. • What are the potential benefits of this project?	• Who are the customers (internal and external) of this process? • Describe the specific outputs of the process. • Use a matrix diagram (or other method) to show which customers receive which process outputs. • Describe the important characteristics of the process outputs and how they will be measured.

(3) Process Definition	(4) Process Assurance

• Identify the inputs to the process.
• Show how the process is currently done—include all variations actually being performed.
• Identify alternative methods to achieve the desired outputs, for example:
  ▪ Brainstorming
  ▪ "Clean sheet" re-design
  ▪ Meetings with other people who do similar processes.
• Agree upon a process flow that everyone will now follow.
	• Validate that the proposed process will accurately and consistently deliver what the customers need. This can be done by:
	  ▪ Structured review of the process by the team
	  ▪ Pilot runs
	  ▪ "Mistake proofing"

(5) Standardization Plan	(6) Results
• Fully document the new process. • Explain how the team members were trained on the new process, and describe the training plans for new team members. • Set up an ongoing measurement system to verify consistent process output. • Set up a review meeting a few months down the road.	• Show how the process is currently running in terms of the process metrics previously specified. • Have you contacted your customers to see what they think of the process outputs?

(7) Problems Remaining	(8) Future Plans
• List any remaining issues. • Did you completely achieve the expected results? • Are there any areas that need to be watched?	• Now that the process is producing consistent results, are these results satisfactory? • Will a quality improvement project be started to continue work on this process? • Will the team now address another problem area?

Source: Personal Communication, Ron Black, Meta-Dynamics, Loomis, CA, January 30, 1995.

Figure 6.15

Quality Improvement Project Storyboard

(1) Why Selected	**(2) Initial Status**
• What is the Problem Statement? • Describe the method used to choose this problem. • Show any customer data that was considered. • Show any linkage to other plans in the organization.	• Provide an overall description of the state of the process before making improvements. • If possible, show one clear overall measure of the process. • In addition to the measure above, show any measures of the intermediate steps in the process.

(3) Analysis	**(4) Action**

• List the root causes of the problem.
• Show any relevant charts/graphs that helped you identify the root causes.
    ▪ Fishbones
    ▪ Pareto charts
    ▪ Control charts
    ▪ etc.
• Describe any other methods used to identify the root causes.
	• Describe the proposed solution to the problem.
	• Explain how the team arrived at these solutions.
	• Provide a schedule for implementation of these solutions.
	• Describe the metrics that will be used to measure effectiveness of each of the solutions.
	• State the anticipated results.

(5) Results	**(6) Standardization**
• Show the results that were achieved. • Use the overall process measures to show total results. • Use the intermediate process measures to show intermediate results. • As much as possible, use the same tools that were used during the analysis phase, so as to compare 'apples and apples.'	• Show the steps you have taken to ensure that the problem does not return. This often includes documentation and training. • Have you shared your results with anyone else in the organization with a similar problem? • Have you set up an ongoing measurement system to monitor the process results?

(7) Problems Remaining	**(8) Future Plans**
• List any remaining issues. • Did you completely achieve the expected results? • Are there any areas that need to be watched?	• Will the team stay together and make another round of improvements to the process? • Will another team work on this process? • Will the team now address another problem area?

Source: Personal Communication, Ron Black, Meta-Dynamics, Loomis, CA, January 30, 1995.

(**Figure 6.16**)

A Self-Assessment Tool for Quality Improvement

(**Instructions**)

For the following items answer *yes* if the item is fully in place, *in process* if the item is in process or there is a formal plan to begin, and *no* if there has not yet been any planning or action.

Item	Yes	In Process	No
1. Number of clients seen each week is accurately known.			
2. Numbers and types of hours of service per client are documented.			
3. Incidents and accidents are kept in a written record and are reviewed at regular intervals.			
4. Individual client data are examined to determine whether goals are being met.			
5. Client needs are formally and regularly examined through a needs assessment.			
6. Quality improvement teams are in place.			
7. Agency leadership has been trained in quality improvement.			
8. Monitoring procedures are set in place for each program.			
9. External review is used in all appropriate programs.			
10. There is a formal procedure for dealing with client grievances and such grievances are reviewed regularly.			
11. Peer review of randomly selected open cases is performed on a regular basis.			
12. Special review is focused on high-volume or high-risk activities.			
13. The agency has set benchmarks, timelines, and thresholds that trigger examination activities.			
14. The QI/PE process examines causes in relationship to meeting goals set by and with clients.			
15. The agency examines aggregate data to see if these goals are being met.			
16. The agency sets goals and objectives to be achieved by clients using the service.			
17. Client satisfaction data are collected and utilized.			
18. When deviations are found in terms of clients or services, there is a procedure for seeking solutions.			
19. Data are collected and analyzed for timely use in planning.			
20. Program improvements are regularly implemented, and come from staff at all levels of the agency.			
21. The agency has a human subjects policy.			
22. The agency has a mechanism for obtaining consent for research.			
23. The agency has review of its research.			
24. The agency has a written policy for conducting research and reviewing research proposals.			
25. The agency has spreadsheet and/or statistical software packages available for staff use, such as Excel, FileMaker Pro, or SPSS.			

(**Figure 6.17**)

JCAHO Timelines
for Implementing Continuous Improvement

(**Phase 1**)   *(Allow a year)*

Leaders educate themselves (e.g., through courses and this handbook) about quality improvement).

A mission statement that identifies quality as an agency goal and commitment is adopted and promulgated.

(**Phase 2**)   *(Allow a year)*

Middle management is trained in quality tools and techniques.

Priorities are established for areas of improvement.

(**Phase 3**)   *(Allow two years)*

Demo projects are initiated across departments.

All staff are trained in quality improvement methods.

(**Phase 4**)   *(Allow two years)*

Projects are initiated across the agency so that all employees are involved in the analysis of processes.

Efforts are integrated.

Cultural change is evidenced across the agency.

Source: Adapted from Joint Commission for the Accreditation of Healthcare Programs. (1992). Performance based evaluation of mental health organizations. Oakbrook Terrace, IL: JCAHO.

- Implement the improvements, being careful to measure their effect on the process; and

- Make sure that you keep the gains you've made, by documenting the new process and training everyone involved.

If the project you have chosen to address is large and complex, the planning method described in Chapter 7 may be the one you need to implement it.

References

Delbecq, A. L., Van de Ven, A. H., & Gustafson, D. H. (1975). *Group techniques for program planning: A guide to nominal group and Delphi processes.* Glenview, IL: Scott, Foresman and Co.

Fraser, M. W., Pecora, P. J., & Haapala, D. A. (1991). *Families in crisis: The impact of intensive family preservation services.* Hawthorne, NY: Aldine de Gruyter.

GOAL/QPC (1994). *The memory jogger II: A pocket guide of tools for continuous improvement and effective planning.* Methuen, MA: Goal/QPC.

Goldman, A., & McDonald, S. S. (1987). *The group depth interview.* Englewood Cliffs, NJ: Prentice-Hall, Inc.

Heath, J. A. (1994). A few good ideas for a good idea program. *Quality progress.* Indianapolis, IN: University School of Social Work, 35-38.

Hoefer, R. (1994). A good story, well told: Rules for evaluating human service programs. *Social Work, 39*(2), 233-235.

Joint Commission for the Accreditation of Healthcare Programs (JCAHO). (1991). *An introduction to quality improvement in healthcare.* Oakbrook Terrace, IL: Author.

Joint Commission for the Accreditation of Healthcare Programs (JCAHO). (1992). *Performance based evaluation of mental health organizations.* Oakbrook Terrace, IL: Author.

Morgan, D. L. (1988). *Focus groups as qualitative research.* Newbury Park, CA: Sage Publications.

Reid, P. N., & Gundlach, J. H. (1983). A scale for the measurement of consumer satisfaction with social services. *Journal of Social Service Research, 7,* 37-54.

Senge, P. (1990). *The fifth discipline: The art and practice of the learning organization.* New York: Doubleday.

The Casey Family Program (1994). *Practice guidelines for clinical case management.* Seattle, WA: Author.

Chapter 7

How Can Planning Make It Happen?

David J. Cassafer

Introduction

Planning is the link between wanting something to happen and making it happen. As illustrated in Chapter 1, the 1990s is a decade of unprecedented change for those of us in child and family service organizations. To successfully implement the changes required of us, we need practical plans and we need to implement them effectively. Chapter 2 presented a good example of planning as applied to the program specification process. This chapter will present a broader planning philosophy, borrowed from leading American and Japanese businesses. We will start by showing how the Plan-Do-Check-Act cycle (which you've already seen in Chapter 1) is the foundation for all effective planning. We will then outline a specific method for developing the plans to accomplish whatever you decide is your agency's most important goal. Finally, we will describe a complementary planning method that helps you manage your "Business Basics." *

The Plan-Do-Check-Act Cycle

The Plan-Do-Check-Act (PDCA) cycle is the essence of good planning. (See Figure 7.1.) This concept is intuitive and so simple, yet ask yourself: How many times have you seen organizations do the following?

- Skip the PLANning stage and jump right into a project without thinking it through first.

---

*   In the language of planning, words sometimes have a slightly different sense than in everyday English. To make things yet more complicated, even within this subculture, different organizations use words differently. To avoid confusion, many of the terms used in this chapter are defined in a glossary at the end of this chapter, Appendix C. Feel free to translate this chapter into the terms with which you are most familiar. For example, some people refer to *mission* as *purpose* or *purpose and direction*.]

Figure 7.1

The PDCA Cycle

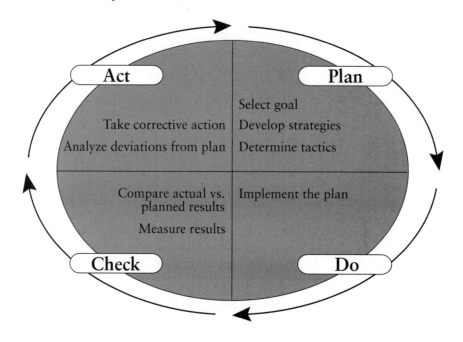

- Spend a lot of time writing formal plans that end up sitting on a shelf, without the agency ever DOing anything.

- Create a good plan, implement it, but fail to actually CHECK the results and compare them to what the plan said was supposed to happen.

- Evaluate the results, but fail to ACT to correct the discrepancy between what was planned and what actually happened.

In the next section we will describe a specific planning method that has proven to effectively implement the concepts of PDCA.

Breakthrough Planning (Hoshin Kanri)

The planning methodology we are about to describe is called Breakthrough Planning because it is very effective at helping an organization focus its collective energy to achieve a breakthrough or other significant goal. It is commonly used to identify, and then achieve, the organization's most important goal for the coming year. It is based on a Japanese method called *Hoshin Kanri*. This term is usually translated as policy deployment, because it helps you deploy (that is, implement) the policies (that is, plans) of the organization. It does this by coordinating everyone's efforts towards a common goal. After the concepts of Breakthrough Planning have been described, we'll discuss the involvement of various members of the agency in the planning process.

As you'll see, with this method there is a spirit of harmony and natural flow. We start with very high level concepts, such as the agency's mission, and end up with detailed tactical steps.

The Breakthrough Planning method has been proven to work in organizations of all sizes. Large corporations use it to ensure that the different parts of the organization are working together towards a common objective, such as a significant reduction in time to market for new products. At the other end of the scale, single individuals use this planning method when tackling a difficult and seemingly overwhelming task. When you implement Breakthrough Planning faithfully, the odds of successfully reaching your goal will go up dramatically. At the end of this section we will review why this method works so well.

One last note before we look at the details of this method: Any time we try to make a change to standard procedures in an organization we are likely to see concern, confusion, and resistance. Chapter 10 will discuss how to deal with these normal human reactions, and will help you implement organizational changes, such as the use of these planning tools.

Mission

We start with the mission of the agency. The mission will be the touchstone against which we evaluate our plans. We must always remember to ask if our plans are in accord with our mission. Below is a sample mission statement that provides a context for developing the plan:

> **Mission:** To promote the well-being of children and, specifically, to strengthen and preserve families in our community.

Situation

The next step is to discuss the situation in which the agency currently exists. Here are some questions to ask:

- What opportunities are in front of us?

- What client needs are currently unmet?

- Do we face any governmental or bureaucratic constraints?

- What is our current workload?

- What is the outside environment like?

- Do we have any mandates from higher up in the organization?

The program specification process described in Chapter 2 will produce useful information to support this analysis. You may also use some of the QI tools mentioned in Chapter 6 to gain an objective understanding of your current situation.

After evaluating the above information, write up a short description (two to five paragraphs) that summarizes the situation the agency is facing. This provides a context for developing the plan. Below is an example of a situation statement:

Situation: The funding available for family counseling services is increasing. There are several counties throughout the state that still do not have access to these services. At this time our organization has been relatively stable, and things are basically under control. We are, however, experiencing some pressure to demonstrate the cost-effectiveness of our services. Our counselors have master's degrees, but other agencies are using people with bachelor's degrees and, therefore providing services at a lower cost. We are also constrained by a cap of $5000 per family. We are currently seeing about an 85% success rate for families who complete our program. However, we are not currently able to intervene effectively in families where drug and alcohol dependency is a problem. We know that many of these families drop out of our program, and their children remain at risk.

Goal

Now, given the agency's mission and the situation statement we've just developed, we choose a goal. Until an organization is experienced with this planning method, it's best to limit yourself to only one goal. (One of the most common mistakes in implementing Breakthrough Planning is to bite off more than you can chew.) The magnitude of this goal should be such that it can be achieved in about one year. Here are some things to keep in mind as you decide which goal to go after:

- It should logically flow from your mission and your situation statement.

- It should be easily understood.

- It should be single focused. (Watch out for the word *and* in the goal statement.)

- It should be outcome oriented unless the goal is a process or implementation goal.

- It should not imply how it is to be achieved. (Watch out for the words *by* and *through*.)

- It should include a clear, unambiguous success measure. (This is often expressed in terms of a measure and a specific target. See the example in the section below.)

Success Measure

Every goal statement needs to be accompanied by a success measure. Having a success measure for the goal (and for each of the strategies) is one of the key reasons why this method works. It forces you to be practical and realistic. It also ensures that participants share a common understanding of what the expected results should be. Below is an example of a goal statement and its success measure:

Goal: Pilot test an addiction treatment program to supplement other family services that will reduce drug and alcohol use by families from 40% to 20%.

Measure: Decreased percentage of substance use among families in which addiction is present.

Target: Move from 40% to 20% by end of fiscal year.

Result Measures vs. Activity Measures

For the high-level goal, we need to measure *results*. We might have defined success as publishing a paper reporting our experiences with this new program, but that would just measure activity. We could say that we did some work (set up a program, ran it for a while, wrote a paper, etc.), but we couldn't say we accomplished anything. Our purpose is to help families, and we want to measure something that resulted from our work—in this case, a reduced rate of substance use. Chapters 2 and 3 provide more information about how to measure results in the context of social services.

In the example, we have a specific goal: 20%. Why was that number chosen? Here are some possible reasons for choosing a specific goal:

- Our own data from past experiences tells us this is realistic, but challenging.

- We have data from other sources (e.g., results reported in professional journals about similar programs) that say this is realistic, but challenging.

- This is an externally imposed goal (e.g., we must achieve this or lose funding).

- Or, lacking hard data or external dictates, we based this goal on the combined experience and best judgment of the directors and staff.

Strategies

Now that we have a clear goal, we need to develop the strategies that will accomplish it. When brainstorming strategies it is often helpful to ask: What are the barriers to accomplishing the goal? Then you can develop strategies to overcome each of them. It's vitally important that all the strategies, when taken together, are sufficient to accomplish the goal they support. One last step is to assign an owner to each strategy. The owner is the person who has the best combination of skills, responsibility, authority, and time to devote to the strategy. As you've probably seen many times over, having an owner ensures accountability.

As with the goal statement, each strategy will have a success measure. Wherever possible we prefer to measure results and not activity. However, this can be very difficult to do. In the subsequent examples you will see that the success measures for these strategies actually measure activity.

Figure 7.2 shows an example of the strategies that together will accomplish the goal: Pilot test an addiction treatment program to supplement other family services that will reduce drug and alcohol use by families from 40% to 20%. To make it easier to talk about the plan, we've given each goal and strategy its own number. As you can see in Figure 7.2, we start with the highest level objective, and number it 1. The strategies supporting it are then numbered 1.1, 1.2, 1.3, and 1.4.

Figure 7.2

Example of Goal and Supporting Strategies

Goal	Owner	Measure
Pilot test an addiction treatment program to supplement other family services that will reduce drug and alcohol use from 40% to 20%	Catherine	**Measure:** Decreased percentage of families where addiction is present. **Target:** Move from 40% to 20% by end of fiscal year.

Strategies	Owner	Measure
1.1 Set up branch office for pilot	Susan	Ready for operation by August 1st.
1.2 Obtain qualified staff*	George	Two people in place by May 15th.
1.3 Develop program for addressing addiction in the family	Kathy	Program defined, approved by directors, and documented by June 21st.
1.4 Fine-tune assessment procedure to better identify addiction situation and drug or alcohol usage	Jarrel	Procedures revised, reviewed by staff, and documented by July 15th.

*Note: This doesn't say *hire* qualified staff, or *train* existing staff, because we don't want to constrain how George accomplishes this strategy.

Deployment

The next step in the Breakthrough Planning process is to deploy or "cascade" the plan. Each of the strategies decided upon in the previous step is now considered to be a goal, and we develop strategies to accomplish it. Figure 7.3 shows an example of how this might be done.

In Figure 7.3 the process or implementation goal necessary to achieve the overall outcome is numbered 1.1. It is the same as strategy 1.1 from Figure 7.2. The strategies beneath it are numbered by taking the number of the goal and adding .1, .2, .3, and so on. In this case we have 1.1.1, 1.1.2, 1.1.3, and 1.1.4.

In Figure 7.4 you can see how the plan might be deployed in a medium sized agency. At the top level of the diagram is a box labeled 1, representing the broad outcome goal that the agency has decided to go after. At the second level are four strategies that, when taken together, will achieve that top goal. As a rule of thumb, three to seven process goal strategies are generally needed to achieve the goal. In this example, we arbitrarily used four.

(**Figure 7.3**)

Example of Continued Deployment of the Plan

Goal	Owner	Measure
1.1 Set up branch office for pilot	Susan	Ready for operation by August 1

Strategies	Owner	Measure
1.1.1 Identify county with greatest need	Michael	Data reviewed with staff and decision made by February 15
1.1.2 Find place for office	Luther	Site identified that provides 2000 square feet, within allocated budget, and located within about 5 miles of identified neighborhoods in need. Ready to move in by July 1*
1.1.3 Hire support staff	Kathy	Staff hired and trained by July 15
1.1.4 Furnish office	Kathy	Done by July 15th

*Note: We have clearly specified what is required, so there will be no confusion about whether or not Luther successfully accomplished his strategy.

The diagram shows that the second strategy (labeled 1.2) has four substrategies that will combine to accomplish it. The box labeled 1.2.2 shows the substrategies that are needed to accomplish this goal. (Each of the strategies at this level will have its own substrategies, but to keep the diagram from getting too busy we are not showing them all.) This process is repeated until we get to the level of tactics, specific tasks done by specific people.

You can see that Figure 7.4 looks like an upside-down tree. As the plan develops, some of the branches will have to be very short, with just one or two levels before getting to tactical details; others may go to three or four levels.

Figure 7.4 also looks like a standard, hierarchical organization chart. If your organization is structured in this fashion, you would probably implement Breakthrough Planning in the following manner:

- The director of the agency delegates one or more strategies to each of the department heads.

Figure 7.4

Cascading Deployment of the Plan

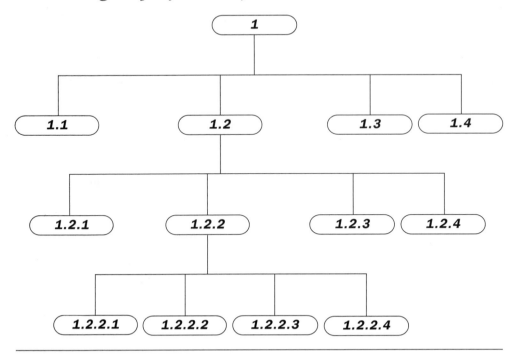

- Each department head develops substrategies and delegates them to the managers in that department.

- This process is repeated down to the level of tactics.

It would be a mistake, however, to think that this planning method only works for hierarchically managed organizations.

In an organization that has a cross-functional, process orientation, the deployment of the plan would look like this:

- The executive leadership of the organization identifies which processes affect the achievement of the organization's goal.

- Strategies are developed for each of these processes.

- A cross-functional team determines the substrategies that are required to make the necessary process improvements.

- Each of those substrategies is then owned by the person most able to implement it, no matter what department that person works in.

- Further levels of substrategies are developed as needed. Again, each of those is given to the person best able to implement it.

Figure 7.5

Example of Strategy and Supporting Tactics

Strategy	Owner	Measure
Develop program for addressing addiction in the family	Kathy	Program defined, approved by directors, and documented by June 21st.

Task	Owner	J	F	M	A	M	J	J	A	S	O	N	D
Research the literature	Kathy	X	X	X									
Develop intervention protocol and methods with staff	Kathy		X	X	X								
Research payers and fee structure	Jim				X	X							
Review progress & initial recommendations with directors	Kathy				X								
Identify support programs	Jim		X	X									
Define assessment and evaluation methods	Kathy			X									
Document protocol/procedures	Jim				X	X	X						
Final review with directors	Kathy					X							

Tactics

Tactics are the final step in deploying the plan—the place where "the rubber meets the road." This stage is a final reality check to see if the plan is feasible. When you actually start seeing who is going to do what, and when they are going to do it, you'll know if your plans were too ambitious for the available resources. Up to this point, you've only focused on the end result. But now you'll see how much time you expect each of the tasks to take. Figure 7.5 shows an example of the tactical implementation of the strategy "Develop program for addressing addiction in the family." You may recognize this diagram as being a modified Gantt chart. (If you are unfamiliar with Gantt charts, see the Glossary.)

As we look at Figure 7.5, we can see that Kathy looks pretty busy. It would be a good idea to look at the other tactical plans and see how busy everyone else is. There might be someone who has a little free time and could help her out.

Regular Reviews

This is the Check step in the PDCA cycle. At regular intervals (usually monthly or quarterly) the plan is reviewed. We always start the review at the bottom level of the plan and check to see if the tactics are being completed on schedule. We then look to see if the strategies above them are producing the expected results. We continue until we are reviewing the strategies directly below the highest level goal. In a large organization this review process could take place over several days, as the owners of each level of the plan review their results with the owner of the strategy one level up. In a small or less formal organization, this could be achieved at one meeting. But even if the whole plan is reviewed at one meeting, we still want to start at the bottom and work up.

For the reviews to be effective, people have to feel free to admit bad news. Dr. W. Edwards Deming, considered by many to be the foremost expert on quality transformation, warned us about this in the eighth of his famous fourteen points: "Drive out fear, so that everyone may work effectively for the company" [Deming 1986].

Fine-Tuning the Plan

Reviewing the plan is not enough, of course. We need to make adjustments to get the plan back on track.

Why are we assuming it's off track? Because the plan that worked perfectly has yet to be written! Between the time the plan was created and the time of the review, several things have happened. We have learned that some of our ideas didn't work as well in practice as we thought they would when we had the planning meeting. People who were working on the tactics of the plan got sick, or left the agency, or didn't have as much time available as they thought. Even if your plan was perfectly conceived and everyone did their part, the world around you has probably changed in the meantime. The bottom line is that we must expect to fine-tune the plan. Often this means making changes to a strategy that's not working—or even throwing it away and substituting a different one. It may mean adding people to a part of the plan that's turning out to be more work than we thought. The important point is to recognize that by making these changes now, we can get the plan back on track and still achieve the high level goal. In Figure 7.6, we see an example of a review form for the strategy: Set up branch office for pilot. A similar review form would be done for each of the other strategies and for the top level goal.

Practical Tips for Breakthrough Planning

Who Does the Planning?

It's very important to have the right people involved in the planning process, and to involve them at the right time. Of course you'll have to make adjustments for your own environment, but there are some guidelines. The agency's executive director, other directors, board members, and key staff members comprise the team that is responsible for starting the plan off on the right foot. They will create the situation statement and set the high level outcome goal. The directors and staff will then create the first-level strategies to accomplish the goal. Each of these strategies will be given to a specific person, who will now treat it as his or her goal. At this point people may work with their own staffs or other associates to create the strategies to accomplish their goals.

It's very important to get the people who will be doing the actual work involved in developing their parts of the plan. As Dwight David Eisenhower once said, "Plans are nothing, planning is everything." Imagine that through some magic,

---

Figure 7.6

Sample Breakthrough Planning Review Table

Plan (Information from original plan)	Do (Progress to date)	Check (Status & trend)	Act (Adjustments to plan)
Objective: Set up branch office for pilot. *Owner:* Susan *Measure:* Ready for operation by August 1.		S=Yellow T= +	
Strategy: Identify county with greatest need. *Owner:* Michael *Measure:* Data reviewed with staff and decision made by February 15.	Done	S=Green	
Strategy: Find place for office. *Owner:* Luther *Measure:* Site identified that provides 2,000 square feet, within allocated budget, and located within about 5 miles of identified neighborhoods in need. Ready to move in by July 1.	Several potential sites have been identified. There may be an opportunity to share space in same building as other social agencies, but we have not yet found a suitable site within the allocated budget.	S=Yellow T= -	We are working to get approval to exceed the budget, but it's not looking promising.
Strategy: Hire support staff. *Owner:* Kathy *Measure:* Staff hired and trained by July 15.	Staff hired, but increased workload in our current offices is affecting the training plan. Support staff are complaining that they don't have time to get their job done, much less train new people too.	S=Yellow T= +	Kathy had overtime pay approved so staff can get caught up and proceed with training the new people.
Strategy: Furnish office. *Owner:* Kathy *Measure:* Staff hired and trained by July 15.	We got a great deal on used office furniture. We're now waiting for an office to move it into.	S=Yellow T= +	

Legend for the Check Column:
S: is overall status expressed like a traffic light, with green (OK), yellow (some concern), and red (in danger).
T: is trend expressed as + (getting better) or - (getting worse.) The trend should be shown anytime that status is not green.

---

the final plan you developed is transported back in time and handed to you just before you began the planning process. Could you take that plan and make it work? Not very likely! A great deal of learning occurs in the process of developing a plan. This knowledge is essential for the implementation phase. In addition, at the same time as people were creating the plan, they were also buying into it. After all, it was their plan! (See Chapter 10 for additional planning strategies from an organizational change perspective.)

It is very beneficial to have a planning facilitator. This could be a respected staff member who has good interpersonal skills, or it could be an external consultant. There are advantages to using consultants. They can be impartial; they have more freedom than staff people to say unpopular things; and, as we've all seen, people tend to listen more to a consultant than to someone in their own agency. Nonetheless, if you have a staff person who has the right skills, who is secure in the job, and who is well respected, there are also advantages to staying in-house. A staff person will always be there when you need help. While they won't be as detached as a consultant, they will have the benefit of understanding the agency—its history, its culture, and its current situation.

Creating the Plan

Here is one way to develop the plan. You can modify this outline to suit your own budget and other circumstances. In this example the majority of the work will be accomplished at a two-day planning retreat. The morning of the first day is devoted to discussing the current situation, writing the situation statement, and choosing the goal. That afternoon the first level strategies are discussed and given owners. On the second day you split into small groups and help each other develop substrategies. Additional people from the agency may join the group on the second day. If possible, cascade the plan down to the tactical level. Near the end of the day all the plans are presented to the entire group.

After the retreat, everyone has one week to think about the plan. If you didn't get a chance to plan down to the tactical level, now is the time to do that. This is primarily an opportunity to reflect on what you've committed to and refine how you're going to accomplish it. If you're not confident that you can deliver on your part of the plan, now is the time to share those concerns. Other people may be able to help you figure out how you can get your part done. If it's just not doable, then your strategy may have to be dropped and other strategies added, to ensure the success of the larger plan.

At the end of the week the planning team meets to go over any changes and conclude the initial phase of planning. The next step is to distribute the plan to the entire organization. It's *vital* that the plan be visible to everyone. This allows everyone in the agency to see how it all builds together. Instead of seeing random pieces, they see a completed puzzle. It's a very powerful feeling to sit back and say: "If I do my part here, then the strategy above that will be accomplished. If that gets done, then the strategy above it is successful, all the way up to the top goal for the agency."

At this point we are ready to begin implementing the plan. As we've already seen, regular reviews of the plan's progress are part of this planning method. For an organization that is using Breakthrough Planning for the first time, we suggest reviewing the plan monthly for the first three months and quarterly thereafter. In addition, it's good for everyone to spend a few minutes each week reviewing the tactical plans for which they are personally responsible.

Why Does This Planning Method Work?

There are four major reasons why this method is so successful:

- *Focus.* We are focused on one major goal. Achieving one significant goal is a lot better than attempting several and not achieving them because you took on too much and were spread too thin.

- *Cascading Deployment.* The plan flows naturally. Each level of the plan helps accomplish the part of the plan above it. All of the pieces fit logically together. People can see how their actions all come together to achieve the organization's goal.

- *Accountability.* Clear, measurable outcome and process goals help to avoid misunderstandings. Each strategy or tactic has an owner who is responsible for it. This forces everyone to think seriously about what they are committing to.

- *Built-In Review Process.* No plan ever works as originally written! Because of the periodic reviews, you will see what parts of the plan are not working and take action to recover while there is still time!

Business Basics (Nichijo-Kanri)

The Breakthrough Plan is exciting and motivating. By definition, we are working to achieve something very important to the organization. It's all too easy to be so focused on the future, however, that we neglect the present. To complement Breakthrough Planning, we need something to make sure our day-to-day tasks are getting done. We do that with the Business Basics Tracking Table. This is very much like the Japanese method called *Nichijo Kanri* (usually translated as daily management). Business Basics are things we already know how to do, but which might get out of hand if we take our eye off them. To create the table, go through the following steps:

- Identify the key activities that keep the agency functioning.

- Select a measure for the activity and a target. (The target is the level of expected performance.)

- Decide upon an action limit. This is a trigger point, which, if exceeded, requires action to review the situation. (The difference between the target and the action limit can be thought of as a grace period.)

- Decide how often the activity needs to be reviewed.

- Describe the data source. (How is the activity being tracked?)

- Name the owner of the activity, or the person who is primarily responsible, if several people do it together.

Figure 7.7 is an example of a Business Basics table. Creating the Business Basics is a very useful exercise. It helps you to decide which are the key activities that must be done and are worth tracking. It may cause the agency to ask some questions that have not been asked for a long time. For example: Who reads that status report, anyway? Does it really have to be done? Even if it is needed, does anybody really care if it arrives more than five days after the first of the month? Would it be OK if it took 10 days? If nothing else, this table documents expectations clearly. Many times people are working to meet expectations that have changed, but those changes were never communicated.

Figure 7.7

Sample Business Basics Table

Activity	Measure, target & action limit	Review period	Data source	Owner
Monthly status reports	*Target:* mailed by 3rd working day of month *Action limit:* 5th day	Monthly	Bill's log	Bill
Invoice processing	*Target:* invoices paid in 45 days *Action limit:* 60 days	Quarterly	Computer report	Mary
Family assessments	*Target:* completed in 7 days of request *Action limit:* 10 days	Monthly	Activity report	Susan
Etc.	*Target:* XXX *Action limit:* XXX			

Remember that the Business Basics table is not intended to track every process in your agency. It should be a tool to monitor the key processes that affect your clients, your other stakeholders, and the agency itself.

Breakthrough or Business Basic?

As mentioned earlier, the Business Basics table is intended to complement the Breakthrough Plan. Remember that Business Basics are things that the organization is already doing with acceptable results. This is not the tool to manage major new initiatives, or to make significant improvements to current processes. These items would be better managed with the Breakthrough Planning process.

Earlier in this chapter you were strongly cautioned to have only one high-level outcome goal for the organization. This advice can lead to the common error of attempting to tackle another major project by including it in the Business Basics table. Please don't fall into this trap. *After* a major project has been accomplished by using the Breakthrough Planning method, it may then become a Business Basic and be tracked as such in future years.

Business Basics and Organizational Structure

In a hierarchically structured organization you would normally select a relatively small set of key Business Basics that will help you track how the major responsibilities of the organization are being met. Each department would then select a set of Business Basics that covers the key responsibilities of that department. In a cross-functional, process-oriented organization, the first step is the same; you still need to identify and monitor the results of the organization's key processes. Since these key processes are not owned by separate departments, but by cross-functional teams, the next step belongs to those teams. They need to identify the subprocesses that make up the key process they are responsible for, and then monitor the results of those subprocesses.

Reviewing the Business Basics

The owners of the various elements of the Business Basics list review their activity at the intervals specified in the review period column. Business Basics that have exceeded their action limits are reviewed during the regular Breakthrough Planning meeting. However since the Business Basics activities are things that you know how to do and have been doing for some time, they are most likely to stay within their action limits and not need to be brought up at the review. If a particular item has exceeded its action limit, you must take steps to address the problem.

Managing Your Business Basics

Agencies don't always give enough attention to their Business Basics. The Basics aren't as exciting as working on the Breakthrough Plan. Unless they exceed their action limits, they probably don't have very much visibility. There is usually very little appreciation for the effort that goes into working on these basics, keeping them running, and achieving the desired results. Successful delivery on your Business Basics, however, is *essential* to the success of the Breakthrough Plan. Experience has shown that if the basics start falling apart the organization will be forced to apply whatever resources are required to get the vital, day-to-day operations back in line. This will almost certainly divert people from working on their portions of the Breakthrough Plan. It is very important to keep a close eye on the Business Basics and to give encouragement and recognition to the people who keep the organization running smoothly.

Conclusion

The most important part of planning is to follow the PDCA cycle. For planning to be more than a meaningless exercise, you must commit to:

- Regularly assessing how well you are implementing the plan and whether you are achieving the desired results;

- Taking action to respond to unanticipated problems; and

- Using the experience gained to plan more effectively next time.

The Breakthrough Planning process helps you to effectively implement the PDCA cycle. But it does more than that. It breaks the plan down into manageable pieces. It allows the organization to focus its efforts on achieving its most important goal. By making the plan visible to the whole organization, it provides a clear understanding of the big picture and everyone's part in it.

Finally, the Business Basics tracking table provides a way to ensure that the day-to-day, critical activities still get done. It's easy to fall into the trap of planning for the exciting future and neglecting today. This tool helps you avoid that trap.

In the next chapter, we review two major accreditation processes and illustrate how applying principles from all the preceding chapters can help the agency gain and maintain licensing, funding, and accreditation.

Reference

Deming, W. E. (1986). *Out of Crisis*. Cambridge, MA: Massachusetts Institute of Technology, Center for Advanced Study.

For Additional Information

Akoa, Y. (1991). *Hoshin Kanri, policy deployment for successful TQM*. Cambridge, MA: Productivity Press.

GOAL/QPC. (1990). *Hoshin planning: A planning system for implementing total quality management (TQM)*. Methuen, NJ: GOAL/QPC.

King, B. (1989). *Hoshin planning: The developmental approach*. Methuen, NJ: GOAL/QPC.

Appendix C

Glossary of Planning Terms

David J. Cassafer

Action Limit—The business basics are processes that are important and are essentially under control, because the agency is already performing in these areas with acceptable results. Because they are under control they are largely ignored. However the results are still monitored, and if they exceed a preset *action limit*, then the results must be reported and action taken. We will need to determine the cause of the problem and work to get the results of the process back to acceptable levels.

Activity Measure—Something that shows work occurred (e.g., research completed, report written, protocol created, program implemented). This can be thought of as a process goal. See Result Measure.

Cascade—To flow from one level to another (see Deployment).

Deployment—This is the process of breaking down the plan into smaller, more manageable pieces. We start with the highest level objective and the strategies to achieve it. We then repeat the process. Each strategy is now being treated as an objective, so we need to develop strategies to accomplish it. This process is repeated until it doesn't make sense to break things down any further.

Gantt Chart—A planning/scheduling chart that shows how long tasks are expected to take and which people are working on each task.

Goal—That which we desire to achieve—the most important thing for the organization to accomplish. At the top level of the Breakthrough Plan, the selection of an outcome goal is based on the mission of the organization and the situation the organization currently faces. In the breakthrough planning process, as the plan is deployed through the organization, when each strategy is assigned an owner, that strategy becomes that person's process goal (see Deployment).

Hoshin Kanri—A Japanese term that is usually translated as breakthrough planning or policy deployment—that is, deploying (implementing) the organization's policies (plans) throughout the organization.

Mission—A description of why the organization exists and what it does.

Nichijo Kanri—A Japanese term that is usually translated as daily management or business basics.

PDCA—The Plan-Do-Check-Act cycle, popularized by Dr. Deming. The acronym summarizes the essential steps in implementing a program of continuous improvement.

Result Measure—Something tangible that happened because of the work we did (e.g., a reduced dropout rate, lowered infant mortality, a greater number of completed interventions, an increased number of clients served.) See Activity Measure.

Situation—A short description of the internal and external environment in which the organization currently exists. This provides a context for choosing an objective.

Strategy—In breakthrough planning, a strategy is one of several necessary steps which, taken together, will accomplish the desired outcome (goal). To accomplish a strategy we break it down into substrategies or into tactics (see Tactics).

Success Measure—A clear, unambiguous way to determine if an objective (or a strategy) was successful. The process of trying to come up with a good success measure can often show that a strategy is ill-defined and needs to be rethought.

Tactics—At some point in the deployment of the plan we get to the tactical level. Tactics are usually specific tasks that can be done by a specific person at a specific time. The simplest definition is that something is a tactic when it's not practical to try to break it down into smaller pieces.

Chapter 8

How Can Evaluation Help the Agency with Licensing, Funding, and Accreditation?

Gary O. Carman

Introduction*

The central theme of this handbook is to encourage child and family service leaders to look forward, to assess where they and their agencies are now and where they will need to be as we approach the second millennium. While previous chapters of this handbook have reviewed current techniques agencies use to evaluate and manage their programs, this chapter describes a context for applying these techniques. This context is created by the standards of national accrediting organizations, which agencies may choose to meet.

Family services on the whole, and the child welfare field in particular, have generally been ahead of the reform movements that began in the late nineteenth century. The development of a continuum of services for children in need of out-of-home care, the call for in-home services to strengthen the family, the adoption movement, the development of service standards, improvements in state licensing programs, and the development of voluntary accreditation programs all began in the hearts and minds of the men and women working in the child welfare field. As noted before in this handbook, the 1990s appear to be a decade of unprecedented change for our field. healthcare reform activity, particularly as it relates to managed care; the rapidly changing nature of the children referred into the child and family services system; and the increasing demand for accountability will profoundly influence the future of this field. The challenge facing the agency leader is to influence the nature and structure of the response to these challenges. The focus of this chapter is program improvement through the process of achieving accreditation. We will describe the accreditation process for The Joint Commission on Accreditation of Healthcare Organizations (JCAHO) and the Council on Accreditation of Services for Families and Children, Inc. (COA). These two organizations review the overwhelming majority of family service and child welfare agencies accredited. Each accrediting organization will be described, the process examined, quality assurance standards explained, and case examples of fam-

---

* Special thanks to Gina Alexander and Nadia Ehrlich Finkelstein for contributing case studies, and to David Cook and Kathryn Gerbino for contributing their knowledge of COA and JCAHO accreditation.

ily and child service agencies accredited by each presented. The chapter concludes with suggestions for agencies contemplating application for accreditation.

Background

Council on Accreditation of Services for Families and Children, Inc. (COA)

The Council on Accreditation (COA) is the accreditation system most frequently used by social service agencies in North America. As of 1995, it had established standards for accrediting over 30 service areas, ranging from Adoption to Volunteer Friendship/Volunteer Relationship (see Figure 8.1).

In 1975, the Family Service Association of America (FSA) and the Child Welfare League of America (CWLA) jointly proposed the establishment of a semiautonomous accreditation council. In 1976, the Office of Child Development of what was then the U.S. Department of Health, Education, and Welfare funded a proposal submitted by both organizations to develop a nationwide accreditation for family and children's services. The proposal identified a number of problems in the child welfare system and presented an array of functions for the new body, which included:

- Assisting funding sources in determining whether applicants met minimum standards of service;

- Encouraging both public and private agencies to move beyond minimum standards;

- Restoring public confidence, which had been damaged by the public exposure of institutional abuse of children; and

- Encouraging the qualitative improvement of social welfare programs.

On the basis of these needs, the proposal specified several uses for accreditation, including the following: (1) funding sources could use accreditation to identify agencies eligible for funding; (2) third-party payers could use accreditation to determine eligibility for insurance reimbursement; and (3) boards of directors could use accreditation to determine the professional quality of services delivered.

CWLA and FSA were also motivated by three forces which, although independent, were pressing reasons for the rapid development of a national social service accreditation system. These forces were:

1. The need of state departments for an accreditation system to meet the requirements of Title XX of the Social Security Act,

2. The difficulty United Way of America was having in developing standards for local service delivery, and

3. The general perception that exclusive reliance on medical accreditation in children's programs by the U.S. Department of Defense (CHAMPUS) was unsuitable for child welfare organizations.

Figure 8.1

Services for Which COA Has Requirements

- Adoption
- Case Management/Supportive Service to the Aging or to Adults or Children with Special Needs
- Child Day Care/Early Childhood Education, Family and Group Day Care
- Co-dependency Counseling
- Community Organization/Social Advocacy
- Counseling Service for Families and Children, Victims of Child Abuse and Neglect and Their Families
- Day Care for the Aging
- Day Treatment/Social Adjustment/Treatment-Oriented Day Care
- Domestic Violence/Rape Crisis/Battered Women's Services
- Emergency Shelter for Abused and Neglected Children/Homeless Individuals and Families
- Employee Assistance Service
- Family Life Education
- Family Preservation Services
- Financial Management/Credit Counseling
- Foster Family Care
- Foster or Group Care for Unaccompanied Minor Entrants or Refugees
- Group Home/Residential Center for Children and Youth
- Group Services for Social Development and Enrichment
- Home-Based Family Support Service
- Homemaker/Home Health Aide/In-Home Aide
- Immigration and Citizenship Assistance
- Independent Living for Youth
- Information and Referral/Crisis Intervention Emergency Telephone Response
- Mental Health Services for Families and Individuals
- Pregnancy Counseling and Supportive Service
- Protective Service for Children
- Resettlement
- Residential Treatment
- Service for Runaway and Homeless Youth and Their Families
- Therapeutic Foster Care
- Therapeutic Residential Wilderness Programs
- Volunteer Friendship/Volunteer Relationship

An independent board of trustees held its first meeting in New York in 1978. In April of 1979, the first onsite review of an agency using the new accreditation standards was conducted. By 1981 the Council had developed its Peer Review System. This system draws on the expertise of volunteer professionals, trained by the Council, to perform onsite reviews of agencies undergoing the process of accreditation. Over the next decade or so, seven other national organizations joined the two founding members. The Council's board of trustees includes representatives from all of the nine sponsor organizations.

In recent years the Council has expanded its board of trustees to include members not affiliated with any of the original sponsors, and has begun to market its expertise in standards development to various public groups (including the State of Delaware, Division of Program Support of the Department of Services for Children, Youth, and Their Families 1987; the U.S. Navy Family Service Centers 1992; and the State of Illinois 1995).

Joint Commission on the Accreditation of Healthcare Organizations (JCAHO)

JCAHO is primarily a reflection of the health profession's commitment to improve the quality of patient care in the United States. Shortly after the beginning of the 20th century, Dr. Franklin Martin, an American, learned about a British system of tracking patients long enough to determine the efficacy of treatment. This system, known as the "End Result System of Hospital Organization," motivated him to seek support for the establishment of an American College of Surgeons in 1913.* Shortly thereafter, the American College of Surgeons formally established the Hospital Standardization Program. The program grew so rapidly in size and scope that it outgrew the capacity of the American College of Surgeons to manage it. By 1951, thousands of U.S. and Canadian hospitals were being surveyed for accreditation.

Support from the broader medical profession was clearly present, and in that year the American College of Physicians, the American Hospital Association, the American Medical Association, and the Canadian Medical Association joined with the American College of Surgeons to form the Joint Commission on Accreditation of Hospitals (JCAH). In 1959 the Canadians withdrew to form the Canadian Council on Hospital Organizations. The U.S. group first developed minimum standards, but revised them completely in 1966 to reflect the JCAH board's consensus that standards must reflect an optimal achievable level of care. These standards were published for the first time in the *1970 Accreditation Manual for Hospitals* [Joint Commission on Accreditation of Hospitals 1990].

Concern for the quality of care provided by health organizations other than hospitals led to the development of accrediting standards for other organizations in the 1960s. This has made it possible and desirable for many social service organizations to seek accreditation under the standards and process established by the Joint Commission. The name was changed in 1987 to the Joint Commission on Accreditation of Healthcare Organizations. The standards were completely revised in 1995 to represent a shift from monitoring individual dimensions associ-

---

*   According to the "Joint Commission History," a fact sheet published by the Joint Commission on Accreditation of Healthcare Organizations in June 1993, Dr. Martin was a colleague of Dr. Ernest Codman, the English physician who proposed the "end result system of hospital standardization" in 1910.

ated with quality to tracking the processes used to improve client outcomes. For the first time, JCAHO required the organization to document a process for systematically measuring, assessing, and improving its performance, and through onsite interviews, observations, and record reviews, evaluate agency performance.

In the seven decades since the first standards for healthcare were promulgated, the system of voluntary accreditation for healthcare organizations has spread throughout the United States and Canada, and is now expanding rapidly to other countries.

Governance and Administration

Council on Accreditation (COA)

The major feature of COA's organizational structure is its relationship with its affiliated organizations. Members of the board of trustees are nominated to the board by the nine affiliated national organizations. Each member serves a three-year term and may be reappointed to a second three-year term, but must then step down. In addition to the members of the board who serve as representatives of sponsoring organizations, the board includes lay members who contribute expertise in areas other than child welfare.

COA has established three commissions, representing the Eastern, Central, and Western regions of North America. Decisions relating to accreditation are the responsibility of the commissions, whose members are nominated by the sponsoring national organizations. The full Council has 13 staff members, including an Executive Director. COA currently accredits over 3,600 programs in more than 600 agencies across North America. Over 500 experienced professionals serve as peer reviewers [Council on Accreditation of Services for Families and Children 1993, p. 83]. The national offices are located in New York City.

Joint Commission (JCAHO)

The Joint Commission is governed by a member board, made up of 24 representatives from the five member organizations, six public members, and one at-large nursing representative. Members, or commissioners, each serve a three-year term. JCAHO employs a staff of over 450 in its Oakbrook Terrace, Illinois, office. Additionally, more than 500 physicians, nurses, healthcare administrators, psychologists, social workers, and related healthcare specialists perform accreditation surveys. The Commission currently evaluates and accredits 8,500 healthcare organizations, including more than 1,000 behavioral healthcare organizations.

Making Application

Council on Accreditation (COA)

The accreditation process begins with the submission of an application form, signed by an agency's board president and its executive director. The two-page application asks for basic agency information. An application fee ($600 in 1995) and agency brochures or a brief description of agency programs and services are sent with the application. In 1996 total COA costs ranged from just over $2,000 for a small agency ($200,000 annual revenue) to $8,000–$10,000 for large agencies ($10 million annual revenue). Fees graduate further for providers with annual revenue over $10 million. CWLA covers the cost of accreditation for its full member agencies; all others pay directly to COA.

All the programs operated by the agency for which the Council has established standards must be included in the Council's review of the agency, so an agency cannot seek accreditation for some of its programs and not others.

The Council acknowledges receipt of the agency's letter of application, outlines the fee for accreditation, and forwards the *Manual for Agency Accreditation* and other materials the agency needs to begin its self-study. The agency has 12 months to complete the self-evaluation phase of the accreditation process. Failure to do so will make the agency responsible for any interim increases in the accreditation fee, and possibly for updating the information submitted in its application. (See Figure 8.2.)

Joint Commission (JCAHO)

The JCAHO application process is quite similar to that of COA. The time frame is identical. The application fee, however, is higher ($1,000), and the application requires considerably more information. CWLA covers the cost of accreditation for its full member agencies. The fee for accreditation varies depending on the scope of the services being accredited. Agencies can expect to pay between $10,000 and $20,000. (See Figure 8.3).

The Self-Evaluation Phase

This phase of the accreditation process presents applicants with two very different expectations from the two accrediting bodies.

Council on Accreditation (COA)

COA requires that the applicant agency respond in writing to each of the Generic and Service Standards sections of its *Manual for Agency Accreditation* [Council on Accreditation of Services for Families and Children 1992], following specific guidelines contained in the manual. Depending upon the number of programs being reviewed, the required documentation may be hundreds of pages long. If the organization is not offering any new programs, future reaccreditation cycles will involve a more focused process in which compliance with a subset of the standards is reviewed.

Instructions for self-evaluation improved markedly in the 1992 revisions of the manual, and should not pose a problem for experienced child welfare administrators. While it is certainly possible for one person or a small committee to respond to the requirements of self-evaluation, to do so would be a serious disservice to the agency. A broad agency effort will both improve the self-evaluation and build staff commitment to the accreditation process.

A major advantage of the COA accreditation system is the requirement that a written self-evaluation be completed and reviewed by evaluators before a site

Figure 8.2

COA Accreditation

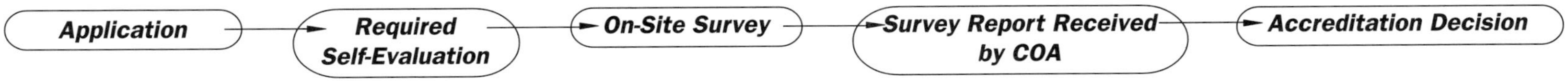

Application → Required Self-Evaluation → On-Site Survey → Survey Report Received by COA → **Accreditation Decision**

Range of Final Possible Decisions

1. Accreditation

2. Deferral

a. If an agency meets the provisions except for limited remediable deficiencies, accreditation shall be deferred until the deficiencies are corrected. The agency will be allowed up to 12 months for correction.

b. If on the basis of material presented, the Service Council is unclear about a particular aspect of agency operation, it may request further information from the agency. The agency will be given up to three months to provide information.

3. Denial

Figure 8.3

JCAHO Accreditation Process

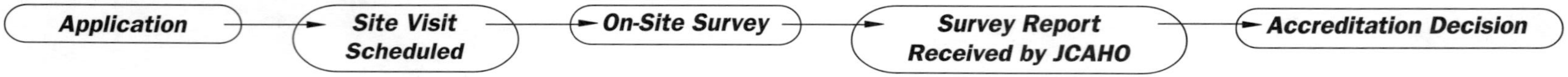

Application → Site Visit Scheduled → On-Site Survey → Survey Report Received by JCAHO → Accreditation Decision

Final Possible Decisions

1. Accreditation with Commendation

2. Accreditation*

3. Provisional Accreditation*

4. Conditional Accreditation*

5. Not Accepted

* If an organization is found to have standard compliance problems that are serious but not serious enough to warrant an adverse decision, the organization is accredited with one or more type 1 recommendations. In this case, an organization is given accreditation status, but must act to remedy the recommendations within a specified period or risk losing accreditation.

visit is arranged. This process, if thoughtfully planned, not only broadens the cross-program knowledge of agency staff, but can also serve as a catalyst for program improvement activities. Applicant agencies find that much preparatory work needs to be done after the self-evaluation phase and before a site visit. The self-evaluation materials and instructions are, with few exceptions, clear and understandable, and leave little doubt of the likely outcome of a site visit. The Council staff readily responds to telephone inquiries seeking clarification on either the standards or the process. It should be noted, however, that the Council's staff is quite small, and a knowledgeable person is not always immediately available.

When the self-evaluation materials are complete, they are mailed to the Council's office for review and distribution to the onsite evaluation team members. There is no specific requirement that a self-evaluation process be reviewed by the chief executive officer before an onsite evaluation visit, but the wise executive will want to know where his or her agency stands before the review team arrives.

Joint Commission (JCAHO)
The written materials provided by the Commission, while generally clear and understandable, may present some difficulties for child welfare or family service agency administrators because of their medical orientation. Although the recent revision of the *Accreditation Manual* [Joint Commission on Accreditation of Healthcare Organizations 1995] makes it more user friendly than previous versions, it is still more difficult to interpret from a child welfare perspective than the COA materials.

Accreditation Strategies

Preparing for the Site Visit
Several key principles are applicable to either accreditation system. The recommendations that follow will benefit both the agency and the evaluators.

- Before the visit, orient your entire staff to the onsite evaluation process and its schedule.

- Set aside a secure, private, comfortable space for the evaluators to work in throughout the site visit. Provide a telephone if possible.

- Equip the evaluators' work space with copies of all the materials they will have to review.

- Identify *one* staff member to coordinate the onsite work, and free up that person's schedule so he or she can do the job.

- Identify significant staff members who will need to be interviewed. If possible, develop an interview schedule in collaboration with the evaluators.

- Identify non agency personnel who will need to be interviewed, and plan a schedule with the evaluators. (Telephone interviews will often be sufficient.)

- When arranging hotel rooms, put a priority on proximity to the agency. Neither accrediting body expects that evaluators will be placed in luxurious accommodations. Hotel rooms should, if at all possible, contain a desk or work table so evaluators can work off site. (A hotel that offers restaurant service is a plus.)

- Arrange transportation to and from airports, if necessary, and to and from the agency. Often, it will facilitate the evaluators' work if an agency vehicle or rental vehicle can be assigned during the period of the onsite evaluation.

- COA does not permit members of the onsite team to offer consultation. Don't ask! JCAHO, however, does not discourage consultation by onsite reviewers. (In fact, the JCAHO reviewer will offer a one-hour workshop on a mutually agreed-upon topic.)

- Agency executives are reminded that the onsite process is a professional activity. The planning of social events is to be avoided.

Quality Improvement through Accreditation

As noted in the introduction to this chapter, the major driving force behind these accreditation systems was the desire of professionals in medicine and child welfare to develop measurable standards of practice and thus improve the quality of care. JCAHO and COA standards were both developed by experts in the field. For example, mental health professionals developed standards related to mental health, and adoption experts developed standards related to adoption.

The standards of both JCAHO and COA require organizations to develop certain processes and to hire individuals in sufficient numbers with specified amounts and types of education. They require that the professionals behave in prescribed ways, and in hundreds of very specific written statements, the standards require the organization to follow specified performance criteria. If the organization demonstrates compliance with the standards, the accreditation body informs the organization of its accreditation status.

Any organization that undertakes an accreditation review will improve the quality of its services even if the process doesn't result in changes of policy or modifications in practice. The organization will benefit from a comprehensive self-evaluation of its programs.

In recent years, however, both accrediting bodies have come to recognize that compliance with a set of standards is not enough, and that the static nature of the process merely represented a snapshot in time of an organization's operation.

The Council on Accreditation

The Council on Accreditation requires agencies to collect and maintain management and service information and to engage in systematic planning for and evaluation of services in terms of the agency's stated goals and objectives. The standards cover the important quality assessment and improvement process that an agency must follow to evaluate its programs, but they fail to focus on the steps an agency must follow to do so. Nevertheless, any agency would be well on the way to developing a continuous quality improvement program if it attempted to meet the standards on quality assurance promulgated by the Council.

The Joint Commission

The Joint Commission introduced a quality assurance process in the late 1970s to emphasize the concept of ongoing monitoring and evaluation, and improved it in 1984. After 1970, accredited organizations were required to have procedures in place for collecting data in a systematic manner and to use the data for evaluating performance. The Commission further revised its quality assurance process in 1988 [Joint Commission on Accreditation of Healthcare Organizations 1991, p. 47]. The process now involves:

- Identifying the most important aspects of care (for example, procedures and treatments) that the organization (or department or service) provides;

- Using indicators to systematically monitor these aspects of care in an ongoing way;

- Evaluating care whenever monitoring raises questions about its quality, in order to identify opportunities to further improve care or to correct problems; and

- Taking actions to improve care or resolve problems and evaluating their effectiveness.

The 1988 revisions required organizations to use the quality assurance process to monitor and evaluate certain aspects of care:

1. Assigning responsibility for monitoring and evaluation activities;

2. Delineating the scope of care provided by the organization (or department or service);

3. Identifying the most important aspects of care that the organization provides;

4. Identifying indicators and appropriate clinical criteria that can be used to monitor these important aspects of care;

5. Establishing thresholds for the indicators at which point further evaluation of the care is triggered;

6. Collecting and organizing the data for each indicator;

7. Evaluating care when the thresholds are reached in order to identify opportunities to improve care or to correct identified problems;

8. Taking actions to improve care or to correct identified problems;

9. Assessing the effectiveness of the actions and documenting the improvement in care; and

10. Communicating relevant information to other individuals, departments, or services, and to the organizationwide quality assurance program.

The 1995 revisions focus on the *processes* of service delivery likely to affect the outcome of care. The revisions define the organization's principal goal as improving the delivery of care. These processes are ongoing and cut across all program activities. They are multidisciplinary and designed to encourage professionals to improve their performance to meet the needs of the people they serve. JCAHO is engaged in a multiyear plan designed to improve the quality of care accredited healthcare organizations provide. The program improvement processes are dynamic, and increasingly focus on a review of the process of improving care.

For two case studies about the accreditation process see Appendices D (COA) and E (JCAHO), located at the end of this chapter.

Choosing An Accrediting Organization

Overview
The overwhelming difference between any agency committed to improving the quality of its service programs and an agency that has made the decision to become accredited by either JCAHO or COA is the relatively public nature of the accreditation process. Once the decision to seek accreditation is made and supported by the governing body, the chief executive officer's feet are held close to the fire by the process underway.

Regardless of which accreditation system is chosen (and some child welfare organizations undergo both) a clock begins to tick; an internal review of all systems is undertaken; and strangers "walk the land" to confirm the organization's capacity to meet the standards of the accrediting organization. All of this, experience has taught us, focuses the attention of the agency leadership. The decision and the subsequent activities are a powerful driving force for change.

Which Accreditation Should You Choose?
The choice of accreditation depends on many factors. It would not be accurate to describe one as better than the other. Many COA and JCAHO standards address similar areas or topics. For a comparison, see Appendix F.

There are, however, some differences to consider if an agency is only going to choose one accreditation system. The COA site review is intended to assure that the agency meets certain program standards. The JCAHO site survey is intended to determine compliance with JCAHO standards. Child welfare organizations with a broad program of services will find that the Council on Accreditation, which has developed a set of standards for over 30 different programs, provides a more comprehensive program review. Council on Accreditation standards have been developed by program experts in each of the different service areas. The language used in framing the written standards and the level of professional expertise they reflect may produce a better fit than the JCAHO standards, which have been developed by experts more oriented to medicine than social service.

For organizations that serve a population with significant mental health problems, the standards of JCAHO provide better risk management analysis than do the COA standards. Yet COA standards may represent a more complete evaluation for child welfare agencies that also offer mental health services, such as residential treatment.

Reimbursement is becoming an increasingly important factor, not only influencing agencies to stand for accreditation, but also influencing their choice of accrediting systems. When accreditation does affect eligibility for reimbursement, it is important to note that the JCAHO accreditation is accepted by more states and insurance companies than COA, and currently, by more federal government agencies. While COA accreditation is rapidly gaining reimbursement recognition across the country, it still continues to lag behind JCAHO. If reimbursement eligibility is an important factor in selecting an accreditation system, agencies should contact: (a) their national association; (b) the offices of either JCAHO or COA; (c) a child welfare agency that has a similar program, and/or (d) the various insurance agencies or medical reimbursement systems to determine eligibility in your geographic area. Agencies are cautioned that some child welfare programs may not be eligible for reimbursement under either accrediting system.

If program improvement is the major factor, then we believe that COA is the best choice. Their knowledge of child welfare and the self-evaluation process that an agency *must* engage in offer a better opportunity for fast program improvement than does JCAHO. While it may be true that an agency undergoing JCAHO accreditation would devise a similar self-evaluation program, the COA materials and procedures actually facilitate a thorough internal review of every aspect of an agency's operation.

The emerging managed care phenomenon is an additional factor to be weighed in considering accreditation. While managed care companies currently place great emphasis on the credentials of individual professionals in determining eligibility to participate in networks, the larger companies are also recognizing the value of the external, independent review that accreditation represents. As managed care companies seek to create expanded networks of providers that offer a wide spectrum of services, broader than traditional healthcare networks, national accreditation will be increasingly important. In addition, as managed care becomes a more significant factor in public child welfare services, accreditation will also play a more important role.

Finally, while JCAHO accreditation costs more in both human and dollar terms, it is good for a term of three years, versus four years for COA. The time and energy spent preparing for and experiencing an accreditation review are not insignificant.

Practical Advice

Hundreds of child welfare agencies are now accredited by either JCAHO or COA. Experienced professionals in many of those agencies have contributed the pointers that follow.

- Involve the governing body in the decision making around accreditation. When a choice between two accrediting organizations must be made, educate them on the advantages and disadvantages of each.

- Find someone you know who has been through accreditation recently and talk to that person. We have found child welfare managers to be both generous with their time and helpful to others seeking accreditation.

- Request literature and purchase the standards from the accrediting organization.

- The standards that seem to give child welfare organizations the most difficulty are the quality assurance standards. If possible, ask other agencies who have successfully completed accreditation to share their written policies and procedures for quality assurance or, for that matter, any policy or procedure that you are developing.

- Call the JCAHO and COA offices for help as often as you wish. They are both very customer focused.

- JCAHO will provide a mock survey at your request through Quality Health Resources, a subsidiary. This can be helpful, even though the mock survey has no exact bearing on the official survey.

- Many professionals offer their services as consultants to agencies undergoing either accreditation. Look for people who are, or recently have been, employed by an accredited agency and who have served as site reviewers. Your national organization or the accrediting bodies can help you identify experienced reviewers.

Regardless of which accreditation you select, we strongly encourage you to perform a comprehensive self-evaluation. Many child welfare organizations have developed multidisciplinary teams to assist in the self-evaluation. This process can serve two purposes. It disperses the workload across the organization, and it increases the understanding of both agency operations and the accreditation process for those staff members involved. When it comes to an activity as important and arduous as accreditation, the more staff involved the better.

Agencies should spend time planning the self-evaluation work process. A form developed to track the progress of agency response to each standard can prove very beneficial. Finally, be aware that the self-evaluation time period, particularly for agencies that are undergoing accreditation for the first time, may well take several months. Six to nine months would not be uncommon.

Accreditation and Quality Improvement

The question posed by the title of this chapter, How Can Evaluation Help the Agency with...Accreditation?, has been obliquely addressed in describing the accreditation process, and particularly COA's self-evaluation review. Accreditation is the one process that requires child welfare managers to apply some of what can be learned from each chapter in this handbook.

Both of the accrediting programs described in this chapter require agencies to define the populations they are serving and the programs developed to serve them. Program evaluation is an area that many agencies didn't pay much attention to in the past. "We know we are helping children, and we shouldn't have to spend time and money proving it."

Sound familiar? Does anyone believe that the days when this view was prevalent are still with us? The fact is, the child and family services field is more under attack now for failing to demonstrate that we make a difference than at any time since the early 20th century [Jones 1994]. Agency administrators have to evaluate not only because it makes inherent sense to know what works and what doesn't, but also because, to remain viable, agencies must be able to demonstrate the efficacy of their services. Evaluations of program services are required not only by both accrediting bodies but also by many licensing authorities. Savas, in Chapter 2, describes just how an agency goes about demonstrating efficacy. She leads the reader through a planning process that establishes a foundation for the evaluation work described in the subsequent chapters.

Davis and Savas (Chapter 3) outline five techniques for evaluating the day-to-day work of a child welfare agency. They list groups of commonly asked questions and provide strategies for collecting information to answer them.

Once an agency understands and demonstrates that it knows who it serves, can define the nature of the services it has developed to meet the needs of the service population, and is prepared to answer the question What do we do?, it is ready for the next steps in evaluation: specifying service outcomes, promoting outcome-oriented case planning (see Chapter 4), and measuring outcome effectiveness.

The Council on Accreditation requires agencies to maintain information in such a way that they can plan, manage, and evaluate their programs effectively. The Joint Commission, as was previously noted, requires an organization to go one step further by using the data gathered from evaluations to improve its performance.

Kluger and Alexander (Chapter 5) list among the top reasons for doing outcome effectiveness studies that they assist in meeting licensing and accreditation requirements. Their turnkey approach to outcome evaluation as a process and the examples they cite are helpful guides for child welfare executives developing or improving their quality assurance programs.

Zirps and Cassafer (Chapter 6) build upon the work of Savas in Chapter 2, offering tools for using the data generated by both process and outcome evaluation. Following the lessons presented in these earlier chapters, an agency will be well on its way to developing a comprehensive quality improvement program that meets the quality assurance standards of both accrediting bodies. The process of accreditation under either system described here offers child welfare professionals the challenge of making improvements to comply with national standards and the recognition that comes with national accreditation.

In the next chapter Benbenishty and Oyserman discuss information systems and their applicability to the child welfare system. Just a few short years ago, only the largest agencies were using management information systems—usually in their finance departments. Today it would be hard to find any child welfare agency that does not, at some level, use information processing technology. Key questions to consider include the following: Are you using information technology effectively? Do you have a master plan for managing information? Are you still using valuable human resources to shuffle paper that could be more efficiently handled by technology? Do you know what a good management information system should look like? These questions and more are addressed in the next chapter.

References

Council on Accreditation of Services for Families and Children. (1993). *Manual for peer reviewers*. New York: Author.

Council on Accreditation of Services for Families and Children. (1992). *Manual for agency accreditation, Volumes I and II*. New York: Author.

Joint Commission on Accreditation of Healthcare Organizations. (1995). *Accreditation manual for mental health, chemical dependency, and mental retardation/developmental disability services, Volumes I and II*. Oakbrook Terrace, IL: Author.

Joint Commission on Accreditation of Healthcare Organizations. (1991). *Consolidated standards manual, Volume I*. Oakbrook Terrace, IL: Author.

Joint Commission on Accreditation of Hospitals. (1990). *Accreditation manual for hospitals*. Oakbrook Terrace, IL: Author.

Jones M. B. (1994, Summer). The past and future of child welfare: Voluntary benevolence, America's history of caring for children in need, Part IV. *Caring, 10* (2), 10–19. Published by the National Association of Homes and Services For Children.

Appendix D

**Case Study
Accreditation Review:
Council on Accreditation of Services to
Families and Children, Inc.**

Gina Alexander

Council on Accreditation Case Study

The organization described in this case study is a statewide child welfare agency providing residential group care, therapeutic foster care, special needs adoption, independent living services, and family preservation and reunification services to children and families. As a relatively young agency (the organization began in 1969), it embarked on the process of accreditation to validate its work against national standards of excellence. Accreditation was seen as an important component of quality improvement as the agency worked for continuous improvement in service delivery and outcomes. The agency leadership chose the Council on Accreditation of Services to Families and Children, Inc. Because the agency offers community-based services without a hospital or on-grounds educational component, the Joint Commission of Accreditation of Healthcare Organizations (JCAHO) was deemed not to be an appropriate accrediting body for its needs. Third-party reimbursement was not a major consideration at the time of accreditation, although accreditation has since proved helpful in positioning the agency for managed care approaches to services and payment.

The Self-Evaluation Process

The agency began the self-evaluation study approximately 12 months before the onsite visit. As in any agency, some staff were more enthusiastic about the process than others. Consequently, the first step was to try to create as much staff ownership in the process as possible by involving staff at all levels and discussing the pros and cons of accreditation. Although new to accreditation, the agency had recently been through a strategic planning process that reaffirmed its mission and established new goals. This process enabled both staff and the board of directors to move into accreditation more easily. The QI concept of cross-functional teams, the ability to work across divisions and disciplines, was vital to making the self-evaluation process succeed. We also sought the assistance of a sister agency that had been through the accrediting process. This helped the agency know what to expect.

Participating staff were selected on the basis of their expertise to facilitate the self-evaluation process for specific areas of accreditation. (Figure 8.1 lists the different areas and services that are covered in accreditation through the Council. Agencies must respond to any standards that apply.) Meetings and discussions were held with representatives from all levels of staff to review the standards and compile information. Two staff members were assigned the responsibility of setting deadlines and pulling all the information together in a central document. Both COA and CWLA staff were available to answer questions and provide assistance throughout the process.

All the standards were entered on a computer file to create a single accreditation document. (COA now has all its standards on software, eliminating the time-consuming task of manual entry. Any organization embarking on accreditation is encouraged to purchase the software.) The document was reviewed by the agency management team. After a final revision, the document was sent to the Council.

While the overall accreditation process was generally well received, it sometimes seemed that the paperwork involved took on a life of its own. Many of the standards are redundant or focused on very specific details of operation; these would benefit from some streamlining. Conversely, as a multiservice, multisite agency, we had to prepare generic responses in such areas as intake and assessment and service planning, despite much variation among services. On the whole, the self-evaluation was an opportunity to take a critical look at all aspects of the agency's functioning, reaffirming what was good and directing us toward areas for improvement.

Quality Assurance

As for many agencies new to accreditation, the Quality Assurance component of the COA standards seemed daunting at first. This component requires the following five elements:

1. *Management Information System:* The agency maintains information necessary to plan, manage, and evaluate its programs effectively.

2. *Planning and Evaluation:* The agency determines whether the agency's services are needed, and evaluates the effectiveness and efficiency of the agency in achieving its purpose and/or mission

3. *Quality Assurance Program:* The agency has a quality assurance program to assure that individual client services meet the agency's expectations for service quality and outcomes.

4. *Remediation:* Action is taken to eliminate or ameliorate problems identified in program evaluation and in review of the individual client services, including as appropriate:

   • Revision of policies and/or operational procedures;

   • Changes in personnel assignments, personnel supervision, or in-service training; and,

   • Modification, addition, or deletion of a program or service.

5. *Client Protections in Research:* When an agency participates in human subject research, the agency exhibits due regard for client privacy and the right of the client to participate on a voluntary basis.

The standards do not provide a step-by-step process for developing a Quality Assurance or Quality Improvement component. However, following the steps toward Quality Improvement, as outlined in the previous chapters of this handbook, will clearly enhance an organization's ability to meet the Quality Improvement standards. In our case, the agency was helped in meeting these standards by its recent development of a clearly defined quality assurance program, which included a newly computerized client information system and the addition of staff with specific quality assurance responsibilities. The agency was also in the process of conducting a program evaluation, which helped in the development of an ongoing evaluation component. Through the self-evaluation process, the agency was able to further refine and enhance its quality improvement processes.

The On-Site Review

Before the review, the Council sent copies of the agency self-evaluation to the selected peer reviewers. Two reviewers came for the site visit. (Usually, an agency our size would have three peer reviewers for the site visit, but shortly before the visit COA experienced a scheduling problem.) The team leader was very experienced as a peer reviewer, while the other reviewer was relatively new to the process. Together, they had experience in each of the services for which accreditation was being sought. The reviewers remarked that their task would have been easier with a third person. The agency approved the site reviewers beforehand to avoid any potential for conflict of interest.

The site visit was scheduled to occur over three days. An entrance meeting was held, with the reviewers, the executive director, staff members, and representatives of the board, to familiarize everyone with what would occur over the next several days. During the visit, the reviewers interviewed staff and board members and reviewed agency records and board minutes, as well as the responses to board member questionnaires and client surveys. The categories of interviews had been previously arranged by the team leader and scheduled by the executive director. The peer reviewers conducted themselves professionally, and were well received by staff and board members. An exit interview was held on the final day with the peer reviewers, executive director, staff, and board representatives. The site review was the culmination of all our hard work and preparation for accreditation.

In the exit interview the peer reviewers presented an overview of the agency's strengths and weaknesses. They were very affirming of the agency and its program of services. We subsequently received a copy of the written report that our reviewers submitted to the Council. The site reviewers make no recommendations to the Council concerning the accreditation decision, but we were notified that we had earned accreditation within four months after the site visit.

Appendix E

Case Study
Accreditation Review:
The Joint Commission on Accreditation of
Healthcare Organizations

Nadia Ehrlich Finkelstein

Joint Commission on Accreditation Case Study

The agency used in this case study is a private nonprofit agency that offers a range of services to children and their families, from intensive residential care for severely disturbed children to group homes, family foster care and adoption, outreach and emergency services, day treatment, special education, and outpatient child and family psychiatric services. The agency is historically rooted in child welfare, and was founded in 1829 as an orphanage.

The agency decided to seek accreditation from what was then the JCAH in order to participate in the development of a residential treatment unit to be licensed by the New York State Office of Mental Health. This program was to be funded by Medicaid which, in turn, required JCAH accreditation.

The Agency Self-Evaluation Process

The self-evaluation process required systematic review of JCAHO standards by agency administrative staff. Over the years there has been a substantial improvement in the documents that familiarize the organization with JCAHO requirements. These have been further adapted to make them useful to administrators whose organizations are rooted in the child welfare system, rather than in the health services delivery system. Most important, however, is that the new standards are realistic, feasible to implement, and of significant consequence for organizations like ours as we continuously improve the quality of client care. JCAHO does not require a written, comprehensive self-study document. The preparatory work involves careful review of where the organization is in relation to standards; documentation of compliance during the site visit; careful revision of agency manuals; a review of personnel folders, clinical records, logs, minutes of board meetings and professional staff organization meetings, plus reports of the committee on quality improvement and other committees; and review of the site to assure full compliance. Attention must be paid to all medical aspects of the program, which include the oversight role of physicians in all aspects of treatment, the operation of nursing staff, the storing and distribution of medications, and appropriate mechanisms for assuring and monitoring effective infection control.

In conducting our self-evaluation, the agency divided the JCAHO manual and turned sections over to those administrators responsible for compliance with specific standards. These administrators then engaged their respective staff in an in-house self-assessment. This process allowed unit or program administrators to identify areas needing remediation and to develop and implement appropriate action plans.

On-Site Experience with Reviewers

It has been our experience that JCAHO is making a very genuine and effective effort to become responsive to the needs of agencies like ours. Just as the standards have continued to change to become more useful and meaningful for a nonhospital setting, so has the choice of reviewers. Reviews early on were handicapped by the fact that reviewers often lacked experience in diverse child caring/mental health settings, and were forced to review our setting against standards designed for hospitals and outpatient medical models. Over time, however, we have found the Joint Commission very responsive to our concerns, and those of other organizations like ours. Our last two reviews were done by people knowledgeable about what we do and how we do it. The experiences were thoroughly professional, and gave us an opportunity to look at our programs and services through the eyes of competent, experienced reviewers. Especially in the last review, the reviewers chosen were professionals who provided services in organizations similar to ours.

In summary, we have the following advice to the field regarding accreditation by JCAHO:*

Advantages

1. Because Medicaid accepts JCAHO-accredited programs, JCAHO accreditation for residential services brings access to Medicaid funding.

2. JCAHO standards have generally been in tune with the increasingly exacting expectations of managed care organizations, and consequently have served to prepare organizations to meet these standards.

3. Commitment to quality improvement and client/customer satisfaction should be fundamental values of human service organizations. The evolving standards of the Joint Commission, especially since the advent of its Agenda for Change, have articulated a clear commitment away from quality assurance to quality improvement. JCAHO has developed a sound framework for the development and refinement of quality improvement processes without demanding that an organization use one particular modality.

---

*   I would like to thank David Cook for his thoughtful review of this section; and for his identification of the advantages and disadvantages of JCAHO accreditation.

4. JCAHO standards are increasingly client centered rather than program or organization centered. This is most notable in the refinement of the 1995 standards, which are organized around client service functions rather than programs or departments.

5. Program evaluation standards of JCAHO increasingly encourage data-based assessment of program and service efficacy, which parallels the growing expectations of funding agencies.

6. The process of preparation for and maintenance of JCAHO accreditation tends to keep organizations "on their toes" and helps prevent entropic stagnation.

Disadvantages

1. For some services, JCAHO accreditation standards require resources that are not available to many programs through the current funding system.

2. The JCAHO standards have historically been predicated upon a medical model of organization that may not be relevant or appropriate to the organizational structure of social service organizations. Most of the support literature and publications of the Joint Commission are also geared toward hospitals. The 1995 standards, however, offer substantial improvement.

3. The JCAHO standards are not applicable or adequate for some types of services, for example, outreach preventive services, emergency foster care services, educational services, and adoption services.

4. JCAHO accreditation is more expensive than COA.

5. JCAHO standards are based on a client disability/illness paradigm that may be at odds with the organization's basic values.

6. The JCAHO accreditation model is derived from an individual patient model rather than a family-centered, family systems, or family preservation model.

7. JCAHO standards are often written in language that does not lend itself to easy understanding, so organizations must expend substantial resources to help staff understand the intent of standards before they can meet those standards.

Appendix F

A Comparison of Accreditors:
    Council on Accreditation of Services
    for Families and Children, Inc., and Joint
    Commission on Accreditation of Healthcare
    Organizations

Process Comparison*

JCAHO	COA
Inclusiveness of Study	
Entire organization/system included in study.	Entire organization included in study; all services must be subject to review. The review can cover up to 47 programs or services.
Preparation for Accreditation Review	
Completion of an application survey. Preparation includes the compilation of data and materials necessary to demonstrate compliance with standards at the time of the surveyor's site visit.	Completion of an agency self-study, consisting of documents and narratives describing agency practice in relation to each applicable standard. Self-study process typically requires six to eight months of preparation. Peer reviewers review material thoroughly before the site visit. Preparation is unique among accreditors in the depth and scope of involvement of governing body, administration, and staff and the degree to which the self-study process serves as a systematic framework for quality improvement.

---

* Adapted with permission from: A Comparison of Accreditors: Council on Accreditation of Services for Families and Children, Inc., Joint Commission on Accreditation of Healthcare Organizations, Commission on Accreditation of Rehabilitation Facilities. *Process, Standards, and External Recognition.* (July 1994).   Oakbrook Terrance, IL: Council on Accreditation of Services for Families and Children, Inc.

JCAHO   *COA*

Personnel Used to Determine Compliance

Paid professional surveyors from various diciplines serving behavioral healthcare providers, trained in the policies and practices of JCAHO.

Professionals serving as peer reviewers are senior management and program staff from agencies similar to those under study. Selected for their expertise and experience and assigned on that basis, with a minimum of eight years experience in addition to an advanced professional degree, and trained in the policies and practices of COA. Cadre of 725 professionals committed to quality service through accreditation who contribute their time.

Determining Compliance with Standards

Surveyors conduct site visit and review agency practice in view of standards, assigning a rating from a six-point scale.

A team of peer reviewers conducts a site visit. The length of the visit is adjusted to the complexity of agency operation, with a minimum of two peers for two days for the smallest agency. The reviewers verify compliance with COA standards using a four-point rating scale. The team compiles a report indicating a level of compliance for each standard and including explicit reasons for ratings of partial compliance or noncompliance. Rating indicators introduce great inter-rater reliability, and a weighting system fully disclosed to all parties provides a framework for decision making.

The Accreditation Decision

The surveyor's report is reviewed and analyzed by JCAHO staff and a determination is made from one of four options:

The report is submitted to an accreditation commission consisting of professionals in the field elected by COA's board of trustees, with no identifying information. There are four options:

1. Accreditation with commendation

2. Accreditation with or without recommendations

1. Accreditation

2. Decision deferred for more information

JCAHO

3. Conditional accreditation

4. Denial of accreditation

An accreditation committee must review certain decisions, such as those that involve denial of accreditation or are challenged.

Duration of Accreditation

Organizations in substantial compliance are awarded accreditation for three years.

Interim Reviews of Provider Compliance

A facility must undergo a resurvey in the event of merger, consolidation, or other changes that might affect the ongoing recognition of the facility as an accredited provider.

The Accreditation Decision

A facility is required to apply for reaccreditation near the end of its current accreditation period.

COA

3. Decision deferred for remediation of deficiencies

4. Denial, subject to appeal

Accredited providers carry the credential for four years. There is no limited or conditional accredited status based on partially meeting the requirements.

A provider must submit an annual maintenance of accreditation report, detailing changes in the organization in the past year or other information that might bear on contined accreditation. The chief executive officer and head of the governing body must sign, attesting to continued compliance to all weighted standards.

COA is obliged to explore any complaints brought against an accredited facility to determine if a change in status is warranted. This review may include another site visit. Policies provide for a probationary status or suspension of accreditation when circumstances found to be present would endanger clients or staff.

A facility is required to undergo a reaccreditation review in sufficient time before its expiration date to assure that there is no break in its accredited status.

External Recognition: JCAHO and COA

Sanction

Both systems are sanctioned or endorsed by a number of independent national professional organizations. Both, unlike some other accreditation systems, which operate within the framework of a membership organization, have independent, third-party review systems free of conflict of interest.

National Consensus-Based Standards

Each has its own process of developing standards, which are based upon input from the field. COA arguably has the most inclusive and participatory process of consensus building, using the professional community represented by the range of professional disciplines to review and refine its standards as a means of arriving at as solid a consensus as possible.

Recognition of Accreditation: JCAHO and COA

These two major accreditors in the behavioral healthcare field, amoung others, have sought external recognition of their credentials as a means of adding value to accreditation and thereby encouraging providers to meet high standards of care. The COA credential is equal to that of other accreditors in every important respect and, as a result, allows providers a choice of the standards that best reflect their history, tradition, philosophy, and orientation. The following is a partial list of those places where COA accreditation has been found to be equal to that of JCAHO in determining the competence of provider agencies. We know of no instance in which, after a full review of the content of the COA's standards as compared to those of JCAHO, COA has not been included. Generally, both accreditors are included after such an evaluation and comparison has occurred. Historically, JCAHO, the oldest accreditor, has been routinely recognized, with the COA accreditation added state by state on an irregular basis.

National

Value Behavioral Health, Inc., one of the largest managed care companies operating in the behavioral healthcare field, requires accreditation by one of four national accreditors for consideration of participation in its service network. COA is one of the four.

Arizona

The Department of Health Services accepts COA accreditation as meeting the requirements for Medicaid certification in the state.

Hawaii

The State Division of Alcohol and Drug Abuse requires that all contract providers be accredited, and has designated JCAHO and COA as the acceptable credentials for meeting the requirement.

Illinois

State administrative code governing participating in Medicaid as a mental health provider includes COA accreditation as equal to that of JCAHO for determining eligibility. Pending legislation will require COA accreditation for secure residential treatment centers.

Kentucky

Providers accredited by JCAHO or COA are exempted from a state requirement that child caring programs undergo self-evaluation every three years.

Maine

Accreditation by JCAHO or COA exempts a provider from the licensing requirements of the State Department of Mental Health and Mental Retardation.

Michigan

United Auto Workers contracts have specified COA and JCAHO as equivalent credentials for several years.

Blue Cross/Blue Shield of Michigan conducted an independent comparison of COA standards and process with those of JCAHO and found them to be equal. Blue Cross/Blue Shield accepts COA accreditation for reimbursement for case management services, substance abuse services, and outpatient mental health services.

Healthplus of Michigan, Inc., an HMO, requires accreditation by COA or JCAHO for a provider to be reimbursed for day treatment services.

The Health Alliance Plan of Michigan, a managed care organization, has formally recognized COA.

The State Center for Substance Abuse Services of the Medical Services Administration requires all contract providers to hold accreditation by COA, JCAHO, or the American Osteopathic Association.

The Detroit-Wayne County Community Mental Health Board requires all contract providers to be accredited by JCAHO or COA.

New Mexico

The Medical Assistance Division of the Department of Human Services includes COA accreditation as one of the means by which a provider can become eligible for Medicaid reimbursement.

Ohio

Accreditation by COA or JCAHO is accepted by the Department of Mental Health as meeting certification requirements for reimbursement for mental health services.

The state Blue Cross/Blue Shield organization accepts JCAHO or COA accreditation as part of its requirements for reimbursement for substance abuse service.

Washington

New regulations governing state funding of substance abuse programs will recognize the accreditation of COA as well as JCAHO as equivalent to state requirements.

Wisconsin

Administrative rules for outpatient mental health and substance abuse clinics recognize COA and JCAHO as equivalent as a baseline for state certification.

Chapter 9

How Can Integrated Information Systems (IIS) Be a Support?

Rami Benbenishty and
Daphna Oyserman

Introduction

Quality improvement depends to a large extent on systematic monitoring of an agency's processes, performance, and outcomes and careful analysis of the information collected. The effective handling of information is therefore essential to most quality improvement efforts in social service agencies [Martin 1993]. Agencies need information about their clients, interventions, and outcomes (see Chapter 2). Timely and accurate information are essential for decision making and planning on all levels (see Chapters 6 and 7).

In order to assess what they should change and where they stand in the quality improvement process, agencies need to gather, store, process, retrieve, and analyze information. These are not easy tasks. Child and family service agencies need new ways to handle them. This chapter discusses the information needs of child and family service agencies and problems that might be encountered in meeting these needs. It offers a conceptual framework that will help you address your information needs and promote quality improvement by designing and implementing an integrated information system. Information technology can support clinical practice, administration, and evaluation in your agency.[*]

The Challenge: Handling Information Effectively

In child and family service agencies, workers on all levels spend a considerable portion of their time gathering data, documenting information, and preparing reports—for their own clinical files; for administrators, courts, supervisors, and licensing and supervising agencies; and for their clients. Managers and administrators process and analyze reports provided by line staff in order to carry on their duties and compile

---

[*] We wish to acknowledge the help of the staff at Lutheran Child and Family Service in Michigan; and especially the great contribution of Rita Turner-Sheerin.

additional reports required by county, state, and federal licensing regulations and by funding agencies. State and federal agencies process information received from child welfare agencies in order to monitor service delivery, identify needs and reformulate policy, regulate funding, and oversee expenditures.

Do most child and family service agencies handle these information needs effectively? All indications are that the answer is a resounding No. Workers spend much of their time documenting their activities and assessments and preparing reports. This time-consuming and frustrating endeavor takes resources away from service provision, and in spite of all efforts, reports are often late, inaccurately completed, or completed only partially. Supervisors, administrators, and managers devote considerable energy to ensuring that paperwork is timely and properly completed so they can meet licensing and funding requirements. Hence, much of the communication between management and line workers focuses on the completeness and timeliness of documentation and reports.

Time, energy, and communication are so focused on paperwork that the central agency goal, provision of quality care to children and their families, seems in danger of being displaced by the goal of meeting reporting requirements. This goal displacement or slippage may be seen as a natural outgrowth of the current process, in which workers struggle to meet information needs and avoid penalties connected to noncompliance with regulations.

Furthermore, despite all these efforts, supervising agencies on the county, state, and federal level are frequently dissatisfied with the quality of the information they receive. While the information found in clinical files may be accurate, the information that moves upward from the agency to the county, to the state, and to the federal government is often inaccurate [Finch, Fanshel, & Grundy 1991]. In recent studies by Harrod in the United States [1988] and Barnes [1994] in the U.K., between 1% and 67% of information items reported to child information systems were in error. On average, more than 20% of the information items in a single short record were in error.

How does this happen? Workers and agencies that are under pressure to provide these reports may compile them hastily, with little attention to accuracy. Because these reports have no clear relation to the everyday work, are compiled in addition to and independently of documentation for the clinical files, and are compiled only because they are required, there is little intrinsic motivation to assure that they are accurate.

Consequently, the information supervisory agencies receive is often out of date and fails to accurately reflect the situation of children and their families. Policymakers, having no alternative source of information, often incorporate these unreliable data into their decision making. Clearly, it is hard to make sound policy decisions under such circumstances.

The Response: Integrated Information Systems (IIS)

Child and family social service agencies invest enormous amounts of time and effort in handling information. Current trends toward managed care may only

---

Figure 9.1

Integrated Information Systems (IIS)

Overall Mission

Support Quality Care

For Whom

All Partners to Care
The Continuity of Care Axis
Continuity of Responsibility

Scope

Monitor
Communicate
Learn from Experience

---

add to this overwhelming task of data gathering, processing, and reporting [Corcoran & Gingerich 1994]. Clearly, unless a significant change takes place in the way child welfare agencies handle information, the problems we see today will only multiply. It is time to change and to move forward.

This chapter describes how to improve the quality of care agencies provide through the use of Integrated Information Systems (IIS). It presents a framework for designing and implementing such systems and describes how they can help your agency provide quality care. This framework should be relevant to child and family social service agencies of all sizes, no matter where they are located, and whether they are public or private.

A Conceptual Framework for IIS

To design information systems for social service agencies we need a conceptual framework. Our conceptual model addresses three fundamental questions: What is the overall purpose of this system? Who is it designed for? What is its scope—what information does it need to target?

Overall Purpose: Support Quality Care

Traditionally, information system design has focused on providing information for managerial and administrative tasks. Management information systems (MIS) are designed so frontline workers collect information for the sole purpose of making it available to administrators. Looking toward the future, we propose that information systems should have a different mission: supporting quality care. This mission differs dramatically from the traditional approach. It requires a new and very different look at how human service organizations harness information. Using this view of information systems, we will identify who systems should be designed for and what tasks they should tackle.

Who Is the System Designed to Serve?

Providing quality services to children and their families requires effective cooperation among many service partners. Therefore, in order to support a quality process, information systems in child and family service agencies should be integrated and designed with all service partners in mind. We conceptualize two basic axes of interdependence among service partners: Continuity of care and hierarchy of responsibility.

Continuity of Care

The first axis refers to interdependence and cooperation within and across agencies that provide services to children and families simultaneously or over time. In a typical child welfare scenario, a family may be subject to a protective services investigation while receiving family preservation services. Over time, some children in the family may be involved with juvenile court, others may be in residential care, while others may be in foster care, moving eventually to adoption services or to an array of aftercare programs. At each point in time, information about each particular child and family member should be available to the frontline worker, to other workers in the agency who provide services to these clients, and to workers and agencies that are either providing services at this point or will be involved with this family in the future. A break in the information flow between staff working with family members to support reunification, foster care workers considering termination of parental rights, foster home licensing workers finding the right foster home for a long-term stay in care, and adoption workers looking for appropriate adoptive families might have devastating outcomes for the family in care.

In order to provide quality care for these families and children, all relevant information must be shared among the various workers and programs within a child welfare agency, as well as among the various agencies that care for this family over time. Information systems for child welfare should encompass and integrate all these elements of the child welfare system, as they are actually partners in care. Later we will address some of the confidentiality issues that typically arise when a child welfare agency considers information sharing.

Continuity of Responsibility

The second axis refers to the line extending from the frontline worker, who is in direct contact with the family, through supervisors, administrators, and managers on the agency level to the county-, state-, and federal-level managers, administrators, and policymakers. Each link in this chain needs certain information, and depends on others to provide it in a timely and accurate manner. In order to provide quality care, frontline workers need to gather relevant information and process it effectively. Supervisors need workers' reports so they can carry out their supervisory role and provide frontline workers with expert feedback in a timely and effective manner.

Agency administrators need workers and supervisors to report promptly and accurately so they can function effectively in their roles and be able to report to supervisory agencies at the county, state, and federal levels. These high-level agencies depend on the flow of information from lower-level agencies to inform their policy and decision making. The quality and timeliness of the information that reaches the top levels of responsibility will have direct implications for the quality of decisions made and policy guidelines established. Furthermore, the effectiveness of practice guidelines formulated at the policymaking level in improving quality of care depends to a large extent on how these guidelines are disseminated back down the hierarchy of responsibility.

A break in information flow reduces the effectiveness of the best policy guidelines and expertise. Frontline workers, who are often novices, need this expertise to guide them in service delivery. As much as high-level agencies depend on frontline workers for information to formulate effective guidelines, frontline workers need the knowledge, expertise, and advice supervisors generate from this information.

Information systems should target all partners along both these axes. They should create a shared language and facilitate information flow between workers and agencies that provide care to children and families, as well as up and down the hierarchy of responsibility.

Scope: Monitoring, Communicating, and Learning from Experience

How will information systems support our efforts to improve quality? By helping us tackle three major tasks: monitoring, communicating, and learning from experience. We will describe each and briefly explain how they relate to all of the partners to care.

Monitoring

Monitoring is the task of gathering and processing information in order to obtain an up-to-date picture of clients, services, and outcomes. For frontline workers in child welfare agencies, the focus is on obtaining an up-to-date account of children and families, their environment, and their circumstances in order to plan interventions and assess their effectiveness. Thus, a worker needs to assess whether a child is in immediate danger of abuse, whether a mother will be able to cope effectively with future stress, and whether a father can play a positive role in reunification plans. Systematic monitoring alerts the worker to acute problems requiring immediate intervention, and helps to set priorities and allocate resources on the basis of client needs, while also ensuring that all clients receive care that meets quality standards and that no one gets "lost in the system."

Supervisors and program directors monitor the caseloads of individual workers and of the whole agency in order to understand the characteristics of children and families in care, the services that workers provide, the outcomes of agency interventions, and any changes over time. This information is essential for quality assurance, training, planning, and identifying trends in clients and in outcomes. Thus, for instance, the director of adoption services needs a clear and timely picture of the number of cases in which the termination of parental rights is being considered, how many children are waiting for adoption, what are the characteristics of children for whom adoption could not be achieved, what services are being provided to children who have already been adopted, for which children adoption was unsuccessful, and why.

Administrators on all levels need to have their "hands on the pulse" for an accurate and timely picture of the agency. Cost-effective management and policymaking require a detailed overview of issues such as the characteristics of families who are being served, the range and frequency of services rendered, the degree to which regulations are being met, the cost of services, and the overall effectiveness of services.

Communicating

The need for communication, or passing of information to partners in care, comes directly from the collaborative effort required to care for children and their families. In order to coordinate this effort it is essential to communicate. Thus, information must flow from protective services to family preservation agencies, to foster care, and to adoption services. To care for a particular child, a worker may need to receive information from a multitude of services and report to other relevant agencies. Provision of quality care requires that workers communicate with their supervisors, with the courts, with families, and with fellow workers.

Communication is vital to provide an unbroken stream of care over time. Workers need to document their observations and assessments so that other workers in the future can understand the family and have a sense of their progress over time. Information should also flow between the agency and supervising agencies, which need the information for a variety of tasks. Supervising agencies must communicate back to direct service providers to inform them of new guidelines and updated expertise.

Learning from Experience

This can be defined as identifying patterns in information that can be used to guide future work. Thus, child welfare agencies need to be able to look at all the data they have accumulated over the years and answer questions such as: What do we know about the chances of reunification in these family constellations? What do we know about the impact of cross-racial placement? What do we know about the effectiveness of this particular intervention to support family preservation? Is this intervention more effective for families who were identified as physically abusive than for neglectful families? Who are the children for whom adoption tends to break down most frequently? Answers to these types of questions are immediately relevant for treatment planning on all levels. Lessons and expertise gained from experience will help guide the course of each individual intervention, as well the design of child welfare services, agencies, and systems.

IIS Design Principles

In the following sections we will describe in some detail the major principles that should guide the design of information systems, based on the conceptual framework outlined above.

Create Your Own Building Blocks for Integrated Systems

Our conceptual framework depicts an ambitious role for information systems. In order to respond to a large array of information needs for a wide range of participants and to continually improve quality of practice, information systems must be very extensive and complex. For any particular child welfare agency the task of designing such a comprehensive system may be overwhelming. Under these circumstances it may be tempting to forgo the customized design of an information system, hoping to find an existing system that addresses all your needs or to have such a system provided by a higher level agency, such as the state or federal government. Our first design principle is that agencies should not wait for such solutions. These integrative systems do not yet exist, and if they are being developed by higher level agencies, they will probably reflect those agencies' needs and requirements, rather than yours.

Instead, we encourage agencies to start by designing systems that address at least some of their most pressing information needs. Each information system should be designed as a component, a module, or a building block from which larger-scale integrated systems can later be developed. Thus, a particular agency may only have the resources to design a limited system that addresses the needs of their family preservation programs. This system, however, should be designed with a keen eye on what kind of information will flow to it from either existing or future protective services information systems, and what information this system should send to the existing management information system (MIS) and to future foster care, residential care, and adoption services information systems. Further, even systems that have a limited focus should consider very carefully what information will be required for accreditation and what information has immediate relevance for planning ongoing operations. (See Chapter 8.)

This design principle is of utmost importance when information systems already exist in a particular agency. For years agencies have been developing systems that addressed their management and financial needs [Bronson, Pelz, & Trzcinski 1988]. In many instances these systems are doing a good job in supporting management, and it is unwise to scrap them. Instead, make sure that relevant information flows to and from these systems effectively. Each bit of information should be gathered and reported only once, and not separately by each system. Design distinct systems that address different needs but are mutually compatible, so that duplication of effort is avoided.

Focus on Frontline Workers

One of the most important implications of this framework is that while it addresses the needs of all partners to care, it highlights the pivotal role of frontline workers in the information systems of the future. In order to improve quality of care and to monitor, communicate, and learn from experience, information systems should encompass all the processes of care frontline workers provide. These systems should clarify, structure, and support assessment, evaluation, decision-making, and treatment planning aspects of the clinical process, and aid in documentation and reporting. This kind of support for frontline workers enables them to base care for clients on the best advice available, reduces their documentation and reporting burden, and improves timely and accurate reporting.

Furthermore, a focus on the information needs of frontline workers creates a solid basis for a system that responds to the information needs of all the other partners to service delivery, supervisors, managers, and policymakers. Frontline workers are directly in contact with children and families. As an essential part of their practice, they gather information in order to make assessments, evaluations, and treatment plans, and then continue to gather information in order to assess the impact of their interventions. This information is important for their interventions, for their court appearances, and for their individual supervision. Because they are personally accountable for each detail, this information tends to be as accurate and as timely as possible. Information systems that are based on this foundation are likely to provide supervisors, managers, administrators, and policymakers with the most accurate and timely information available.

Systems that eliminate duplication in data gathering and reporting by frontline workers will not only save resources but also eliminate many errors and delays. Supporting the frontline staff lets workers know that the complex tasks they carry out are worthy of support, that the detailed information they gather is important, and that agency resources are being used to support them. This will restore the balance of power in an agency, so that it supports not only the decisions of management and administration but also the decisions and everyday work of the front line [Flynn 1990, Mandell 1989].

Structure and Support the Process of Services

It is common to focus on the products of information systems, the data and the reports, and to see data entry into these systems as only a means to an end. We suggest a major shift in focus. The design of an information system for your agency is a tremendous opportunity to support the *process* of services. Information systems should facilitate effective functioning by structuring the service delivery process and supporting it.

Workers, especially the less experienced ones, are often overwhelmed and confused by the demands of data gathering, documentation, and reporting. They face multivolume manuals, friendly advice, and (often conflicting) instructions, all providing prohibitive amounts of detail. Frontline workers function in complex and varied circumstances. They see children of all ages in a wide range of family situations and difficulties. Even experienced workers may not have the expertise to make assessments and judgments in each particular case. Most frontline workers are novices who do not always handle information gathering and processing tasks efficiently. These tasks form a maze that only the most experienced staff can navigate comfortably. All the others will appreciate a map, and if possible, a friendly hand.

Thus, an important design principle is to support workers by *moving expertise to the front line*. The system should be designed so that every worker can benefit from expert advice that has been integrated into the system. Consider, for instance, protective service workers. An information system should be designed to let them know what information they need to fully describe a particular incident: the participants involved; the nature, history, and circumstances of their involvement; the characteristics of the family, including the supports currently available and potential supports that can be accessed; and the strengths as well as problems in the family system. If sexual abuse may be involved, the information system will direct the worker to gather information regarding this specific kind of abuse. When there are directives governing eligibility for services or mandatory reporting to authorities, this information should be immediately visible, so that even a worker who has never handled such a case before will comply with requirements.

The information system should lead the workers through the initial phases of data gathering and reporting, as well as structure, clarify, and remind them of the next steps. There are many other ways in which you can use your agency's information system to inform, tutor, guide, and advise workers throughout the process of providing care. For instance, you may want to have online a guide to assessing suicide risk for adolescents. Supports of this type will go a long way to bolster workers' functioning, reduce mistakes, and ensure that best practice principles are guiding even the most novice workers.

Provide Maximum Access, but Maintain Confidentiality

An information system tuned to the needs of all partners to care and focused on frontline workers should be decentralized and accessible to all: support staff, workers, supervisors, administrators, and managers. It should allow each team member as much control and flexibility as possible in entering information, retrieving it, and generating reports. This will allow workers to provide quality care with the best support available.

Decentralization is connected with empowerment. Workers should be empowered through the design process to identify and explicate their needs. When the system is in place, they should feel that their access to information increases their competence and effectiveness. Empowered workers will provide the best care.

While ensuring maximum access, we must attend carefully to confidentiality. It is important to guarantee that information is accessible only to authorized staff. Computer technology available today can help you build a password system that compartmentalizes information, so that only workers who need certain information will have access to it. Identify which information items require better protection than others. For example, there may be legal directives on how to protect the anonymity of parents involved in voluntary adoption, whereas information on foster parents may need to be open to the public.

Strike a balance between access and confidentiality. If you follow our advice to provide access to as many partners as possible and to empower frontline workers by providing them access to information, you will find it difficult to emphasize confidentiality. This is a tough balancing act, to be addressed differently by each particular agency. Our advice is not to build a complex system to protect confidentiality too early in the design process. Add barriers to access only when you have a good understanding of how the information can be shared by as many relevant and authorized personnel as feasible.

It seems clear that we are only in the early stages of discussing the implications of IIS for confidentiality. As we move forward in our efforts to integrate information technology in direct practice, we will revisit these issues time and again.

Structure and Form of IIS That Support Practice

A simple way to picture information systems is to focus on four components: data input, database (data repository), data processing, and output generation. Before we deal with these components one at a time, it is essential to emphasize their interdependence. Whenever we plan data input we should plan with output requirements in mind (for example, the type of reports we need); whenever we design a database structure we need to know what data are available, how these data will be processed, and what kinds of outputs we will need to generate from this database. Furthermore, all our work, including data entry, storage, processing, and reporting, should be governed by our mission, our conceptual framework, and our design principles.

In the following sections we will briefly describe each of the four components of the IIS. This review does not require a high degree of computer literacy, so many of the more technical details are not addressed. Readers interested in technical details should consult the appropriate resources. The present review is based on the current widely available technologies; future innovations and new technologies may require considerable modifications of how information systems are structured in the future.

Data Input

Apply Teamwork to Data Entry

One of the important questions facing child welfare agencies that consider information systems is: Who will enter the data into the computer? Today's systems are often designed so that support staff, often temporary and part time clerical aides, do data entry. This practice goes against the basic idea of using IIS to support the process of care. When support staff enter data, the impact of the system as a tutorial and guide to practice is lost. Data entry should be done by practitioners involved in direct care.

Insisting that practitioners enter data raises many practical issues with regard to the typing skills of workers, time allocation, the underutilization of dedicated and capable support staff, and access to computers. Our recommendation is to think in terms of teams or units, comprising direct care workers, supervisors, and support (clerical) staff. Each member will enter the kind of information that he or she is most capable of handling and that will contribute most to quality care. Thus, frontline workers will be interacting with the computer while entering information, so that they will be guided by the advice the system provides. Nevertheless, some workers may find it cumbersome and too time consuming to enter many paragraphs of handwritten notes into the computer. Support staff may do a better job of typing these notes. In other instances, support staff may be responsible for finding information on issues such as funding, addresses, or dates of service. They should be able to enter this information in the most convenient way for them. Agencies will find their own optimal blend of responsibilities with regard to data entry. The information system should allow this flexibility.

Network the Agency Computers

One important implication of the idea of teamwork is that several workers may need to enter information about the same child and family. When computers are not connected, it is extremely difficult to move information between computers; to ensure that all the users who work on separate, stand-alone computers share the same information; and to prevent duplication or contradictory data. It is much more efficient to connect these computers through a network [Hudson

1993]. Computer networks allow several users working from different computers at the same time to share the program and the database, so that all updates and data entries are immediately available to all the users. The software that operates in a network environment assures that at any given moment in time only one user can change a given information item, and all the others can only view this information. As soon as this change is completed, the information item is "released" and can be accessed by other users.

Consider vacancy control. One practitioner views the list of available beds and assigns a child to a family. This, of course, results in a change in the vacancy list. When all the computers are networked, the next worker who scans this list will see a completely up-to-date vacancy list and will be able to make an assignment based on accurate information. Networks may seem more expensive to create and maintain than a series of stand-alone computers, but they are definitely more effective and efficient, and provide benefits that far outweigh their relative cost.

Avoid Duplication

An IIS is a great opportunity to avoid redundant data entry. Your information system should have the ability to transfer and move information, so each information item will be entered only once. This does not happen automatically, however. You'll have to identify all the cases in which duplicate information is being collected, documented, and entered today, and to plan data entry procedures that will prevent unnecessary repetition.

Keep It Simple and Friendly

The interface you provide workers will determine to a large extent whether and how the system will be used. Keep it as simple and as friendly as possible. If you need to provide a week-long training before new workers can operate the system, you have missed the target. Aim for an interface that requires a much shorter training period, preferably the kind of training that can be provided by a fellow worker on the job.

Many volumes have been dedicated to interface design issues. In this chapter we can only offer some basic advice. You can keep the interface simple by using language that is familiar to the worker. Provide instructions on the screen rather than in a manual. Keep the interface consistent: Use the same colors and the same key strokes and/or icons throughout the system, so that workers will feel competent to approach elements and modules they haven't used before.

One powerful way to simplify the interface is to use standards that have already been established and are familiar. For one example, all the programs based on Windows™ use a set of conventions that are familiar to regular users. By using this interface you will be capitalizing on the experience that many workers have already acquired. Some people prefer a Graphical User Interface (a GUI). Whichever you choose, be careful not to overload the worker with too many unfamiliar icons and symbols.

Another important consideration when you design an interface is the overall organization of the information system and the ease of navigating it. The IIS for a child welfare agency may grow to be large and complex. It is important to help workers understand its structure and organization so they can reach their destinations easily. You may want to use a main menu that depicts all the tasks workers will need to address. Each task a worker picks may break down into subtasks. You may want to provide a picture of a typical work flow, so the worker can go through the various phases of this flow. You may even create a "desktop" that resembles the worker's real desk top (without the clutter, of course).

Whatever the format, it is important to respond to two important navigation needs: clear structure (organization) and flexibility. You need to provide structure, and information about the structure, so that workers will have clear guidance about where they are in the process and what are the next possible steps. You need to provide flexibility so that workers can break out of a task easily and move to a different task without having to go through an endless series of screens and steps.

Provide Structured and Intelligent Data Entry Interface

There is a tendency to design data entry interfaces by merely translating the forms in an existing manual into a series of computer screens. This approach is unacceptable. Because the purpose of an information system is to support quality care, data entry should be designed to support and ensure a quality process. The interface should be planned as a tutorial, guiding the worker through the process, offering advice and instructions, pointing out what options should be considered, and preventing errors.

The system should prevent a worker from entering an out-of-range number, such as age 61 for a child in care, by indicating that this is probably a data entry mistake. Consider a permanency planning application. The system should respond to the age of the child the worker enters by branching to a set of screens that present the information needed for permanency planning for children of that age. If a worker is indicating a permanency plan of adoption for a 16-year-old who is a temporary ward of the court, the information system should respond that policy guidelines do not permit this plan for temporary wards, offer expert suggestions on reasonable options for children of this age and status, and provide some means of learning how to proceed if this specific 16-year-old is in fact going to be adopted.

To design a workable interface, agency staff should imagine an expert supervisor walking through the process with a novice frontline worker. This will ensure that the system provides all the necessary instructions, hints, and tips; that procedures and guidelines will be followed; and that errors in data entry will be detected and prevented before they become part of the database.

Support Varied Data Entry Formats

The interface should allow as many different data entry formats as will be needed by all partners to care. The common entry formats that every system should support are described below.

- *Single choice lists.* This format presents the worker with a fixed list from which he or she is able to select only one choice. Such lists may reflect the only alternatives permitted by current policy guidelines, the best options as suggested by experts, or the only available alternatives (such as a list of the agency's staff members). This allows standardization of information, because all workers can check an option only from a shared single list. This also allows for the generation of reports and analyses important to administration and management.

- *Multiple choice lists.* This format allows the worker to select several options from a list. It allows standardization and best use of expertise as above, but at the same time enables the workers to describe complex phenomena that have several attributes simultaneously. For instance, there may be more than one reason for a referral; workers should be able to check all appropriate reasons, rather than trying to determine which one they should report.

- *Numbers and dates.* Numbers and dates should be entered with appropriate formats and checks for legitimate values. Entering data on number of siblings, income, or phone number requires a numerical format. When a date is required, such as a court date, use the month/day/year format to prevent undesirable variations that will cause difficulties when generating a list of all court dates. When you expect that workers will not have full dates (e.g., date of birth for parents), use more flexible formats, allowing partial data entry (e.g., only year of birth) and testing for out-of-range values.

- *Text and open-ended text.* Text is necessary in conjunction with lists as well as when lists are not available or are considered inappropriate. Lists function to organize and categorize observations, easing the transition from observation to assessment. Text should be entered as a means of documenting the specific and unique characteristics of a case, allowing for accountability by setting up a framework to document the basis for each categorical assessment.

  Note the importance of *open-ended text*. Because IIS are designed to support the process of care, workers must have the means to enter information in as much detail as they find necessary to describe the unique characteristics of specific cases. Some management information systems do not permit this type of data entry. Integrated information systems should not only allow open-ended text, but also support it. Word processing and spell checking facilities should be integrated into the data entry so workers find it easy to give as many details as necessary.

  Certain elements of the information child welfare agencies need do not fit into the traditional categories listed above, and cannot be entered into existing databases using traditional keyboards. Recent technological developments will help create interfaces to accommodate these less traditional forms of data entry.

- *Electronic data input.* As more and more agencies adopt computerized information systems, the opportunities to transfer data electronically are growing. Imagine an intake unit that makes referrals to child welfare agencies. This unit may be using a system that contains information on a child and a family. When the child and family are referred to another unit, the information can be copied onto a disk and sent to the appropriate unit, which will copy this information into their system, saving the resources and discomfort involved in asking for and documenting the same information again and again. Today's technology allows us to achieve this process through phone lines and networks in simple, automated ways. Tomorrow's technology will make communication between systems even easier. Of course, all this can be achieved only when the two units exchanging information are congruent in terms of the specifications of the data being transferred. Your information system should support this type of input.

- *Hand-written text*. For child welfare agencies, there are many advantages to using interfaces that do not require typing on a keyboard. Practitioners who interview families and children on home visits may find that writing notes on a pad is more efficient and more acceptable to families than typing on a computer keyboard. Furthermore, when input from families and children is needed, it is much easier to ask for handwritten notes than to ask them to type into a computer. Today's technology is fairly accurate in interpreting handwritten text. We can expect significant improvements in this area in the near future.

- *Documents*. Documents such as a physician's assessment of a child may be useful in assessing the child's status over time. Being able to scan these documents and make them a part of the child's record can facilitate health monitoring. Today, the technology is quite expensive and rather limited in its usefulness because of a lack of clarity in some scanned images. Progress in this area, however, is very likely, and this form of input should be considered seriously.

- *Pictures and other nontext information*. Some of the most valuable information for workers in child welfare agencies is not in the form of text at all. For protective service workers, pictures of a child's body when she or he is admitted to the emergency room are worth many words. Children's photos may also be valuable for adoptive services, or for any category of workers who need to see changes in children over time. Children's drawings of themselves and of their families at various points in time may tell the true story of permanency planning.

Databases

Use Relational Databases

Computers store information in databases. This chapter offers a short, nontechnical introduction to databases in general and relational databases in particular, along with some basic terminology.

The information in a database is contained in *records*. Each child may have his or her own record of demographic information. Each record can be visualized as a line or a row. Records have a fixed structure: They are divided into distinct *fields*, each containing information on a different issue. A series of records that have identical structures forms a *database*. Consider the example of a database containing demographic characteristics of children in care. Each record in this example has the following fields:

Field Name	Field Structure
1. Child's first name	Text, up to 20 spaces
2. Child's last name	Text, up to 20 spaces
3. Child's I.D number	Text and numbers, 9 spaces (the first should always be a character)
4. Gender	Number, one space (1=female; 2=male; 9=unknown; no other number allowed)
5. Date of birth	Date format (month/day/year) (if unknown leave blank)
6. Physical description	Open-ended, unlimited text

Information on each child can be entered into these fields, creating one record per child. Two records describing two children have identical structures (each has 6 fields and each field has a predefined structure) but different information. A series of such records forms a database of client characteristics.

Note that in this example each child will have one record. If the child's physical description changes over time, there is a need to go to the record, erase the data in that field, and enter an update. But in other areas this may not be a good idea. In many instances we would like to keep a record intact and *add* records if necessary. Take the example of periodic progress notes. Children will have different progress notes for every period. In order to trace a child's progress in care, it is essential to keep a history over time for each child. Thus, the database of progress notes may contain information on several children, each having several records.

Sometimes it's not easy to decide whether we need to maintain a history of changes in a certain area. Consider the issue of parents' address. In many agencies, practitioners consider an address as an information item that should always be kept up to date, with no need for a history. Whenever they get address change information they erase the old address and enter the new one. In other agencies, however, practitioners may think that it's important to trace the history of address changes, and that the number of placements a child has had is clinically useful information. They will add a new record each time the address changes, keeping the old one in the database.

Child and family social service agencies need to gather and store many kinds of information. For technical and practical reasons, it is not advisable to create one database that holds all the information. Instead, it is common to have a series of databases, each containing information on a different subject. Thus, for instance, an agency may have separate databases for each of the following areas: demographic information on children and families, funding information, medical records, court reports, foster families' background information, progress notes, and more. The question then becomes: How can we relate information from several databases to provide a comprehensive picture of all aspects of a particular child and family? The most common answer is to design *relational databases*, databases that are interlinked.

In this case, each database contains information about a certain topic, but also some identifying information that is common across databases. A child's demographic record can be related to his or her medical record through a child identification number that appears in both databases. By sharing certain key identifying information, all databases can relate to each other, and are in fact one relational database.

Child welfare agencies should be especially interested in *how* databases interrelate. These agencies need a way to relate databases so that each child is identified individually and as a member of a family. This is because some analyses and reports must be child-based, while others focus on the family as a whole. A database should be designed so that not only children but families and siblings can be tracked in care. Furthermore, when they plan identification keys, agencies must consider what keys other information systems use and how they may be interfacing with them in the future.

The implication of these technical details is that even nontechnical people at a child welfare agency need to be aware of the choices they can make with regard to the database structure. The design of databases is quite complicated, requiring technical expertise not usually found in our agencies. The final decision about database structure may involve some technical considerations the computer people introduce, but the main driving force should be the agency's practitioners and administrators. They need to ask themselves a series of questions on how their needs can best be translated into a database structure.

Data Processing

Process Information at the Level of the Individual Client

Processing information on the individual level will yield valuable insights with regard to a particular child and his/her family. There are many ways in which this can be accomplished.

Translate Information into a Narrative

The information entered into a database is stored in various formats: numbers, dates, codes, text, and open-ended text. When a practitioner or a supervisor needs this information, it's important to be able to translate all these codes into a comprehensible narrative. Thus, a practitioner may have entered the code 1 to indicate that the child is a male. The information is stored in this form. When workers need this information, the code should be translated automatically back to the word *male*.

Information on a list of services provided to the child and family may be stored as a series of codes, each indicating a specific service. To make this information useful for practitioners, the series of codes should be processed and transformed to yield a list of services in plain language.

Provide Summary Scores and Overall Assessments

In some instances family service agencies may use a structured instrument to make a complex assessment. A checklist may be used to describe a child's behavioral problems [e.g., Benbenishty 1991] a family risk level for abuse, or a multidimensional assessment of family functioning [e.g., McCubbin & McCubbin 1992]. These checklists consist of many items that together give a comprehensive picture. Integrated information systems that use these instruments should process them and generate summary scores for individual clients. These scores can be graphed to provide a pictorial representation of the scale [Benbenishty 1991; Hile 1989], and can also be compared over time, as discussed below.

Compare Data over Time

Child and family service agencies often target certain behaviors or situations and provide services in order to change or improve them. The integrated information system should process information to determine whether there was indeed a change over time. Thus, for example, when certain family communication patterns are targeted for change and are assessed periodically, the way the IIS processes the information should allow practitioners to assess whether any improvement is evident over time in the communication patterns of a particular family.

Process Information at the Level of the Group of Clients

Identify Groups of Clients: The information stored in a database permits agencies to identify and examine groups of clients. These groups are identified by selecting only those records that share certain characteristics. Thus, for example, supervisors and managers may be interested in the groups of children who (a) have been released for adoption; (b) have been waiting for more than six months; and (c) are still in foster homes. In another example, administrators may be interested in finding out which children (a) are under three years old and (b) were born with addiction symptoms.

Describe Groups of Clients, Services Provided, and Outcomes Achieved: Agencies need to be able to describe their clients, services, and case outcomes. Then information on clients can be summarized to reveal the distribution of variables. This analysis will inform you of client characteristics such as the age distribution of children in care—information that has direct relevance to service planning. Similarly, the distribution of training needs of foster families will help the agency plan training for these families. Information on the relative frequency with which various services are provided and the average duration of certain programs is an important source of feedback on service delivery patterns. The distribution of length of time in care, number of disrupted placements, and percentage of reunifications within a year of placement can all shed light on outcomes.

Make Comparisons

This type of information processing provides important information on:

- Differences between groups. Summarizing the same information on two or more groups allows us to identify dissimilarities between groups.

For instance, comparing males and females on placement type will show whether boys are placed with relatives more frequently than girls. Similarly, tabulating type of placement by type of social work contact will show whether you are providing different services to children who live with unrelated foster families than to children who live with relatives.

- Changes over time. Comparing the same information item at different points in time provides the opportunity to detect changes over time. Compare "snapshots" of clients' status before and after intensive treatment to see if any improvement can be identified [Corcoran & Gingerich 1992, 1994]. One valuable comparison would be the contrasting of parenting skills before and after parenting classes.

Another valuable comparison is among sets of information collected at several points in time. A series of assessments permits the detection of trends. Consider an agency that maintains records of reasons for referral. Comparing referrals made in each of the last several years may allow us to see an increase over time in the percentage of children who were sexually abused by family members. This will have clear implications for service planning [see Usher 1993].

- Associations and predictors. Comparisons are useful in identifying relationships and predictors. For instance, comparing the rates of successful reunification between families with different parental characteristics may provide important insight. Do certain parent characteristics known at intake predict certain outcomes? Similarly, a cross-tabulation of case outcomes by type of services (e.g., whether intensive casework was offered to parents to facilitate reunification) will help to identify any signs that certain services are related to case outcomes.

Data

Provide Reports for All Users

Report generation is a central function of information systems. In agencies, these systems can relieve workers from the time-consuming and error-prone task of report generation. A key design issue is the information system's ability to serve all users rather than focus only on management needs. The IIS should be accessible to all partners to care and should provide reports that address the particular and specific needs of each user.

Practitioners will need reports that focus on their individual clients and their individual caseloads. They will need reports required by courts and other supervising agencies. They will also need reports that serve as reminders of planned activities, such as medical appointments and court dates. Caseload reports can help practitioners prioritize effectively. Thus, a list of children sorted by assessment of risk can help the worker focus on the most urgent cases [Rapp & Poertner 1986].

Supervisors need access to all the reports used by each of the workers they oversee. Further, they need reports that will allow them to supervise several workers and get a picture of more than one caseload. Lists of reports due will facilitate communication with these workers and lead to timely reporting [see Bhattacharyya 1992]. Administrators and managers also need reports covering various groups of clients. These staff members will frequently require summary reports and statistics. Reports should also be generated for partners to care outside the agency. Thus, supervisory agencies may need lists of children and families served, services provided by the agency, and funding information.

Automate—Provide "Canned" Reports

Having entered information into the system once, workers should be relieved of the need to enter the information numerous times in order to create different reports. Reports should all be generated from the same set of relational databases. Automate report generation as much as possible. Reports that are needed on a regular basis should be pre-defined in the system ("canned"), so that generating them will be very easy. Defining a large but limited set of reports will allow your agency to design these reports with great care and invest time and effort to ensure content and style.

Facilitate Ad Hoc Report Generation

An IIS in a family services agency should provide flexibility in report generation. In addition to producing the standard set of reports, staff should have the ability to design and generate any new reports that they may need. This report generation facility should have a friendly interface, so that even workers who know very little about computers and programming will be able to generate reports. Several software packages can create an interactive interface that queries users about their needs, then generates a report that can later be modified as needs evolve. New reports can be saved for future use.

Make Report Generation Accessible to All Staff

For IIS to support care, report generation must be accessible to all workers. Practitioners should be able to generate their own reports, examine them, make any changes in the data, and reproduce the reports. This will give them the kind of autonomy and control that support their sense of ownership and responsibility. Workers who can design and generate their own reports may be motivated to look more deeply into their caseloads and identify areas in need of improvement.

Use a Variety of Formats

Because the IIS responds to a wide range of needs and users, it requires a range of report formats. Some common ones are described below.

Narrative

These reports translate information stored in the database to text. Sophisticated programs can generate sentences and paragraphs that contain the information in a case file. This text can then be formatted as required by reporting guidelines,

(**Figure 9.2**)

*An Example of a Narrative Report**

Initial Service Plan 01/04/94 - 02/04/94

(**Identifying Information**)	(**Race**)	(**DSS#**)	(**MA#**)

Children

Sherman Smith (Male)   African American   V1111111Q   77777777
D.O.B. 08/04/91
Placement Type: Foster Home

Jimmie Dock (Male)   African American   V1111111Q   77777777
D.O.B. 04/25/93
Placement Type: Foster Home

Parent(s)

Mother: (birth parent of Jimmie, Sherman)
Ursula Smith, D.O.B. 05/15/72
Race: African American
999 Navada, Detroit, MI 48219

Father: (birth parent of Jimmie)
Jimmie Dock Sr., D.O.B. 1940 (exact date unknown)
Race: African American
9999 Forest, Detroit, MI 48999 - 313/555–9999

Father: (birth parent of Sherman)
Michael Johnson, birth date unknown
Race: African American

County of Commitment or Referral: Wayne
Date Entered Care: 01/04/94
Report Dates: from 01/04/94 to 02/04/94

(**Adjudication of**)	(**Date**)	(**Current Status**)
Sherman	03/16/94	TCW**
Jimmie	03/16/94	TCW**

Next Court Date: 02/16/94. Type: Pretrial

---

* These are segments of an actual report. Names and personal details were changed to protect
   confidentiality.
**Temporary Court Ward

Figure 9.2 cont'd.

Initial Service Plan 01/04/94 - 02/04/94

Reasonable Efforts Provided by the Department of Social Services

2) *Family Involvement in Present Problem*
Ursula Smith's nature of involvement consists of: neglect of health/hygiene, neglect of medical needs, neglect of supervision, and abandonment.
The contributing factors to her involvement include: substance abuse, poor parenting/coping abilities.
Mother is a known drug user and has left the children alone.
When they were transported to the hospital by the police to meet with the child abuse officer, mother stated Sherman had fallen the night before (Jan. 1, 1994) and she did not realize how bad the head injury was.
Both children reportedly had a bad odor related to uncleanliness.
She is willing to engage in therapy.

3a) *Likely Harm to Children if Separated from Parent(s) or Guardian(s)*
Bonding with parent/s may be jeopardized and socioemotional development in the family will suffer discontinuity.
  b) *Likely Harm to Children if Returned to Parent(s) or Guardian(s)*
The children will be at risk for neglect.
Mother is crack addicted and recently entered Harbour Lights treatment program.
Until completion of the program mother is not physically able to care for children.

5) *Health/Legal*
Ursula Smith has a highly severe substance abuse problem.
She is crack addicted per self-admission for a period of approximately two years.
Intervention consists of: Drug treatment.
Currently at Harbour Lights residential treatment program. She admitted herself after children were taken into care.
She has signed a release of information for LCFS.
She is allowed to visit her children with an escort at LCFS weekly.

6) *Social Support Network*
The social support network consists of friends and relatives.
Ursula's relatives, her mom and her Aunt Sonia, will be supportive to Ursula if she is drug-free.
Mr. Dock, Jimmie's father, is as supportive as possible considering he is married to another woman.

Figure 9.2 cont'd.

Initial Service Plan 01/04/94 - 02/04/94

Placement Selection Criteria

a) *Current Placement and Date Placed*
Sherman is currently placed in the licensed foster home of Kelley, William
& Helen.
Date placed: 01/02/94

Jimmie is currently placed in the licensed foster home of Glaspie, Ora Lee.
Date placed: 01/04/94

b) *Case Plan and Goal of Permanence*
The permanency planning goal for Sherman is to return home.
The child is to be reunited with mother.
This goal is to be achieved by 11/02/94.

f) *Placement with Siblings*
Siblings are not placed together.
Neither foster home could accommodate both children at time of place-
ment due to their licensing capacities.

g) *The Children's Racial, Ethnic, and Cultural Identity, Heritage, and Background*
The current placements are racially congruent with the children.

h) *Family's Religious Preference*
This information is presently unavailable.

i) *Least Restrictive Placement*
The current placements are the least restrictive, most family-like placements
available to meet the children's current needs.

Expected length of stay in placement 6 to 9 months.
Anticipated next placement: With mother, if all parent/agency agreement
goals are met.

Recommendation

Sherman should remain in care until P/A agreement can be successfully fulfilled.
Jimmie should remain in care until P/A agreement can be successfully fulfilled.
It is expected that the mother, Ursula Smith, will cooperate.

with the appropriate headers and special printing features such as underline, bold, and various fonts. It is possible to automatically generate a text report that is indistinguishable from manually generated reports (see Figure 9.2).

Lists and Column Reports

Reports of this type are very useful for management and administration. They present information on a group of cases. Information on each case is presented in a series of columns, each containing a different field. The reports can pertain to all cases or to a subgroup only (by defining inclusion criteria); can be sorted by one or more keys (e.g., by gender and age); and can be broken down by one or more variables (e.g., list of children in care broken down by worker, and the same list broken down by supervisor and worker).

Summary Statistics

Certain reports provide information that summarizes data on cases and fields. Thus, the median length of stay can be computed and presented, along with other relevant statistics such as the average number of office and home visits, the overall number of serious incidents reported last month, and the average number of children in a caseload. Reports of summary statistics can provide complex information that helps in decision making. Thus for instance, presenting the number of disrupted adoptions per region can help identify trouble spots.

Graphs

Figures and graphs can summarize complex data in an easy to understand format. A pie chart that breaks down social workers' activities by type can communicate very effectively the sad fact that paperwork is the largest slice of the pie (see Figure 9.3).

Client progress can be charted on bar graphs or line graphs that describe a child's situation at several points in time. For instance, in Benbenishty's study, social workers used the Child Behavior Checklist [Achenbach & Edelbrock 1978] monthly to assess the situation of children in residential care. Bar charts were used to describe the child's "problem profile" every month, as well as to describe changes over the last six months. (For details of the study and examples of graphs, see Benbenishty [1991].)

Most database software packages have the capacity to generate graphs. Under certain circumstances, however, it may be more efficient to move the data to computer programs designed specifically to produce graphs. This will produce much higher quality graphs, but will take more time and resources than the automatic generation of a set of graphs by the IIS.

Electronic Data Output

Because child welfare agencies are links in a chain of services, they need to be able both to receive and to send data from and to other partners, such as referral

---

Figure 9.3

Time Spent by Practitioners

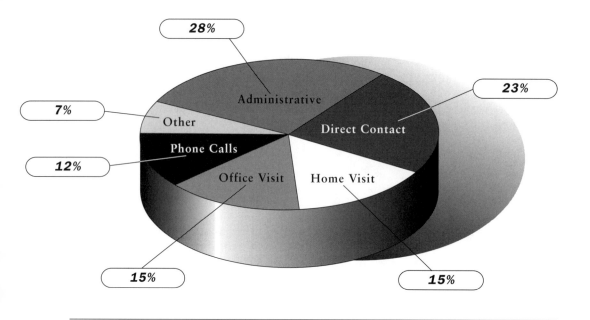

---

services, funding agencies, the state's department of social services, and the courts. Thus, for instance, an information system should be able to fax messages to all partners who need to receive a particular paper report.

Furthermore, an agency's IIS should have the capacity to send reports that can be read and utilized by other information systems, within and outside the agency. This could be achieved in many ways, depending on the technical arrangements between the various computer systems involved. When cooperation and compatibility between systems are minimal, reports can be translated into a very simple format that can be read by all of today's computer systems (known as "flat ASCII") and downloaded to disks. When systems are integrated, information and reports can flow directly from one database to another via phone (or data) lines, preserving all the information and requiring no additional processing. Progress on the "information superhighway" and use of the Internet will no doubt add to the range of possibilities.

Support Staff Members' Use of Reports

Providing users with an array of reports helps them carry out their jobs more effectively. Be very careful, however, not to overwhelm users with reports. Do not provide more reports than they can possibly digest at any one time. Make sure that users understand the reports and know how to interpret them.

Dumping a stack of computer-generated tables on a practitioner's lap will not be helpful. Each report should be designed with an understanding of its intended user's ability to read tables and graphs. It is good practice to introduce each type of report to the users, explain what it contains, give examples of possible interpretations, and warn against common mistakes in using it. This education process may take resources, but it infuses the agency with expertise that will benefit service delivery on all levels.

Conclusions: The IIS and Quality Improvement

The design and implementation of an information system should be an essential and integral element of quality improvement in every child welfare agency. When you think of quality improvement, think of your IIS; when you think of your IIS, think how it can and should have an impact on the quality of your agency. You can think of this relationship in terms of both process and product.

The process of designing and implementing an information system will be immediately relevant to quality improvement [Poertner & Rapp 1987]. To design an IIS you will need to analyze your agency's needs and practices in depth. This will allow you to identify areas of strength and weakness, ambiguities about policies, and disagreements among staff members. As you move to introduce changes in your agency you will want the IIS to reflect these improvements. To be able to modify the information system you will need to clarify, to yourself and to others, exactly what you want and how certain practices will change.

An Integrated Information System designed to respond to the needs of all levels of the agency is an effective means to create and to strengthen a team approach. The IIS design is driven by frontline workers, as well as by administrators, managers, support staff, and funders. As you use the IIS, encourage and value feedback from all staff members. This in turn will contribute to an agencywide drive toward improvement. Along with other organizational changes you are making to improve quality, you will need to consider organizational changes that maximize the benefits from your IIS.

As the information system becomes functional, the information and analyses it provides can become key factors in quality management. Information on clients—their strengths, needs, and characteristics—will be most valuable for planning future services. Accurate and timely accounts of the services the agency provides are important for self-evaluation and for assessing the areas in need of improvement. Outcome information is one of the key issues for any quality improvement effort. The IIS will provide you with detailed information about outcomes that you have targeted as most important (see the Check phase in the planning process described in Chapter 7). You will be able to describe these outcomes, compare outcomes in different areas and programs, and compare outcomes achieved by various client groups. Furthermore, you will be able to check whether, indeed, outcomes improve over time (see Chapter 5 for ideas on how to study your agency's outcomes). As you consider this information, you may also be able to evaluate the extent to which your information system is cost effective. Are the costs involved in the process of design, implementation, and maintenance justified by the benefits the system provides?

Finally, integrated information systems to support quality care and child and family service agencies' quality improvement efforts share a central quest: continuous improvement. An information system should always be seen as the best interim solution. Remember that the target is always moving. Whatever we accomplish will give us a better starting point to address higher level goals.

The environment in which your agency operates changes continuously, so you need to adjust continuously. Your information system should be improving continuously. The more you work on improving quality, the more ways you will find that the integrated information system can help you.

Initiating and sustaining a quality improvement drive is a formidable task. The design and implementation of an IIS, as part of this effort, is not an easy task either. Yet, the advantages you can gain by embarking on this journey are enormous. It is time to move ahead. It is time to take advantage of the technology of the end of this century to address the challenges of the next one.

The final chapter discusses some possibilities for facilitating the kinds of organizational change that will be necessary for agencies to implement information systems and other essential components of program evaluation and quality improvement.

References

Achenbach, T. M., & Edelbrock, C.S. (1978). The classification of child psychopathology: A review and analysis of empirical efforts. *Psychological Bulletin, 85,* 1275–1301.

Barnes, C. (Coventry City Council Social Service Department, U.K.) (1994). Accuracy of information in a social services client record index. Paper presented at the International Expert Meeting on Client Information Systems and Social Reporting: Building an Interorganizational and International Frame of Reference, Brussels, Belgium.

Benbenishty, R., & Oyserman, D. (1991). A clinical information system for foster care in Israel. *Child Welfare, 70*(2), 229-242.

Benbenishty, R. (1991). Monitoring practice on the agency level: An application in a residential care facility. *Research on Social Work Practice, 1,* 371-386.

Bhattacharyya, A. (1992). Tickler: An automated system to monitor assessment dates for psychiatric care. *Computers in Human Ser*vices, *8,* 87-119.

Bronson, D. E, Pelz, D.C., & Trzcinski, E. (1988). *Computerizing your agency's information system.* Newbury Park, CA: Sage.

Corcoran, K., & Gingerich, W. J. (1992). Practice evaluation: Setting goals, measuring and assessing change. In K. Corcoran (Ed.), *Structuring change: Effective clinical practice for common client problems,* pp. 28-47. Chicago: Lyceum.

Corcoran, K., & Gingerich, W. J. (1994). Practice evaluation in the context of managed care: Case recording methods for quality assurance reviews. *Research on Social Work Practice, 4,* 326-337.

Finch, S. J., Fanshel, D., & Grundy, J. F. (1991). *Data collection in adoption and foster care.* Washington, DC: CWLA.

Flynn, J. J. (1990). Issues in the introduction of computer and information technology in human services. *Computers in Human Services, 6,* 21-33.

Harrod, J. (1988, Winter). Collecting accurate information about child abuse. *CUSSN Newsletter, 24*–27.

Hile, M. A. (1989). Two automated systems for behavioral assessment of clients with mental retardation or developmental disabilities. *Computers in Human Services, 5,* 183-191.

Hudson, W. W. (1993). The future of social service computing. *Computers in Human Services, 10,* 1–7.

Mandell, S. F. (1989). Resistance and power: The perceived effect that computerization has on a social agency's power relationships. *Computers in Human Ser*vices, *4,* 29-40.

Martin, L. L. (1993). Total quality management: The new managerial wave. *Administration in Social Work,* 17, 1–15.

McCubbin, H. I., & McCubbin, M. A. (1992). Research utilization in social work practice of family treatment. In A. J. Grasso, & I. Epstein (Eds.), *Research utilization in the social services*, pp. 149–192. New York: The Haworth Press.

Poertner, J., & Rapp, C. A. (1987). Designing social work information systems: The case for performance guidance system. *Administration in Social Work, 11*, 177-190.

Rapp, C. C., & Poertner, J. (1986). The design of database management reports. *Administration in Social Work, 10*, 53–64.

Usher, L. (1993). Building capacity for self-evaluation in family and children's services reform effort. A presentation at the annual meeting of the American Evaluation Association.

Chapter 10

Making It Happen:
Strategies for Organizational Change

E.C. Ted Teather, Kathryn A. Gerbino,
and Peter J. Pecora

Introduction*

This chapter will address the knowledge, skills, and actions needed to promote the types of organizational change that can implement an outcome-oriented, consumer-driven approach to quality improvement and program evaluation. The four main topics addressed in this chapter are: (1) a framework for managing complex organizational change, (2) team building, (3) working with entrenched opposition, and (4) using a systems approach to manage change.

Previous chapters have outlined the essential components of a practice model that can lead child and family service agencies effectively into the next decade. The model is a blueprint for transition, with special attention paid to processes that improve quality. The major elements of these processes are summarized below:

- An understanding that, for the most part, problems in an organization aren't with individuals, but rather with systems—and people are often unaware of those systems [Schenkat 1993]

- A broad-based vision for the future created with input from all stakeholders

- Constancy of purpose and a clear set of core values and principles. (These must be imbedded in the structure and culture of the agency to inform and guide daily practice.)

- An agency-wide commitment to understanding and anticipating customer needs that leads to continual examination and recreation of services that meet or exceed those needs in a timely, affordable manner

*   The authors wish to thank Gerald D. Zaslaw, Executive Director of Vista Del Mar; Robert L. Roy, Executive Director of the Children's Farm Home; and Thomas M. Luzzi, Associate Executive Director of Parsons Child and Family Center, for their consultation in the preparation of this manuscript. David Cassafer helped broaden our change perspective by providing essential linkages to the quality improvement literature.

- A learning culture, where every process is studied and quality is viewed as a technology that can be systematized and taught [Pines 1990]

- Opportunity and desire for people at *all* levels to learn and to contribute, "continually expanding [the agency's] capacity to create the future" [Senge 1990]

While there is consensus on the rationale and key elements of transforming an agency, there is no one best practice model, and no cookbook recipe for success. Available resources, agency traditions, a mission, a vision, and values, all shaped by local needs, must guide the adaptation of theory into practice for each unique setting. The role of the leader in the family service agencies of the future is that of designer, steward, and teacher, constructing the agency culture and shaping its evolution [Schein 1985].

To guide change in the practice environment and to assist in the implementation of key elements for success, a growing number of child and family social service agencies are implementing aspects of quality improvement (QI) and the more specific techniques of continuous quality improvement (CQI) or total quality management (TQM). The incorporation of these elements requires a significant organizational transformation, which typically takes place over a period of years, although a more radical and time-limited transformation, "Reengineering," has been urged by Hammer & Champy [1993].

Why should agency leaders be interested in these new models? The motivation for their adoption arises from and is reinforced by several sources. National and state accrediting and licensing bodies (the Joint Commission on Accreditation of Health Care Organizations, the Council on Accreditation for Services to Children and Families, and state and county welfare agencies) increasingly require demonstration of best practice and a process for reviewing and improving the outcomes of services to clients. (See Chapter 8). Title 19 Medicaid funding and the "mixed payer market" are examples of the necessary pathways for accessing new funding resources. The advent of managed care systems introduces a gatekeeper function in the delivery of care, and emphasizes reducing costs and improving efficiency through time-bounded, carefully monitored services. Increased competition from those agencies that have moved forward by embracing these new ideas is another motivator.

Finally, there are heightened demands to increase accountability while decreasing costs, without compromising quality of care. These demands dictate that an agency's economic survival will require increasing productivity and employees who strive continuously toward the improvement of quality and services. These realities impel leaders of child and family service agencies to change the context and form of agency practice.

Administrators and staff members place a high value on providing the best possible services. This valuing is a powerful motivator. When the authors asked directors of residential treatment centers "Why are you changing?," one factor stood out: the desire for their programs to be delivering the best possible service and an unwillingness to be associated with a program that did not make sense in light of current information. They reported as their primary motivator a desire to direct programs of which they could be proud.

A variation on this theme was introduced by the associate executive director of a large child and family service agency in upstate New York. "Our mission compels us to offer the best possible services to our clients. We simply must employ any reasonable strategy that increases the likelihood of improving services and outcomes for our children and families. Yes, I want to feel proud of our agency, but that is definitely secondary to the drive to do the best we can for the people we serve."

Those agencies that are among the best reflect best practice both in terms of program components and of the processes that produce, maintain, and alter those components. Pursuing a standard of best practice based on an outcome-focused service model promises many benefits: higher productivity, improved quality of service, empowerment in the work force, enhancement of job dignity, employee self-esteem, and job satisfaction. Agencies have to change; while we have visions of best practice, what limits agencies' ability to bring about best practice is how they engage in the change process. How can an agency implement and institutionalize processes that support continual change? We are redesigning both *how we decide how* to deliver services and *how we deliver* those services.

This chapter will explore the leadership principles, knowledge, and skills involved in effecting a fundamental shift in program emphases and practices to reflect best practice initiatives. It will be useful to leaders who are involved in moving child and family, juvenile justice, or mental health agencies toward a more outcome-focused service model rooted in the new quality improvement philosophies and methods. The central premise of this concluding chapter is that new forms of leadership are essential to the restructuring of all human service agencies.

A Framework for Managing Complex Organizational Change

Premises

First, quality improvement need not wait for optimal conditions. Leaders who wait to cover every exigency may find themselves waiting forever. Can you remember any time in your organization's history when everything was in perfect order? Neither can anyone else!

Second, the transformation of the organization establishes a long-term social contract for change. In most instances, it will take at least three years of constant work to redesign less than optimal systems and processes and an additional two years to see visible and significant benefits. Staff members need to know that the change process won't go away, that they can't outwait it, that they and the organization are into it for the long haul. Staff must view their best response as enthusiasm for, or at least compliance with, the proposed change process. Letting people know up front that change is not negotiable reduces the impact of nay-sayers and resisters.

Third, failures may occur, and that should be seen as OK. Change is a complex and demanding task for leaders, individuals, and organizations. The object is not to try to reduce risk so initiatives never fail (this is impossible), but rather to ensure that when failure occurs we fail intelligently. Only through learning from our mistakes can we continually improve. Remind your staff that transformation is a journey and not a destination. Along the way, there will be more than a few bumps in the road, and you will meet them together. See for example the following, part of a full-page ad that United Technologies ran in the *Wall Street Journal*, which was reprinted in John Bonstingl's book, *Schools of Quality* [1992].

<hr>

Don't Be Afraid To Fail

You've failed many times, although you may not remember....You fell down the first time you tried to walk.... You almost drowned the first time you tried to swim, didn't you?.... Did you hit the ball the first time you swung a bat?.... English novelist John Creasey got 753 rejection slips before he published 564 books.... Don't worry about failure.... Worry about chances you miss when you don't even try.... [United Technologies 1981]

<hr>

The sections that follow will guide you in creating a vision for change in both programs and management processes. You will be assisted in finding the time to incorporate new ways of doing things into the culture of the workplace and in identifying the principles, knowledge, and skills you'll need to introduce, maintain, strengthen, and sustain the transformation you are about to embark upon.

It has been said that the quality of an agency is dictated by its top management. The quality throughout cannot be better than the quality at the top, as the people on the line can only produce the design of product and service prescribed and designed by agency leaders [Deming, cited in American Association of School Administrators 1991]. If you are at or near the top management level in your organization, the ball is in your court! If you are a leader or supervisor, but not in the top position in your agency, then you must learn to "manage up." Managing up means obtaining vital buy-ins from your boss through open communication about vital concerns and issues of quality improvement.

You may not be able to wait for your boss to lead these efforts. Rather, develop the skills you need to move forward and build alliances that will make future requests, particularly for additional resources, more likely to be forthcoming [Capezio & Morehouse 1993; Patti 1974; Resnick & Patti 1980].

Vision: Knowing Where You Want to Go

As the queen tells Alice in the classic story *Alice in Wonderland,* if you don't know where you want to go, then any road will get you there. The first factor in orienting for change is to articulate the program vision that is guiding the change effort. Without an overall picture of what the end state of change should look like and why it's crucial, the process itself is difficult to plan, and implementation is vulnerable to program drift.

Articulating the vision involves providing a clear rationale for the new program model, as well as identifying a clear plan for change and giving staff members the skills, resources, incentives, and supports for program refinement. Consider the interdependent relations among the various key elements illustrated in Figure 10.1 [American Productivity and Quality Center 1993].

Figure 10.1

Managing Complex Change

Vision	Skills	Incentives	Resources	Plan ⟶	Change!!
	Skills	Incentives	Resources	Plan ⟶	Confusion
Vision		Incentives	Resources	Plan ⟶	Anxiety
Vision	Skills		Resources	Plan ⟶	Gradual Change
Vision	Skills	Incentives		Plan ⟶	Frustration
Vision	Skills	Incentives	Resources	⟶	False Starts

Source: American Productivity and Quality Center, 1993.

What is especially valuable about this matrix is that it describes the relationship between key elements for change and the negative results that occur when any one element is not adequately addressed. For example, without an overall vision that guides the change effort, plans may not be articulated to staff or may be too shortsighted, resulting in mass confusion as implementation barriers are encountered. Unless staff members are given the specific skills they need to implement change efforts, their anxiety will increase to unacceptable levels and interfere with what should be an exciting, empowering, and positive time of change. Organizations may begin with a clear vision and most of the other elements in place, but without a specific, well-considered plan, there will be many false starts as implementation roadblocks or unexpected problems arise [David Cassafer, personal communication, February 4, 1994]. Setbacks like this damage management's credibility and make people doubt that there is a real intention to move forward.

Creating the Time for Change

Quality improvement activities such as vision development, goal setting and planning, skill building, and program implementation take time. Lowering time barriers to allow agency staff to be involved in shaping these activities must be a primary goal for agency leaders. But of course, programs and services for clients must continue while change moves forward within the organization. We simply can't "close for inventory" and reopen when we're fully ready.

The leader must be receptive to the reality of staff members' lives. A dictum that reform will be added to the seemingly overwhelming tasks staff already must accomplish trivializes the change effort and leaves less time for everything else they are already responsible for. Changing programs and processes will require some flexibility from everyone.

We can't create more time. So how do we find the time to successfully engage staff in the process of transforming our agencies? There are three prerequisites to creating time for change:

1. Develop the ability to reallocate priorities;

2. Abandon every policy and practice that does not contribute to the new mission, vision, and values; and

3. Focus; avoid multiple, competing reforms that would divert time and attention from goals consistent with the new mission.

Creating time for change requires agency investment. Resources must be provided to create some reduction in workload, so staff members can participate in the process while the agency continues to operate. Involvement of staff must also reflect the lengthy time frame of transformation. Change of this magnitude will occur over a long period of time, and there may be no tangible gains for the first few years. Leaders must keep staff mindful of the long-term nature of the process.

Planning for the time necessary to make the transition will involve not only freeing staff for specific training or meetings, but also building in time to try out new ideas, time to receive ongoing support and assistance, and time for practice, observation, data collection, review, and revision. As staff move through the change process, the skills that move the changes forward must be constantly monitored and addressed through relevant training. Top management must remain consistent in the messages they give when scheduling for these events, and consider which staff members need access to one another, when, and how often. Every activity in the workday is competing for time. Staff will measure and gauge management's commitment to the change process by how well top leaders integrate and prioritize the activities that are fundamental to the restructuring process [Purnell & Hill 1992].

Agencies have successfully created time for the change process by reducing client contact time, changing the focus of existing meetings, reducing the length and number of meetings, and rescheduling the work day to free people for common meeting times. Use overtime, release time, and, more rarely, time outside of usual working hours. It is important to place a strong emphasis on the efficient use of time [Purnell & Hill 1992]. Above all, recognize that time is precious, that its usage must be prioritized, and that the change activities are critical.

During the change period it is vital to guard against any perception that clients are not being cared for. Central services must be attended to while pointing to the promise of the new mission. Failing to do so will provide additional support for resisting the change.

Building in the time for change is one of the first tasks of the successful change agent. Leaders can help their agency to throw off old ways of doing things, much as a crab sheds its shell when it has become too tight and constrains growth. The old shell served its past purpose admirably, but it simply can't accommodate the new form. Abandoning unproductive behaviors, unlearning skills that have become obsolete, and cultivating new values and dispositions are all essential to change. This is especially true for agency administrators, who must lead through example and staff reinforcement, not just through exhortation. "Discarding unproductive and inhibiting behaviors and attitudes can contribute as much to restructuring as acquiring new ones" [National Leadership Network Study Group on Restructuring Schools 1991]. Recapturing the time from these activities and putting it to use in those that move the agency forward is a prerequisite to the entire initiative.

Developing New Knowledge and Skills

A transformed view of leadership for organizational change suggests that:

"The people work *in* a system.
The manager should work *on* the system
To improve it...
with their help."
[Tribus and Tsuda, cited in American Association of School Administrators 1991].

What knowledge and skills does it take to work on the system and to design that work to include collaborative input? Knowledge and skill categories critical to success that will be addressed in the following sections include:

- Creating a sense of urgency,

- Recognizing the personal aspects of the change process,

- Building teams,

- Managing conflict,

- Understanding and predicting team dynamics,

- Working with entrenched resistance, and

- Using a systems approach to manage change.

Creating a Sense of Urgency

The goals of child and family service agencies—to provide vital supports that help children and families improve their functioning or achieve other objectives— have never before paralleled those of industry, where profit and the bottom line are preeminent. The human service agency as an accountable industry is a relatively new metaphor. Our choice of metaphors both reflects and influences our representation of reality. Today, agencies are borrowing from business and industry and applying techniques successful in business to human service agencies. Client outcomes become products; therapy and interventions become services; funders and all family members become customers. Unfortunately, if they are not carefully designed, these quantifiable measures of success can easily become too mechanistic.

Much of what we know about continuing quality improvement and outcome-focused systems, particularly their effect on the quality of the finished product and on profitability, was established in the corporate world. Clinicians and managers have drawn concepts and expectations of benefits from this model and transferred them to human services. There may be fundamental differences, however, not only in the language clinicians use to conceive of and describe their work, but in the very nature of human service intervention that make wholesale transfer of this technology impractical, and indeed, likely to fail, without significant modifications. (See Appendix A, Chapter 1.)

Yet, to experiment with and accept radical change, people need to feel a sense of urgency. They need incentives to become proficient with methods to improve performance [Keller 1983]. It is the job of the leader to communicate this sense of urgency as the new vision is developed and the rationale for change is communicated [Bechard & Pritchard 1992; Kettner et al. 1985; Rothman et al. 1981]

While many practitioners are aware of the national call to redesign service delivery or risk disaster, almost all of us believe this may be true in someone else's hospital, clinic, or treatment program. Practitioners are largely satisfied with their work and how they accomplish it. Many human service agencies do not feel the sense of impending disaster that may be a necessary spur to radical innovation. But local and federal cuts in human services funding and increased competition among agencies are rapidly changing this perception. Faced with either going out of business or embracing new methods and strategies of continuing quality improvement, agencies have moved with dispatch to facilitate the change.

Leaders must provide information to those affected by change to support their claims that redesign is not only desirable, but necessary, and that the benefits for clients and staff outweigh the emotional stress and hard work of engaging in a change process.

Leaders may point to external stressors and expectations for a rationale to improve practice, but one of the most effective strategies is to engage the principle of creative tension. Creative tension occurs when we are able to clearly see and articulate where we want to be and what we want to be able to do for our clients (a vision) and when we tell the truth about where we are now (current reality). The gap between the current reality and the ideal vision generates a natural tension [Senge 1990, p. 3]. This tension can only be relieved in one of two ways: by drawing the current reality closer to the vision, or by lowering the standards the vision implies to match the current situation. If our choice is to be the former, a clear and accurate grasp of both the vision and the current reality is essential.

The impetus for change, then, need not come solely from the urgency of compliance with external accreditors or other "outsiders." Rather, it can spring from professional pride, the value base of the participating professions, and the natural drive people have towards self-actualization. When an agency changes to meet regulations or to comply with someone else's imposed goals, it soon reaches a plateau. That is, once people have reduced the threat or complied with the requirements, they feel free to stop improving. When the driving energy is their own vision and their quest is to improve services for those they serve, the motivation is intrinsic and potentially sustainable for the long haul.

As goals are approached, visions are continually readjusted upwards, and improvement becomes a continuing and unending way of working within the agency. The model for organizational change and the maintenance of the evolving organization supports the continued evolution of best services to clients. This critical element, that of shaping an organization's culture toward one of generative learning and intrinsic motivation to improve, rests with top management. The first skill the leader of a continually improving human service agency must acquire is the ability to build a foundation of purpose and core values.

Recognizing the Personal Aspects of the Change Process

Change is a highly personal process. If individuals have not changed, then the organization has not changed. As innovation is introduced, people experience three progressive levels of concern : (1) self-concern, (2) task concerns, and (3) impact concerns [Loucks-Horsley 1990].

Each of these stages involves feelings, knowledge, and behavior as they relate to the change being introduced. A breakdown at any one of these stages can cause change to derail, and can keep people from developing the new ideas, attitudes, and skills critical to the success of the innovation. The leader can help by understanding the personal process of change, and by providing the information and support people will predictably need as they enter each of the three phases of the process.

Self-Concern

In the self-concern stage, people ask how this change will affect them. Self-concern needs must be addressed and resolved, or at least minimized, if initial and forceful barriers to change are to be overcome. Creating awareness, as well as providing information about the characteristics, probable effects, and requirements of the change process, helps people prepare to meet the demands of the changes about to be implemented.

In this first phase the individual is concerned with three things: (a) the demands of the innovation; (b) his or her adequacy to meet those demands; and (c) the role he or she is expected to play as a result of the innovation [Hall & Loucks 1978]. The transition through this stage is facilitated by leaders who articulate the values that will frame the change process, articulate the reward structure of the organization, inform staff of their role in decision making, and attend in advance to predictable conflicts with individuals whose self-concern is demonstrably tied to current program structures.

Innovation cannot be viewed as something that is being done *to* people in the agency, but rather as something the people in the agency are striving to accomplish together. Rewards and incentives must be provided along with personal support as staff members struggle to learn how they will fit in and to comply with the expectations generated by participation in quality improvement efforts.

Managers often rely upon the intrinsic rewards generated by staff members' knowledge that these new ways of doing things are improving services for clients. However, these proofs may be years away and difficult for line staff to see or measure in their daily struggle to be there for clients. The opportunity to meet during the work day and to receive appreciation and acknowledgment for their participation, financial compensation where appropriate, and the help of relief workers and flexible scheduling to ease their additional responsibilities, particularly during the intensive awareness and information stages, are essential if staff are to overcome their self-concern needs.

Task Concerns

The second stage is that of task concerns. People need to know how to be successfully involved in the change process, what the expectations are for their performance under these new rules, and what outcome measures and objectives are guiding this innovation. Ongoing and consistent leadership from top management is critical to overcome task concerns. Discussion and resolution of these issues is essential. Everyone must feel the constancy of purpose; be able to articulate the agency mission, values, and visions; and know how they can personally contribute successfully. Orientation of new employees and ongoing training for all employees to gain and refine the necessary skills are critical in this process.

Without the prerequisite skills and information, staff will be frustrated and even resistant. In a system that relies upon the contributions of every member, skill acquisition and refinement will not only reduce task concerns, but also lead to strengthened self-esteem and job satisfaction.

Impact Concerns

Impact concerns must be addressed if change is to be maintained. All the parties involved in the change must come to believe that the new system actually works for the better; that it has a positive impact on colleagues, on relationships, and on client outcomes. Staff need ongoing feedback about the effectiveness of both their own work with clients and the organizational change process.

Involvement and empowerment of staff introduce the need for them to own their decisions. Currently, failure to make the right choice or the best organizational decision may be laid on someone else's doorstep. If clinicians and practitioners are able to overcome their issues of self-concern, task concern, and impact concern, they will be considerably less worried about assuming ownership for choices. The leader must model risk taking, and reinforce the fact that risk taking is valued and there are no penalties for having failed intelligently.

Building Teams

Leaders of agencies that survive in the rapidly changing world of the future will be those who can build teams and build people. Several factors contribute to the dynamics behind this declaration. The first of these is the increased span of control each supervisor has in overseeing the work of subordinates. Cost-cutting measures, including downsizing and improved communication systems, have made the old strategy of direct supervision to monitor and control employees nearly obsolete. At the same time, workers of the 1990s place less and less value on their jobs as life satisfiers. This shift in the work ethic makes authoritative control less likely to succeed in the future than in the past. The desire to participate in decisions that affect us in the workplace has become almost universal. Participation has moved beyond something desirable to something like a right for employees [Harvey & Drolet 1994].

Workers today expect more autonomy, and by virtue of the changing face of the workplace, employers require them to demonstrate greater self-motivation and initiative.

The traditional Taylorian vertical hierarchy and command structure [Taylor 1972, p. 93] is giving way to a flatter organizational pattern, one in which teams play a vital and fundamental role in accomplishing the work of the agency. The manager's role has shifted and will continue to shift from planning and inspecting the work of subordinates to assuring that plans are followed and tasks completed. Just as managers are responsible for their own unique roles and relationships with others, so are subordinates. In this environment, subordinates are viewed as process managers in their own right. Through team efforts that cross program and department lines, staff members are motivated to make important contributions to the organization and to society [Baker & Hunter 1989].

What does it take to establish teams capable of both understanding and influenc-

ing an organization at a systems level? Contemporary definitions of team building should not be confused with old stereotypes of "motivating the troops" with
cheerleading exercises. Organizational teams take a variety of forms: improvement teams, task forces, project teams, action research teams, and quality circles.
The focus of these teams is on improving quality through collective problem solving.

The belief underlying the creation of teams is that all of us are smarter than any
one of us; that is, groups are better than individuals at making high-quality decisions. In recent research studies, groups outperformed the most proficient individual group member 97% of the time [Michaelsen, Watson, & Black 1989].

Effective teams have the following characteristics: group power, inclusiveness, commitment, and healthy relationships. Additionally, they provide the opportunity for
staff members to speak out and demonstrate active listening skills [Gastil 1993].

Group power stems, in part, from true jurisdiction over the agenda and real influence over the outcomes. Power in this context cannot be limited to "input"
sent up the agency ladder to higher levels of administration. Inclusiveness is the
principle that those significantly affected by a decision need to have input in the
decision making process. For human service agencies, this implies the involvement of internal team members who understand existing processes across programs that are being continuously examined, and who have a high level of credibility with their colleagues.

Since it is impossible to gather together all of those who may be touched by a
team's decision, Gastil proposes that those *profoundly* affected be members of
the group; those *significantly* affected be involved through an ongoing information exchange; and those *marginally* affected at least be provided the opportunity
to express their points of view before implementation. This perspective must be
incorporated into the value statements that shape the change process. It provides
defensible guidelines for inclusion on teams and helps to avoid problems created
by staff either not wanting to be involved in anything or claiming the right to be
involved in everything. Teams should also include external stakeholders, whose
perspective may not be as narrow or as vested as that of internal members. Their
greater objectivity may bring a fresh perspective; they can raise concerns that
internal members too close to the process may not even see [Hammer & Champy
1993, p. 110]. These external members may be agency staff (external to issues or
programs being examined) or people from the outside such as funders or clients.
It is the synergy of committed people working from a variety of perspectives that
produces ideas of high quality and innovative change.

Commitment to common goals provides the focus for the team. These goals include enhancement of agency mission, both vision and values, as well as commitment to the change process through team effort. Effective team dynamics include
open and honest communication, active listening, the ability to resolve the inevitable conflicts that arise when people work together, the willingness to understand and adapt to the diverse backgrounds of other members, and the maintenance of motivation among all members of the team [Chang 1994].

Managing Conflict

It is impossible for a leader to build teams, empower staff, or enhance outcomes for the agency without being able to manage conflict. However, managing conflict should not be confused with avoiding conflict. Conflict is a necessary component of organizational growth, a process with positive consequences. Change cannot occur unless staff members struggle with one another over matters of control, ideas, values, goals, and resources [Coser 1956]. Effective management of this struggle is central to the emergence of a new consensus, one that embodies and supports program and organizational change.

People are problem-solvers; we need conflict in order to survive. Conflict between what is and what could or should be (creative tension) can lead to the attainment of high organizational goals [Harvey & Drolet 1964]. It is in reflecting upon and managing conflict that individuals and teams create positive change. Managing conflict requires a sensitivity to early cues that conflict is bubbling just under or on the surface, an understanding of how conflict can escalate, and the development of a set of strategies to defuse and redirect conflict to functional outcomes. Harvey and Drolet [1964, p. 82] classify conflicts into five types:

1. Value conflicts;

2. Tangible (resource) conflicts;

3. Interpersonal conflicts;

4. Boundary conflicts (involving violation of turf or roles); and

5. Perceptual conflicts (involving different understandings).

Conflicts cannot be resolved unless there is agreement about the nature of the disagreement. It is critical that beginning positions be listened to, and that team members hear each other. The skills of "perspective taking" [Johnson & Johnson 1987] and active listening are central. It is also useful for team members to collectively understand their individual and group "controversy behavior" [Johnson & Johnson 1987]. Is the focus on win-lose or on perspective taking? Is the concern with conflict avoidance or problem solving? If conflict is allowed to escalate, people develop adversarial responses. Win-lose scenarios dominate, colleagues become opponents, positions harden, communication narrows, and people abandon their pursuit for mutual goals. Positions further solidify when there is emotional involvement and attachment to adversarial positions.

Conflict resolution begins with an understanding of individual and group controversy behavior. It requires perspective taking and agreement on the nature of the disagreement and its relationship to a situation of concern or a problem to be solved. Then resolution can proceed, with a careful analysis of the situation or problem. What type of conflict is this? Who are the players? What is the content of the conflict? Are factors within the organization contributing to the problem? What might be some beginning goals for conflict resolution? What resources are present, and what barriers? What are the "sunk costs"—in other words, how much has been invested in the status quo [Patti 1974]? What is the reward structure? What specific objectives and activities can be set? How will we know whether or not progress is being made?

It is critical that all team members be working on the same disagreement in the same stage of problem solving. If they are not, problem solving will not proceed. The resolving of conflict should be a somewhat orderly problem solving process, which begins with specialized knowledge and skills related to conflict resolution.

Problem solving is one of the most popular conflict resolution strategies. It requires some initial trust building activity between parties, which provides the basis for resolving disputes. Old perceptions and beliefs must be brought into the open and subjected to continual examination. The nature and content of the problem must be clearly understood by all parties—and open for frequent redefinition. Next, participants generate a wide variety of possible solutions. After examination of all available options, consensus is sought and obtained for a solution that everyone can agree to, abide by, and live with [Johnson & Johnson 1987, pp. 102-105]. As a final stage, participants agree on a process for monitoring the solution, the person(s) responsible for that activity, and dates for reporting progress.

Specific activities to resolve conflict might include decisions to expand resources (often organizational conflict can be traced to people competing for the same money, time, or staff); to restructure the way the organization is arranged (transfer or terminate an employee, change a job description, alter who reports to whom, redesign the organizational chart); or to bring in a human relations consultant to mediate a dispute.

Understanding Team Dynamics

Teams, like individuals, grow and change over time. Understanding and predicting team changes over time will help both members and leaders weather the stress and tension that come with the agency's change process. Five stages of team development have been identified: Forming, Storming, Norming, Performing, and Adjourning [Tuckerman & Jensen 1977]. The members' needs, and consequently the leader's role, shift during each stage.

During the "Forming" stage, the leader must help the group to establish ground rules and guidelines. These should include clear norms for behavior related to communication and inclusion, the scope of the team's responsibility, team membership, constraints or restraints under which the team must operate, and a timeline for expected outcomes.

In the second phase, "Storming," teams begin to struggle with emerging conflicts and find ways to work together productively. Leaders must actively facilitate clear communication, model and teach conflict resolution skills, and do some cheerleading. This is when groups are most stressful and potentially most creative. Challenges must be framed as investments in the process, strong statements of interest, and indicators of competency and a willingness to assume leadership. Team members must also be provided with the skills they need to collaborate, gather data, and problem solve.

As team members gain confidence and practice, they enter the "Norming" phase. Stress decreases as the team acquires a history of working together and ironing out differences, and begins to develop a routine for working together. The danger in this stage is that people become complacent or reticent to introduce conflict; they want to focus on enjoying each other. The leader's task is to help them move through this phase, continue to voice differences of opinion, and focus on the task the group was convened to manage, while applauding the growing trust level. This is typically accomplished by increasing the scope and responsibility of the group, as well as increasing their authority and accountability.

Figure 10.2

Team Development: Stages, Behaviors, Tasks, and Skills

Stages	Members' Behavior	Leader's Tasks	Leader's Skills
1. *Forming:* People volunteer or are recruited to work together on a common task.	Questioning the leader about the group's purpose, appropriate behaviors of members, and leader's role Attributing in-team status to members on the basis of outside-of-team information Obeying the leader Discussion patterns are jerky, and there are long periods of silence	Provide structure regarding boundaries of the team (such as the frequency and place of meetings, the organization's reason for forming the team, time lines for achieving the team's task) Offer guidance in setting directions for the accomplishment of the task Solicit each member's opinion and ideas Encourage dialogue	Awareness of a personal leadership style Effective communication Thorough knowledge of the fit between the team's task and organizational goals
2. *Storming:* Individual and subgroup differences of opinions, values, skills, and interests start to surface.	Expressing opinions and disagreements Exploring the degrees of individual power and challenging the leader's role and style Attending to and avoiding the team's task Emergence of cliques and bonds	Discuss the team's decision-making process Model appropriate awareness of self and others Provide the team with the resources necessary to accomplish the task Help the team to establish procedures and norms for the resolution of conflict	Management of different values, behaviors, and skills Awareness of personal strengths and limitations Use of process and content

Stage			
3. *Norming:* The team focuses on the need for order and guidelines for how to work together.	Stabilizing the team's purpose, authority relationships, individual levels and types of participation Exhibiting in-group humor Emergence of informal leadership Establishing procedures for the resolution of conflict and the accomplishment of the task	Adhere to the team's established structure and procedures Ensure that the team's actions are in accordance with what the team *really* wants to do Infuse the team with enthusiasm and energy Reward individual and team efforts Acknowledge and reinforce the informal leadership Protect the team from outside interference	Mentoring Management of agreement Balancing work with play Buffering the team from ongoing operations
4. *Performing:* The team delivers the completed task.	Producing results: alignment of members' energies and interests with the team's task.	Vigilance: attend to the team's need for fine tuning its skills and attitudes Develop mechanisms for the continued monitoring of the team	Visioning Listening with the "third ear" Evaluation
4. *Adjourning:* The original need for the team no longer exists.	Assessing process and product Dissolving the team	Publicly acknowledge the team's accomplishments	Positive regard of self and others

Source: Jensen, M.A.C. and Tuckerman, B.W. (1977). Stages in small group development revisited. *Group and Organizational Studies, 2,* 419–427. New York: Sage Publications, Inc.

In the final stage, the team attains a "Performing" level. Risk taking has increased, conflicts are resolved smoothly, and members are productively engaged in successful problem solving. Upsets to the calm of this period occur, however, when time constraints, audits, or external reviews create new stressors. Stress is also induced by the gain or loss of group members, either of which immediately alters the stage of group development while posing new inclusion challenges. During periods of group disagreement or crisis, the leader's role is to monitor, educate, adjust, and work with the team until it is able to regain its balance.

The authors have purposefully connected the term *leader* to an organizational context, and have developed the paradigm of a single responsible person appointed to this position. In team development, however, leadership is essentially situational, and varies according to the work to be done. Is the focus on attending to interpersonal matters or completing a task? Is participation enhanced by the provision of personal support or by clearer definition of the task? Are there special knowledge or skill requirements unique to the task at hand? Who best facilitates the team at different stages of group development? The formal leader's commitment to inclusion, to power sharing, and to the facilitation of situational leadership are central to effective team functioning, as he or she calls upon a variety of individuals to assume the position of team leader pro tem.

Working with Entrenched Resistance

If the change process is implemented *with* the staff rather than done *to* the staff, resistance can be substantially reduced. However, if resistance continues and impedes the ability of the agency to move forward, what actions should the leader take? This issue is a difficult one for human service practitioners to confront, as our professional training typically does not prepare us to handle this type of conflict in positive ways. Fortunately, there are a variety of practical strategies for using and managing resistance [e.g., Coser 1954; Fisher & Ury 1983]. A difficult issue can be made more manageable by attending to three basic principles.

First, a clear rationale for the change process must be established, with input from all stakeholders. It must be written, widely disseminated, and discussed within the agency. Staff must perceive that the reason for change is to better meet the needs of clients, that the goals are consistent with the established agency mission, and that the plans were derived with input from all those interested in agency outcomes. In many cases it is also true that the financial health of the agency requires changes in both client services and management processes.

Second, the performance of staff and managers must be evaluated against clear performance standards that support the mission and goals of the agency. The practice behaviors the new model calls for must be clear, unambiguous, and codified in practice guidelines or policies that maximize worker discretion and creativity while establishing a foundation of performance expectations. Expectations for involvement and for practice must be specific, and clearly stated in job descriptions.

Third, staff who are having difficulty making the necessary changes require assistance. If the difficulty results from a skill deficit, then training in how to accomplish the task is required. If training is provided, a strategy for monitoring and evaluating changes in performance must be determined, written, and agreed upon. If the individual cannot or will not perform in the required fashion, he or she must be assisted to leave. (See Mager and Pipe [1970], and Pecora and Austin [1987] for strategies for analyzing performance problems.)

Terminating Staff

There are ethical, personal, and financial considerations involved in terminating administrators or staff. Clients must be attended to, and steps must be taken to ensure that service is only minimally disrupted. Clients and therapists must be helped to terminate in ways that maintain client gains. Applicable formal statements of professional ethics must be followed. Many professional organizations, such as the Child Welfare League of America and the National Association of Social Workers, have published personnel standards that address the basic principles to be followed in the termination of employees. If appropriate procedures have not been followed, the director and the agency may be vulnerable to formal proceedings on behalf of discharged employees.

Even more importantly, terminated employees require personal support, career planning, or personal counseling. The agency should assist in identifying and providing the necessary services. Agency personnel practices and all applicable laws must be strictly adhered to if the agency is to do right by the staff member and avoid costly litigation [Coulson 1981; Morin & Yorks 1982].

Remember that the discomfort of letting go an employee who cannot or will not adapt to agency direction and practice is followed by relief for all concerned. The relief for the director is almost immediate. Other administrators and staff members may have some lingering difficulties based upon personal relationships. Even those terminated eventually experience considerable relief, as they find work in settings where they feel more valued.

It is not unusual for persons who voluntarily leave or who are terminated to take legal action against the agency. The wise director anticipates such activity with the board, and is absolutely clear about and in compliance with relevant legal guidelines.

Helping administrators or staff members to change or leave is a difficult task for human service professionals. But it is not the employee you terminate who can hurt you or the agency; it is the one you should have terminated but didn't. Everyone knows who these individuals are, and like a ripple on a pond, their negative impact spreads to thwart major efforts at improving the quality of the organization. It is necessary to carry out this function in a caring and professional manner, while providing the best possible service to clients.

Using a Systems Approach to Manage Change

Reform requires more than mere tinkering. Change in any single part of the system effects change in all of the other parts. Therefore it is critical to view the organization in its entirety as changes are being planned. The leader needs to solidify a broad view, and to recognize the interrelationships of the parts to the whole, both as the organization stands today and as it is envisioned in the future. Fragmented improvement, implemented in a piecemeal fashion, seldom accomplishes the goal of improved services to clients. A systems perspective and approach can accomplish these goals.

Fundamental change in a human service organization requires that the leader ask *why* do we do what we do and why do we do it the *way* we do it. Before answering either of these questions, leaders must first ask *what* has to be accomplished and *how* it has to be done, trying to take nothing for granted and attempting to get past all the existing assumptions, which may be obsolete or even incorrect [Hammer & Champy 1993].

The process must provide for an early education of the system's pacesetters. The board of directors, management, line staff, and funders (private, corporate and public) must all learn about and support the concepts of the change process. A general buy-in to the process will smooth implementation glitches and lead to greater involvement of these critical stakeholders. Board members' support is essential to change efforts. Losing either their support or their involvement may bring a disastrous and swift end to both the process and the tenure of the director!

Often a board will hire a new director with the idea that agency practice should be refined, but with little clarity about the actual refinements needed or how to achieve them. Considerable energy must be invested in educating the board about the differences between "good" practice and current agency services. The vision must be shared at the highest level. The board must also be kept fully abreast of change activities and their consequences.

Engaging the board in strategic planning and goal setting is one way to cement its involvement. Another is to remain focused on the activities and tasks that the board identifies as its central issues. At the same time, the director must prepare the board for the conflict and tension that inevitably surround the change process and the additional outlay of resources that will be required to initiate and sustain the process. The stress of the future must be anticipated and viewed as a sign of moving ahead. Finally, the director must give clear and repeated reminders that it may take years, not weeks or months, for change to be accomplished and enculturated.

It is entirely likely that board members from the corporate world will be involved in similar restructuring efforts in their own businesses. Strategies, successes, and glitches can be shared.

The support of key management personnel and a management structure capable of providing support for the director's change activities is imperative. The organizational change process can be isolating as well as stressful; core management staff must be cohesive and actively supportive of each other. Key staff must share the practice philosophy and commitment required by the new processes of staff empowerment and the service delivery model that results from that input. If they are not supportive of the proposed changes, the process is hampered, if not undermined, from the onset.

At least six formal system management structures require scrutiny when engaging in the change process. These structures are central to what the system is and might be.

1. The personnel policies and procedures of the agency require attention. Which management and service forms do the policies and procedures support? How are participation and practice defined? What are staff being asked to do? What time commitments are prescribed? How are people hired, promoted, or fired in relationship to these definitions?

Major revisions are often required if these policies are to support a new approach to doing business.

2. Assuming that staff roles are correctly described and structured to support the current organizational goals and structures, what new job descriptions and what kinds of restructuring are required? Defined staff roles must quickly reflect changing organizational requirements as well as new service delivery forms. It is important to be prepared to communicate to staff their part in the new model; to help them see how they can fit in [Bridges 1991].

3. What are the current patterns of supervision, training, and consultation? Who is teaching and reinforcing what with whom? If these patterns do not fit with the change goals, major shifts will need to be made. It is not uncommon for agencies to retain revered consultants well past the time when their managerial and practice frameworks are no longer relevant to the new ways.

4. As discussed in Chapters 1 & 9, integrated information systems should be designed to meet the need for data-driven decision making at the program and agency levels [Bronson 1988; Caputo 1988]. The information system should be capable of providing information about service delivery inputs, processes, and outcomes that can be used to refine services. If not, the leader needs to identify the changes needed and how they will be made. The development of an information system can help the quality improvement implementation process, through facilitating the invention, introduction, and reinforcement of various forms for recording worker and client activity. The information system not only generates data that provides line staff and administrators with feedback about service delivery processes and outcomes, but also reinforces the bottom line that practice must be outcome driven.

The process of designing information systems is significant. It provides the reason to develop working teams that cut across agency boundaries and are involved in the process of selecting what information is desired and how various process or outcome variables should be measured. Four activities must occur concurrently: defining service delivery, creating empowering management processes, constructing a new culture, and designing a feedback system—one that holds the promise of continuing service refinement.

5. Once the change process is underway, clear guidelines for employment decisions must be developed. A process for interviewing to determine potential employees' acceptance of and likely support for the agency's mission, values, and vision must be codified and used by every department charged with the responsibility of recommending employment. New staff must be hired who are committed to advancing the organization's goals and whose internal values and goals are not in conflict with the agency's new direction.

6. Finally, those on the front lines of the "battle for change" must open and maintain external lines of support. The personal and professional support of friends, key consultants, mentors, and other external groups should be planfully identified and utilized.

In thinking about the agency as a system, it is impossible to overstate the importance of attending to leaders and staff members who like, respect, and provide professional support to the top agency administrator and the other members of the change group. Too often a disproportionate amount of time and energy is invested in those who resist change, a focus that results in souring the mental health of both the director and the critical supporters. In any agency change process, approximately 20% of the staff will be excited and provide leadership; 60% will be watchers, who move when an impetus is given; and 20% will resist all efforts at change.

The authors are convinced that during change processes, upper management typically spends 80% of its time and energy on the 20% of staff who resist and impede change. We would achieve far better results if we reversed that ratio, and spent as little as 20% of our efforts on the resistant few. The 20% who are excited are the real potential change agents. They stand on the extreme edge of risk-taking; they are the paradigm shifters who can see new ways to do things and lead the change process. When the leader supports and facilitates their risk-taking, and the watchers see that no harm comes to those risk takers—that change is both attainable and rewarded—the watchers are likely to join those out in front of the movement toward change. Suddenly, the 20% who resist and thwart change become a distinct and generally voiceless minority. It is wise not to increase their impact through disproportionate attention.

When the agency culture transforms the workplace to one where staff are energized and focused on improving the quality of services to clients, those who do not conform are either reduced to silent coexistence or they leave the agency by choice or termination. Resistors and nay-sayers simply can't fit in with a climate where staff are empowered, reinforced, connected, and pursuing common professional goals. Attending to those staff who are making the shifts requires focused effort. It involves activities such as public praise, written and verbal thank yous, positive informal communications, the assignment of important tasks, ongoing support, promotions and salary increases, and active assistance when anything interrupts the implementation of new ideas.

The Outside Environment

Any discussion of the organization as an entity would be deficient if it did not attend to the role of the external environment. Every agency has an established reputation in its own community, with both supporters and detractors. Changing management and service practices must be constantly communicated to the relevant practice communities (administrator groups, community practice forums, NASW members); to members of local or national like-minded networks who are influential and supportive of the change efforts; to supportive funding sources (foundations, county or state officials, accrediting bodies); to critical neighborhood entities such as schools; to current and potential referring agencies; and to the region's professional schools (schools of social work, psychology, or education).

Conclusion

Agency leaders are simultaneously involved in two major change efforts: to implant quality improvement processes while enhancing service methods. Each becomes a vehicle for the other. Quality improvement processes require the agency's mission, values, goals, and service methods to be clear. All staff must be empowered to develop that clarity. The continual improvement of service methods to meet current definitions of best practice requires a way to make change possible. Quality improvement strategies contribute to that process. We believe that undertaking the change process strengthens management and services with resultant gains in empowerment and self-esteem for both our staff and our customers—simultaneous outcomes that promise to be truly exciting.

References

American Association of School Administrators. (1991). *An introduction to total quality for schools: A collection of articles on the concepts of total quality management and W. Edwards Deming.* Arlington, VA: Author.

American Productivity and Quality Center. Organizational Change Tables [Mimeograph]. Houston, TX: Author.

Baker, E. M., & Hunter, W. G. (April 1989). The chief executive's role in total quality: Preparing the enterprise for leadership in the new economic age. Paper presented at the Conference on Quality, Madison, WI.

Bechard, R., & Pritchard, W. (1992). *Changing the essence: The art of creating and leading fundamental change in organizations.* San Francisco: Jossey-Bass.

Bonstingl, J. J. (1992). *School of quality: An introduction to total quality management in education.* Alexandria, VA: ASCD.

Bronson, D. E., Pelz, D. C., & Trzcinski, E. (1988). *Computerizing your agency's information system.* Newbury Park, CA: Sage.

Capezio, P., & Morehouse, D. (1993). *Taking the mystery out of TQM: A practical guide to total quality management.* Hawthorne, NJ: Career Press.

Caputo, R. K. (1988). *Management and information systems in the human services.* New York: Haworth Press.

Chang, R. (1994). *Success through teamwork.* Irvine, CA: Richard Chang Associates.

Coser, L. (1956). *The functions of social conflict.* New York: The Free Press.

Coulson, R. (1981). *The termination handbook.* New York: The Free Press.

Fisher, R., & Ury, W. (1983). *Getting to yes: Negotiating agreement without giving in.* New York: Penguin.

Gastil, J. (1993). *Democracy in small groups: Participation, decision making and communication.* Philadelphia: New Society Publishers.

Hall, G. E., & Loucks, S. (1978). Teacher concerns as a basis for facilitating and personalizing staff development. *Teachers College Record, 80,* 41.

Hammer, M., and Champy, J. (1993). *Reengineering the corporation: A manifesto for business revolution.* New York: Harper Business.

Harvey, T. R., & Drolet, B. (1994). *Building teams, building people: Expanding the fifth resource.* Lancaster, PA: Technomic.

Johnson, D. W., & Johnson, F. P. (1987). *Joining Together.* Englewood Cliffs, NJ: Prentice Hall.

Keller, G. (1993). *Academic strategy: The management revolution in American higher education.* Baltimore: The Johns Hopkins University Press.

Kettner, P., Daly, J. M., & Nichols, A. W. (1985). *Initiating change in organizations and communities: A macro practice model.* Monterey, CA: Brooks-Cole.

Loucks-Horsley, S. (1990, September). What we know about change in school: An interview with Susan Loucks-Horsley. *The Developer, 1* (National Staff Development Council), 6.

Mager, R. F., & Pipe, P. (1970). *Analyzing performance problems, or "you really oughta wanna."* Belmont, CA: Lear-Siegler/Fearon-Pittman.

Michaelsen, L. K., Watson, W. E., & Black, R. H. (1989). A realistic test of individual versus group consensus decision making. *Journal of Applied Psychology, 74;* 834-839.

Morin, W. J., & Yorks, L. (1982). *Outplacement techniques: A positive approach to terminating employees.* New York: AMACOM, A Division of the American Management Association.

National Leadership Network Study Group on Restructuring Schools. (1991). *Developing leaders for restructuring schools: New habits of mind and heart.* Washington, DC: U. S. Department of Education, Office of Educational Research and Improvement.

Patti, R. J. (1974). Organizational resistance and change: The view from below. *Social Service Review, 48* (3), 367-383.

Pecora, P. J., & Austin, M. J. (1987). *Managing human services personnel.* Newbury Park, CA: Sage Press.

Pines, E. (1990, May 29). The gurus of TQM. *Aviation Week & Space Technology, Advertiser Sponsored Market Supplement,* 33-34, 36.

Purnell, S., & Hill, P. (1992). *Time for reform.* Santa Monica, CA: Rand.

Resnick, H., & Patti, R. J. (1980). *Change from within: Humanizing social welfare organizations.* Philadelphia: Temple University Press.

Rothman, J., Erlich, J. L., & Teresa, J. G. (1981). *Changing organizations and community programs.* Newbury Park, CA: Sage Press.

Schein, E. (1985). *Organizational culture and leadership.* San Francisco: Jossey-Bass.

Schenkat, R. (1993). *Quality connections: Transforming schools through total quality management.* Alexandria, VA: ASCD.

Senge, P. (1990). *The fifth discipline: The art and practice of the learning organization.* New York: Doubleday, 4.

Taylor, F. (1972). The principles of scientific management. In F. Taylor (Ed.) *Scientific management.* Westport, CT: Greenwood Press.

Tuckerman, B. W. & Jensen, M. A. C. (1977). Stages in small group development revisited. *Group and Organization Studies, 2,* 419-427. Newbury Park, CA: Sage Publications, Inc.

For Further Information

Bardach, E. (1977). *The implementation game: What happens to a bill after it becomes a law.* Cambridge, MA: MIT Press. A classic book that vividly describes the gamesmanship and other barriers to successful policy and program implementation.

Bridges, W. (1991). *Managing transitions: Making the most of change.* Reading, MA: Addison Wesley. A concise but practical model for helping organizations manage the change process, with helpful checklists.

Johnson, E. W., & Thompson, F. P. (1987). *Joining together.* Englewood Cliffs, NJ: Prentice Hall. This is a particularly useful reference for understanding and working with groups. The chapters on communications, creative conflict resolution, and managing conflicts of interest are particularly helpful.

Joint Commission on Accreditation of Healthcare Organizations (JCAHO). (1990). *Chemical dependency and mental retardation/developmental disabilities services.* Volume I: Standards; Volume II: Scoring Guidelines. Oakbrook, IL: Author. Contains a comprehensive overview of QI activities and processes as they relate to human service providers.

United Technology. Twelve original copyrighted messages are available at no cost to nonprofits by writing to United Technologies Corporation, Hartford, Connecticut, 06101.

About the Editors and Authors

Gina Alexander is vice president of The Villages of Indiana, Inc., a statewide child welfare agency. She holds an M.S. in education and an M.S.W. from Indiana University. Much of her work has been in program development and administration in child welfare and children's mental health, with particular emphasis on developing an outcomes orientation for these systems. She is currently serving as co-principal investigator for the Odyssey Project, CWLA's multistate longitudinal study of children in out-of-home care.

Rami Benbenishty, Ph.D. is with the Paul Barewald School of Social Work at Hebrew University in Jerusalem. He wrote the chapter in this book while on sabbatical at the Merrill-Palmer Institute, Wayne State University. Dr. Benbenishty is interested in clinical judgment and decision making, and has developed information systems in the areas of family treatment, foster care, and residential treatment.

Gary O. Carman holds a Ph.D. from Syracuse University in special education administration. For the past 20 years he has been chief executive officer of the Julia Dyckman Andrus Memorial, Inc., a children's residential treatment center in Yonkers, New York. Co-author of a number of books on child welfare and special education program evaluation, he serves on several national boards concerned with children's issues, and chairs the American delegation of the Institut Internationale Education Speciale. His chief current interest is the interface of quality improvements in child welfare agencies with mandated managed care.

David J. Cassafer, B.S., is a Quality Program Manager with Hewlett-Packard where he has worked for the last 16 years. He has used the quality improvement strategies he advocates both as a line manager, directly resposible for business results, and as a quality coach, helping other teams to improve their processes. His current reponsiblities include post-project reviews, which he has worked to transform from a required formality into an effective tool for organizational learning.

Sally M. Davis, a research analyst for the Montgomery County Public Schools' Department of Educational Accountability, conducts program evaluations and quality improvement projects. She developed her contribution to this book while she was director of evaluation at the Child Welfare League of America and CWLA staff liaison to the National Council on Research in Child Welfare. She holds a master's degree from the Catholic University of America.

Nadia Ehrlich Finkelstein, ACSW, earned her M.S. degree at the Columbia University School of Social Work. She is a child and family services management specialist engaged in consultation and training on program design and the implementation of family-centered child welfare practice. She is on the editorial board of *Residential Treatment for Children and Youth* and a life fellow of the American Association of Children's Residential Centers. Her extensive publications include *Children and Youth in Limbo: A Search for Connections.*

Mark W. Fraser, M.S.W., Ph.D., currently serves as interim director of the Jordan Institute for Families at the School of Social Work, University of North Carolina, Chapel Hill. In addition, he holds the John A. Tate Professorship for Children in Need. He also leads the Carolina Children's Initiative, an early intervention program for high-risk elementary school children and their families. He has written numerous articles and chapters on delinquency, violence, family-based services, and research methods. He is a co-author of *Families in Crisis* (1991) and *Evaluating Family-Based Services* (1995), and the editor of *Risk and Resilience in Childhood*, scheduled for 1997 publication.

Kathryn A. Gerbino holds a Ph.D. in program evaluation. She is the assistant executive director of Parsons Child and Family Center, Albany, NY, and is a graduate professor at the College of St. Rose. At Parsons, which has a staff of more than 400 and an annual budget of $18 million, she oversees all the clinical programs. A consultant and frequent presenter at the state, national, and international levels, she is currently working on projects that deal with the process of change and innovation, particularly as it applies to managed care.

Miriam P. Kluger holds a Ph.D. in applied psychological research and evaluation from Hofstra University, Hempstead, NY, and is senior vice president for research and planning at the Village for Families and Children, Inc., Hartford, Connecticut. Before joining the Village staff she was a health care analyst at Queens Hospital Community Mental Health Center, Jamaica, New York, and a project management course developer and public relations researcher for AT&T. *Innovative Leadership in the Nonprofit Organization: Strategies for Change,* which she co-authored with William Baker, was published by the Child Welfare League of America in 1994.

Ruth W. Massinga, M.S., is chief executive officer of The Casey Family Program, a private operating foundation based in Seattle, Washington, that provides long-term family foster care to nearly 1,400 children in 13 states. She currently chairs the board of the Family Resource Coalition and sits on the boards of the American Humane Association, the National Center for Children in Poverty, and the National Commission on State and Local Public Service. She has also served as secretary of the Maryland Department of Human Resources, president of the American Public Welfare Association, and a member of the National Commission on Children.

Daphna Oyserman is a research scientist at the Merrill-Palmer Institute, Wayne State University, Detroit, Michigan, and an adjunct associate professor at Wayne State. She holds a master's degree in social work from Hebrew University, Jerusalem, Israel, and a Ph.D. in social work and social psychology from the University of Michigan. Her ongoing studies focus on the impact of social context on the well-being of children and youths.

Glen Paddock, Ph.D. is director of clinical practice at The Casey Family Program and adjunct professor of family psychology at Seattle Pacific University. His teaching and training promote the application of an outcome-oriented conceptual framework and critical thinking skills to clinical case management and program service development.

Peter J. Pecora, M.S.W., Ph.D., has a joint appointment as the Manager of Research for The Casey Family Program and Associate Professor, School of Social Work, University of Washington, Seattle. The co-author of a number of books on child welfare practice, administration, and evaluation, he has provided consultation on evaluation of child welfare services to the U.S. Department of Health and Human Services and a number of national foundations. Currently, he is working on projects to refine outcome measures for evaluating family social services, implement quality improvement systems, and develop independent living assessment approaches.

Sue Ann Savas earned her M.S.W. from the University of Michigan and has been managing program evaluation at Boysville of Michigan for eight years. The agency presently offers a spectrum of services throughout Michigan and northern Ohio, with a staff of 620 serving 2,000 youths and their families yearly and an annual budget of over $30 million. Ms. Savas' work has focused on program specification and the use of computerized information for practice and management-based decision making. She has consulted with a number of private and public organizations, has presented at several national conferences, and volunteers as a peer reviewer for the Council on Accreditation.

William R. Seelig, M.S.W., is president of Seelig & Company, a professional service firm that consults with child welfare, behavioral healthcare, and business organizations. He has held leadership positions in both child welfare and behavioral healthcare, where he specialized in the design and development of integrated systems to serve children and families. Currently, as a consultant to agencies preparing for managed care, he is developing business alliances and related management services providing strategic and reinvention planning services, as well as for groups of providers seeking strategic partnerships to serve local, regional, and statewide markets.

E. C. "Ted" Teather, M.S.W., is an associate professor at the University of Washington School of Social Work. He chairs the Concentration on Children, Youth, and Families, and teaches courses in individual, family, and group practice. He is also involved with faculty from four other University of Washington graduate programs in identifying and teaching the knowledge and skills required for effective collaborations. He consults extensively on both clinical issues and organizational development. Much of his time as a consultant is spent assisting residential agencies in their efforts to embrace new and challenging program realities.

James J. Traglia, A.C.S.W., is the executive director of the New England Home in Boston. He was formerly the deputy chief executive officer and chief operating officer of The Casey Family Program, deputy secretary of the Maryland Department of Human Resources, executive director of the Maryland Department of Employment Security, director of government affairs for the American Public Welfare Association, and a director of public sector marketing for the UNISYS Corporation.

Fotena A. Zirps, Ph.D., is an associate professor at the Florida Mental Health Institute, University of South Florida (USF). She currently coordinates the Special Studies piece of the Comprehensive Community Mental Health Services Program for Children with Severe Emotional Disturbances Evaluation. In addition to her work in mental health, she has worked directly with a number of child welfare agencies in the roles of researcher, consultant, and trainer. She has worked with CWLA as a consultant in quality assurance and program evaluation. She began her career as a researcher in the area of special education. Dr. Zirps currently teaches social policy in the School of Social Work at USF.

National Council on Research in Child Welfare
Quality Improvement and Evaluation Committee

Chair:

Fotena Zirps, University of South Florida, Florida Mental Health Institute, Tampa, FL

Members:

Gina Alexander, The Villages of Indiana, Bloomington, IN

Carole Bausell, Woodbourne, Baltimore, MD

Jennifer Boyd, Child Welfare League of America, Washington, DC

Gary O. Carman, Julia Dykman Andrus Memorial, Yonkers, NY

Sally Davis, Montgomery County Public Schools, Rockville, MD

Sally Flanzer, National Center on Child Abuse and Neglect/ACYF, Washington, DC

Kathryn Gerbino, Parsons Child and Family Center, Albany, NY

Miriam Kluger, The Village for Families and Children, Inc., Hartford, CT

Peter J. Pecora, The Casey Family Program, Seattle, WA

Sue Ann Savas, Boysville of Michigan, Clinton, MI

William Seelig, Seelig & Associates, Campbell, CA

Index